DR. DIRT

The Best of His Tall Tales & Short Essays

JEROME A. KESSLER, M.D.

iUniverse, Inc.
New York   Bloomington

Dr. Dirt
The Best of His Tall Tales & Short Essays

iUniverse books may be ordered through booksellers or by contacting:

iUniverse
1663 Liberty Drive
Bloomington, IN 47403
www.iuniverse.com
1-800-Authors (1-800-288-4677)

The front and back cover photographs were taken by Patty Petrik.

ISBN: 978-1-4502-6295-8 (pbk)
ISBN: 978-1-4502-6296-5 (ebk)

Printed in the United States of America

iUniverse rev. date: 11/1/2010

Contents

Introduction

I hate long introductions, so will keep this short. I am the son of a landscaper who became a doctor, spent 25 years in the medical profession, and then went back to landscaping. People wondered if I was crazy to give up the big bucks and glory of being a doctor in order to dig holes, mow lawns, lay sod, and do other landscaping duties. I am a bit crazy, after all, and was willing to give up the stressful lifestyle of doctoring in order to be "just a landscaper," and also try my hand at creative writing.

But I will always be a doctor. I still dream about patient care scenarios, and I try to help people in need. It is a part of personality. I have many fond memories of the people I met and cared for – and include anecdotes of those experiences in my writing. And I will always be a landscaper – even after my arthritic knee doesn't allow me to do this kind of work anymore. That is just one example of the dichotomies that govern our lives. We are all more than what we do – and we are always both this and that, parent and child, male and female, young and old, good and bad, and so on.

My first book, *Crazy Like Me: Memories and Musings of a Retired Small Town Doctor* (CLM), explored some of these life paradoxes. It was a tongue-in-cheek semi-fictional memoir. I hate to give the plot away, but the book explored the reality of the fact that "everybody is a little bit crazy… some more and some less." It never made it to the "Best Seller List," but did sell a respectable number of copies in my geographic region.

CLM helped launch my career as a landscaper *and* a writer. Since my main character was a landscaper, the local newspapers thought I was marketing myself as a landscaping expert. They asked me to write a "landscaping advice" column. I sarcastically named my weekly column "Dr. Dirt", and started cranking out weekly columns … Before long I ran out of things to say about landscaping topics, though, so I started writing about the philosophical meaning of "Good Dirt" and other farfetched topics. My editor received positive feedback on my articles, so he let me write about whatever I wanted. My column now includes items of great diversity: humorous anecdotes, book reviews, feeble attempts at poetry, personality profiles, sentimental reflections, psychology, politics, spiritual matters, medical topics, and so on, and so forth.

Readers have suggested that I compile a "Best Of" collection of my newspaper columns. This book is an attempt to respond to those requests – and an attempt to satisfy my own need to put my thoughts down on paper. I was going to call this book "Best of Dirt" or "Tall Tales and Short Essays". It probably doesn't matter what I call it, though. Some people are going to like it, and others aren't. Many people won't bother to read it at all. But if you do, you will realize that *Dr. Dirt* contains many slices of life that you will enjoy, and many topics that you can relate to.

Most of the stories and articles in this collection have been previously published. They contain the date they were originally published, and knowing that may help you to realize that the news, as such, goes in cycles. Occasionally there are references to local or temporal matters that are no longer important. But remember that it's not what changes in the world that matters – it's the changes inside us that are most important.

Many articles in this collection have been revised from their original format. Some of the stories in this collection have not been previously published. These entries of verities and balderdash are organized in sections of somewhat related material. But don't feel obliged to read this book in any particular order. Life only seems to travel in a straight line … It is okay to let our minds jump from one topic to another in a circular (and even random) manner.

I am indebted to Russ Wells and *The Roundup* for giving me a chance to write. He has had to put up with my "duds" as well as my more readable columns. I am, of course, also indebted to my mom. She recently passed away. Mom was my original inspiration for writing. She was a typical mom who took care of us "Kessler kids" through thick and thin, and made our home the kind of place that all kids should come from. My wife also deserves recognition. She is occasionally the good-natured target of my spoofs, is always classy, and is truly the love of my life. It would be impossible to mention all the other people (friends and family members) who have also been important. Suffice it to say that I appreciate that God has put all of you into my life, and I remain – as always – grateful for everything the good Lord has done for me and my family.

Section 1:
Seasons

Autumn Passing

(3/31/2009)

Autumn came the other day. But it seems like it was springtime just a few weeks ago. Whatever happened to summer? The long, cold, bleak winter will be with us before we know it. And winter seems like the season that never comes to an end. The passing of these seasons are truly milestones in our lives. They come without much fanfare, and then sneak away in a manner that makes us think they might not be that important. These changes are sometimes welcomed, and sometimes not, and they occur whether we want them to or not.

Why am I reflective? It's because I'm a year older – that's why. And at this stage in my life, I realize that I've got fewer birthdays in front of me than behind. If I don't occasionally reflect on these matters, then they will pass even more quickly.

Harry Chapin, in his song *Circle*, describes changes in this manner: "All my life's a circle; sunrise and sundown; moon rolls through the nighttime; till the daybreak comes around. All my life's a circle; but I can't tell you why; season's spinning round again; the years keep rollin' by … It seems like I've been here before; I can't remember when; but I have this funny feeling; that we'll all be together again. No straight lines make up my life; and all my roads have bends; there's no clear-cut beginnings; and so far no dead-ends."

From the beginning of time people have celebrated the changes we are now going through: passage of day into night, passage of winter into spring, and passage of young age into old. These *seasons* of our life might feel like they are "good or bad," but they are really just the stuff that makes up our life. No matter what these changes are, they have to be accepted. So we must try to enjoy the rainy days as much as the sunny ones. And when the autumn of our life comes, with the winter chill that follows, be comforted with the knowledge that winter death has always been followed by rebirth in the springtime.

Trick or Treat

(11/4/2009)

I hope everyone had a nice Halloween. In recent times the holiday has evolved into an economic stimulus package for costume shops, candy makers and pumpkin growers. It's not a bad thing – but having extra candy lying around is not good for my waistline.

The ancient Celts believed there was a border between the living and the dead, and this division is most permeable on Halloween. On the ancient festival of "Samhain" (as Halloween was once known) friendly and not-so-friendly spirits crossed from "the Otherworld" into the land of the living. It was a time to honor family members who had passed away; and Halloween is "the Eve" of the religious feast of "All Saints Day". Wearing scary costumes was how you could keep *unfriendly spirits* from bothering you.

As a kid, I always imagined *ghouls* to be evil demons that robbed graves, ate human flesh, and reveled in activities that were *ghoulish*. Although this concept is revolting, it is amazing how many people love watching horror movies that depict this scenario. "Night of the Living Dead," for example, was a 1968 budget film that has been viewed by *zillions* of people, and has grossed 42 million dollars in ticket sales. It was the first zombie movie. The horde of undead relentlessly broke down walls, overwhelmed their victims, and then feasted on flesh – until the victims themselves rose to join their ranks.

I now know that flesh-eating monsters are just a myth … Or are they? We are, if you haven't heard, in the midst of a "Swine Flu" epidemic. This virus is uniquely attacking young people, may require "intensive care" for its victims, and occasionally kills people. Last year we were similarly obsessed with the notion that "Bird Flu" was going to be the next Plague. And equally gruesome was talk a few years ago of "flesh-eating bacteria." These colorful names grab the nation's attention, scare the *bejesus* out of us, and then crawl back into our collective unconscious … And what, I ask you, ever happened to all the talk that AIDS was going to wipe out life as we know it? You should know that AIDS is still around, and remains a huge threat: it has killed over 25 million people, and 20-30% of people in sub-Saharan Africa carry the deadly AIDS virus. (Data from Wikipedia.com)

This past Halloween I was reminded that we are not completely safe. No, hoodlums didn't vandalize my house, zombies didn't stalk me, and we didn't notice any dead bodies lying around. But when we returned from western Montana last week (after visiting prospective colleges with my youngest son) we were perplexed by the presence of many tiny flying insects in our home.

What were they? I didn't think my dog had fleas – but I treated him with "anti-flea" shampoo anyway. The more I thought about it, though, the more irritated I got with these tiny invaders flying around my home. I eventually found the "breeding grounds" of these unwelcome visitors: it was a stinky rotten banana that had fallen behind the pots and pans. *Fruit flies* had invaded my home, and I went on a quest to kill them.

The fruit flies have been successfully eradicated. But what other monsters, I wonder, lay in the dark recesses of our world? We *should* be afraid of potential threats – both big and small. Maybe the Halloween "frame-of-mind" isn't so crazy after all. Even if we don't see any zombies, we should remember that there *really are* goblins in our world; bad things *can* happen; and goodness should not be taken for granted.

Landon Smith & Ian Kessler, 2010

Bad Day

(4/29/2008)

I should've stayed in bed last Tuesday. When a branch hit me in the eye, I had a premonition that it would be a *bad day*. "I hope it's not going to be one of *those* days," I told Joel, my son and helper.

"Don't *let it* be a bad day," he replied.

The naïveté of youth, I thought. He has not learned the Laws of Nature. But I tried to follow his advice. A few minutes later, I slipped on some loose boards, and fell flat on my face … It was another omen! I should've just called it a day.

I planned to do more trimming, but – since it was windy – decided to postpone that job. After unloading two loads of brush at the dump, Joel and I headed for home. "We can work there," I said.

There's always something around our house that needs fixing. I had lately been refinishing my basement, and I asked Joel to help me put in some wall paneling. His end bumped a water pipe. He noticed a "cute" little stream of water coming from the pipe joint, which soon turned into a gusher. Seconds later we were in the middle of a flood, with the separated ends of the pipe dangling in the air.

I didn't know what to do, but reached for the "fix-it" tool I use most often – duct tape. As Joel held the loose ends of the pipe together, I tried to tape them back in place. Three rolls of tape later I realized there wasn't enough duct tape in the world to fix this problem.

My son tried to hold our make-shift repair together (with towels, etc.) while I worked on the shut-off valve. It had been stuck for years, but I hoped to have a surge of *superhuman* strength in this crisis … I did manage to turn it. "Thank God!" I said. But I turned and I turned without anything happening. With the force of a fire hydrant, the water kept gushing out …

"Joel, get help! Call the city and tell them to turn off the water! Call 911. Hurry! Tell them our shut-off valve doesn't work. And call RestorX. We've got a mess here!" And we did indeed have a mess. The water was 2-3 inches deep by now, and the flooding had spread to adjacent rooms. "Turn on all the water faucets. It might lower the pressure down here … Do we know a plumber?" I asked. "Better yet, go get Bryce."

Bryce is our neighbor. Everyone should have a neighbor like Bryce. He is truly a "jack of all trades." He knows about all kinds of stuff: electricity, automobiles, small engine repair, and – most importantly – plumbing. And he's always willing to lend a helping hand.

As I was waiting for help to arrive, I wondered how all this would turn out. If it wasn't so pathetic, it would have been comical. A middle-aged man, soaking wet, was squeezing a broken pipe ... a pipe that had an aneurysm of duct tape wrapped around it, but with a hemorrhage that could not be stopped.

I prayed a dozen *Hail Mary*'s. The water kept coming. Despite the disaster, I felt a surprising calm. I also felt a tingle of electricity in my arm. Maybe this would be the final chapter in my life. "It must be the meter. It probably won't kill me," I said with apathy; "but who knows?" My son ran to the circuit breaker box, and turned off the main switch.

Greg Anderson, from the City Water Department, got there as soon as he could. The street shut-off valve was stuck. He tried again and again and eventually did get the water turned off. I could feel the pulsations in the pipe slow down and eventually stop. "Thank God," I said aloud. And then I looked around ...

"What a mess!" I said. My son had been building a dam around the area, but it wasn't holding. He used towels, then coats, then anything he could get his hands on. When I saw my wife's good clothes in the dam, and more in his hands, I told him that was enough. The dam did slow the flood somewhat, though.

Will and Jason (from RestorX) came with all their gear. Their vacuums started sucking up the water. I was surprised how quickly the lake that was my basement became just a wet floor. Wet carpet and paneling had to be removed, though. Several hours later, the place looked like a battle field – but the bleeding had stopped.

Bryce and I worked on fixing the damaged pipe. The faulty shut-off valve was replaced. Pipes were soldered back in place. Once again, Bryce had come to my rescue. Thank you, Bryce. You're truly a saint.

My wife wasn't as angry as I thought she'd be. "At least you weren't electrocuted," she said. "*That* would've been *even more* expensive. And it looks like you'll be redoing your den after all." I'm not certain about that, but I do know how fortunate I've been. Thank you, everyone, for helping me through a *bad day* – one that could've been a whole lot worse.

Thanks for Nothing

(12/02/2009)

The past year has been a difficult one for the American people. It's a fulfillment of the old saying: if we didn't have bad luck, we wouldn't have any luck at all. It reminds me of the lyrics from an old Cat Stevens song:

"Trouble – Oh trouble set me free, I have seen your face, and it's too much for me. Trouble – Oh trouble can't you see, you're eating my heart away, and there's nothing much left of me... Trouble – Oh trouble can't you see, you have made me a wreck, now won't you leave me in my misery." (*Trouble* 1984)

There's always trouble. Difficulty, it is said, provides more of an opportunity for growth than does comfort or success. But who wants *these kinds of* opportunities for growth? Not even Job, with all his faith, went looking for trouble. But he did not complain when trouble found him. "Though he slay me, yet will I trust him." (Job 13:15a)

So why should we be grateful? We've had to listen to several nasty political debates coming out of Washington. The situation in Afghanistan has deteriorated. A psycho Islamofascist recently killed 13 people in Fort Hood, Texas. The economy has stabilized somewhat, but the unemployment rate is still over 10%. Who in their right mind can be grateful with all this stuff going on?

Many Americans have a "thanks for nothing" attitude this year. And a bad attitude can be contagious. It's hard to be grateful when you don't have a job, or if you don't feel good about the job you have. If you're worried about your finances, then you don't spend as much. And in our "consumer society" over 50% of the GDP comes from personal spending. Retail establishments depend on the Christmas shopping season to put them "in the black" for the year. If retailers flounder, then they lay off workers, spend less on capital improvements, order less from wholesalers, and so on, and so forth.

Attitude is extremely important. A much quoted statistic, the University of Michigan Consumer Sentiment Index (MCSI), reflects how Americans feel about the state of the economy and their personal finances. The MCSI asks people how things are now as compared to one year ago, and also asks them how they think things are going to be one and five years in the future. Most importantly, it asks people if they feel good enough to go out and buy major household items. This index has been low throughout the year, but is starting to improve in recent months. The *best* economic indicator, though, is not what people say but what they do.

The "Average American" has rescued our economy numerous times in the past – and will probably do so again in 2009 and 2010. Even if this hasn't been a year that we'd like to remember, it might be a good time for our country to *move on* with the issues that concern us. There are still many things we can be grateful for: our life, despite health concerns, is certainly better than the alternative … We can also be grateful for our family, friends, national resiliency, and individual freedoms. Even the right to complain, if that's what you are into, is something that should not be taken for granted. Americans complain too much, it seems, but they always come through in the end. The period between Thanksgiving and Christmas is a good time to *get over* the petty irritations that bother us. Easier said than done, of course. As Americans, though, it is our responsibility – and our opportunity – to turn "Black Friday" into a "White Christmas" of holiday goodwill.

Turkey Day, 2009

Turkey Weekend

(12/02/2008)

Thanksgiving came and went without incident. Our family travelled to Fargo, and spent the weekend with my wife's family. It was nice. As I was there, I realized that I am an official member of the Holm (my wife's maiden name) family – and therefore related to her siblings, their spouses, their kids, and so on. It's just a matter of time, I figure, before I'm related to everyone in the North Dakota. That's how Scandinavians are, but that's another story …

While we were in Fargo, my wife did some Christmas shopping. The Friday after Thanksgiving is called "Black Friday" because retailers depend on brisk holiday shopping in order to break even for the year. Let me repeat that – in order to break even for the *entire* year. They need shoppers to buy gifts (and other paraphernalia) in order to avoid having a "red" year. Such is the challenge of being of being a retailer.

My wife and her family went through the newspaper flyers on Thursday to decide where to go on Friday. Many stores advertised phenomenal deals on selected items – but they only had so many items in stock. As a result, some highly motivated shoppers set up tents in the parking lots – so they could be the first to snatch up deals. Other shoppers set their alarm clocks so they could join the frenzy when store doors opened at 4 a.m. And the gimmick worked.

"Half of Fargo," my wife said, "was out shopping at 4 a.m."

"It was nuts," my brother-in-law said. "Mass hysteria is alive and well in Fargo, North Dakota."

It is interesting to note that my wife and her siblings were part of this group of "crazy" early morning shoppers … In the meantime, I was comfortably sleeping. Upon hearing about their experience, though, it did seem to me that the "American consumer" was poised to once again rescue our country from its economic woes.

The Thanksgiving holiday, which started with the Pilgrims in 1621, is a big part of our culture. President Abraham Lincoln proclaimed it an official holiday in 1863. And eating turkey is a part of Thanksgiving tradition. Believe it or not, Benjamin Franklin wanted the turkey, and not the eagle, to be our national bird.

Celebrating a holiday that "gives thanks" is as appropriate this year as any. Even though we all have concerns (about the economy, the war in Iraq, etc.) it is a typically American characteristic to maintain a "can do" attitude about the problems we face. In the last century, American ingenuity and determination has helped the world overcome many obstacles.

And so, my fellow Americans, remember that we need "consumer confidence" to lead us out of our economic recession. I encourage everyone (except my wife) to roll up your shirt sleeves, fight the lines at the stores, and exercise your God-given right to max out your credit card. Be a little reckless. We've only got 4 weeks left to Christmas, and we need everyone's cooperation to make this a successful holiday season.

Holiday Craziness

(12/09/2008)

Did you hear about the Wal-Mart worker who got trampled to death on "Black Friday" by a crazy mob of shoppers in New York? Check out the *New York Daily News* internet story and pictures for a report on this incredible event. A fellow employee said:

"I look at these people's faces and I keep thinking one of them could have stepped on him. How could you take a man's life to save $20 on a TV?"

Shopping madness affected many parts of the country. My last column talked about some "crazy Norwegians" in Fargo who also went nuts – but in a more subdued manner. My in-laws said they heard a chorus of "excuse me's" as people were trying to take advantage of the bargains. North Dakotans, it seems, are a lot more civilized than New Yorkers.

Focusing too much on gifts can cause stress for both the buyer and receiver of material goods. While shopping is on everyone's mind, it is important to remember that Christmas is not just about gift-buying, partying, and contrived happiness. Many people, in fact, feel anything but festive at this time of the year.

People who are alone, have recently lost a loved one, or are not able to afford a big Christmas may feel left out. They may experience "The Holiday Blues." Symptoms of this malady include sadness, loneliness, and disappointment. And existing mental health problems – like Depression, Anxiety and Alcoholism – all get worse at this time of the year.

Christmas is supposed to be about the birth of our Lord. It is meant to be a time of joy, good will, and gatherings of family and friends. If Christmas falls short on any of your expectations, then you may be at risk for Holiday Depression.

In order to reduce your chance of getting the Holiday Blues, make sure you participate in your church's Christmas celebrations. Don't try to "be everything to all people." Have reasonable expectations, stay within your budget, eat healthy, get enough sleep, and avoid excessive use of alcohol. Try also to spend time with people whose company you enjoy – and those who love and/or appreciate you. If you're feeling low, take an inventory of the good things in your life. And give yourself a pat on the back for your positive attributes.

If you haven't made plans for Christmas day, consider joining the gang at the "Community Christmas Dinner" in Sidney, from 11 a.m. to 2 p.m., at the St. Matthew's Parish Center. This is the 11th consecutive year that the

Knights of Columbus, under the culinary direction of LeRoy Strasheim, have sponsored this event. Good food and fellowship are sure to be found. This gathering continues to be a good example of what Christmas is all about.

Inside Out

(12/04/2007)

Last month I was riding my bicycle on the river paths in Bismarck. I couldn't help but admire how many nice homes there were. I'm sure some of the houses there cost over a million dollars. Since it was just a few weeks before Thanksgiving, gratitude should have been on everyone's mind. And then I realized that a car was following me. I soon discovered that it was a security agent following me in his squad car. The neighborhood surveillance equipment must have identified me as a "suspicious character" in their high-brow community.

I politely pedaled my way back to the public access road. "Riff raff" like me should stay out of their neighborhood. I presume they thought I coveted their material goods and lifestyle. Regular people (like us landscapers) must appear to be on the outside looking in. But advertisers want us to long for things we don't have – the newest video game, a luxury car, fancy clothes, etc. It's as if America needs us to be envious consumers in order for our economy to prosper; and people need *things* in order to be happy. And the Christmas season has become more about shopping than it is about the birth of our Savior.

It's no wonder that so many people get depressed at this time of the year. The reasons for feeling down around Christmas are numerous. They range from fatigue (from excess holiday activity) to financial concerns (from maxing out our credit cards) to family tensions. Experts say the common factor to these "Holiday Blues" is when people have unrealistic expectations.

People often remember an ideal holiday from years gone by, or buy into the Hollywood notion that the Christmas season is supposed to be perfect. And perfection is impossible to achieve. Another factor that can cause the Holiday Blues is the memory of a deceased loved one. The poignancy of a loved one's absence is especially felt around the holidays – as well as on the anniversary of when a parent, spouse, or child died.

Sometimes I appreciate how fortunate I am. I have a roof over my head, food in the refrigerator, and a warm place to sleep. While this is part of the recipe for contentment, it's also important to be loved – and to feel connected to people. But I realize many people don't have this connection. It's like being a pauper in a land of plenty. It feels like you have nothing and other people have everything.

The next time you see someone who appears to be on "the outside looking in," imagine what it's like to be in that situation. Imagine the emptiness.

Imagine having nothing. You might even want to imagine what it was like to have nowhere to stay in Bethlehem – even though your wife was pregnant, and about to give birth. And out of the emptiness comes compassion. Say Hello to that person you rarely speak to. Shake their hand and wish them well. Perhaps you can even invite them into your home. Inviting an outsider in helps you as much as it helps the other person. It changes you from the inside out, which is what Christmas is all about.

Andy's Christmas Carol

(12/23/2009)

Andy was a good boy. He was also a smart and handsome boy. Tragedy struck his family, though, and his upbringing was handed off to one disinterested relative after another. As destiny would have it, he became a malcontent. But his intelligence and ambition enabled him to become a successful businessman. He acquired money and worldly goods. He regularly took inventory of these things – not for their own sake, but for what they said about his standing in society.

When Andy was a child he felt "less than" others. He hated feeling that way. To combat these feelings he worked longer and harder than anyone else. Business success went to his head, though. He liked to think he was "better than" others. He didn't have time for anyone, not even his wife and children – so they divorced him. Being king of his imaginary world was lonely, but it was better than being a "nobody".

Andy's image of success would have been perfect had it not been for his unconscious mind. Could it be that he had a conscience? a soul? Whatever it was, it was trying to get his attention. He couldn't sleep. Not even booze and pills could drown out what his dreams were trying to tell him.

In one recurring dream, he saw himself as a young boy, playing with a broken toy, but happy nonetheless. The toy was taken away from him by a shadowy black figure. He cried until he had no more tears. Then he was silent, and alone. And that's how the dream ended.

In another dream he was at his workplace, attentive to the details of his latest money-making scheme. He laughed at the notion that his success depended on another person's failure. His laughter echoed down the empty hallways of his imaginary world. And then the dream ended.

In the third dream (and they occurred one after another) he was an old man, bedridden, and wanted a simple drink of water. His thirst was exquisite. His mouth was painfully dry. He called for help, but nobody answered – apparently it was the servant's day off – so no one came to his aid. Andy's voice became raspy, and weak, and then was heard no more. And that's how the dream ended.

Andy's dream trilogy occurred more and more frequently. And memories of his youth, and his losses, tried to enter his conscious mind – especially when he walked by children playing games and having fun. He would have felt remorse had he not been so good at squelching his feelings.

Andy's office was the only one in town that didn't decorate for Christmas.

Around town Andy was heard to say "Bah, humbug" out loud, and people said he was a modern-day Scrooge. And so he was. But Andy was deaf to gossip. He knew people were jealous of him for having the best business in town.

Bob, Andy's top clerk, requested a few days off for Christmas. Andy said: "If you take more than one day off, you won't have a job to come back to." That was harsh, but Andy knew that Bob was lucky – in these times – to have a job at all.

That same night Andy's dreams were more vivid than ever. They seemed so real that he was able to reach out and touch his loneliness. The emptiness of his miserable life weighed down upon him as it never had before. But that night he also had a dream where he was joking with co-workers and then having dinner with Bob – his trusted employee and only semblance of a friend.

Andy awoke from his slumbering. He thought about his dreams, knew what he had to do, and did it … In the same way, we all "go to sleep" emotionally at various times in our life. We are fortunate if we have family and friends to shake us up, tell us what we need to hear, and get us back on track. And if we don't have anyone who is willing to take that chance, at least we have our dreams – and they tell us (as if we really did have a soul) that it's time to "wake up," have a fresh cup of coffee, and go into the world with a renewed purpose, and a renewed willingness to "do the next right thing." (Allegory adapted from the Charles Dickens' 1843 novel, *A Christmas Carol*)

Christmas

I'm not an expert on religion. Your pastor and priest have gone to school to learn about this stuff – so you should ask them if you have any questions on these matters.

To me, the holiday season should be about spirituality more than it is about religion. It is the time of year when many people relax their guard, inhale the refreshing breeze of "good will" that is in the air, and attend the church of their choice. It's easier to appreciate the season if there are children around – either yours or others. But everyone was a child once, so you might be able to remember how it was … In today's society, however, the "reason for the season" seems to have been lost.

Christmas Day should not be about opening presents in a selfish and materialistic manner. Our commercial society has exploited the "gift aspect" of this practice to their advantage. But in many ways, it is anticipation that exceeds the gift itself. Do you remember what that is like? Unfortunately, many plastic toys look great in the package, but fail to interest the child a few days later. Some toys are definitely used more than others, though – a favorite doll, Lincoln Logs, and Legos are good examples. Toys that are fueled by imagination have more staying power than those that run on batteries.

You need to have the mind of a child to appreciate Christmas. Kids can picture how a favorite toy will give him (or her) hours of enjoyment. Boys believe they're an engineer when they play with their toy train. Girls believe they're a princess when they play with their doll. (I played school, hopscotch, and dolls with my sisters – but that's another story.)

The imagination of childhood is something that we, as adults, need to re-awaken. How else can we understand Christmas? Since none of us were in Bethlehem 2000 years ago, we need to imagine what it was like. The Jewish world had been anticipating the Messiah for centuries. When "the good news" was finally pronounced, many people were skeptical – in the same way that many in our society are skeptical about Christmas and related topics. It's hard to embrace things that have been cheapened by commercialism. Some people are skeptical of all things, though – both good and bad. I suspect they have "thrown out the baby with the bath water …"

The Scrooge in me says: "Bah … humbug!" The reality is that many people will not have a happy holiday. Health problems, financial insecurity, and loneliness can make it hard to be joyful at this (and other) times of the year. The weight of the moment can dominate all our thoughts. You can't see the beauty of Christmas if you wear "sunglasses" that cloud your perspective. These are the times, more than any, when people appreciate acts of kindness from others. It doesn't take much. A simple "Hello" or "Merry Christmas" may be all that it takes.

Many people do nice things at this time of year. Even Scrooge (from *A Christmas Carol* by Charles Dickens) became kind and generous – after the "spirits" showed him the need. Acts of kindness are part of the miracle of Christmas. You don't need to receive an expensive present to know there is something special going on. It's the realization that God loves us enough to send his only Son, and that has allowed a glimmer of light to enter into our dark world. The glimmer turns into a beacon. And the beacon of light in the eyes of a child on Christmas morning is a reminder that there is Hope in our world. Hope brings Faith; and the joyful acceptance of Christmas gives birth to our own redemption.

Kessler Home, 2009

Gray Beard

(12/23/2008)

Well, it's that time again. Like it or not, we're all supposed to make resolutions for the New Year. We're supposed to work on "self improvement." We're also supposed to make the world a better place. Let's see what we can do …

The fact that we're all one year older complicates the issue. In recent years, for example, you may have decided to "look before you leap" Is this the result of prudence? Or is it arthritis? Or maybe you have decided to "think before you speak." Is this wisdom? Or is it dementia?

Sometimes we make subtle changes that have more to do with advancing age than wisdom or prudence. I'm not saying they're bad; it's just the way it is. And we make these changes without even realizing we've made them. Several years later, though – if we look back – we can laugh at the changes we've made. Our goals and preferences, for example, may have changed in these ways:

Jogging is out. Walking is in. Power Ab exercises are out. Kegel's exercises are in. Mustangs are out. Minivans are in. Trips to Las Vegas are out. Trips to Wal-Mart are in. Get rich quick schemes are out. Certificates of Deposit are in. Sky-diving lessons are out. Funeral insurance is in. Long-slit skirts are out. Slenderizing outfits are in. Speedo swimsuits are out. Incontinence pads are in. Wild parties are out. Church gatherings are in. Brandy Manhattan's are out. Hot fudge sundaes are in. Carbohydrate loading is out. Low-carb diets are in. Prozac is out. Viagra is in. Steamy R-rated movies are out. Charlton Heston movies are in. Ceiling mirrors are out. Bathtub safety rails are in. Afternoon romantic interludes are out. Power naps are in. Philosophical discussions are out. Talking about your kids is in. Joining the Peace Corps is out. Retirement planning is in.

Leigh Anne Jasheway, the author of *I'm Not Getting Older (I'm Getting Better at Denial)*, has put it this way: "If you choose to be angry and depressed about aging, that's a long time to be angry and depressed. I plan to get less serious and less inhibited every year. By the time I'm 85, not only will I wear purple, I'll wear a purple velvet g-string. I don't care what the people in my retirement community think! Of course, I'll wear it on my head because I don't believe in being uncomfortable."

The book sounds interesting. Because of my age-related laziness, though, I haven't actually read it … Excuse me, I'm not really "lazy" so much as I'm "conserving energy."

And that, my friends, is the key to successful aging. We need to rephrase these age-related issues. We need to cast a favorable light on the changes we've made in our lives.

I have decided, for example, to have a gray beard, and let my hairline recede a bit, in order to appear wiser. I will allow my belly to bulge in order to appear affluent. I will grow a double chin in order to appear professorial. I will take on, by will power alone, the appearance of an older man. I will try to look like a retired doctor – one who loves to garden. I don't want to look like a young whippersnapper. I hereby resolve to look like a distinguished (and eccentric) author of books, articles and poetry.

This is easier than I thought it would be. New Year's resolutions are a piece of cake. Just be myself, and then tell the world that's exactly what I intended. The world, in fact, might be a better place if we quit pretending to be something other than who we really are. This point is summarized with the immortal words of Dr. Seuss:

"Be who you are and say what you feel, because those who mind don't matter and those who matter don't mind."

Gray Beard, 2008

Sneako-Lutions

(12/30/2009)

This is the time of year when every columnist worth his salt writes something about "New Year's Resolutions". I must not be worth my salt, because I refuse to do that. I have in the past, but columns of *that type* are inevitably ignored or read with *ennui.*

2010 might be a good year to learn one new word per week, however. "Ennui" – for example – means "extreme boredom." It sounds like "on we." It is a good word to use when you're trying to impress pets. Learning two new words per week would be even better. But "Sneako-Lutions" (my word for "sneaky resolutions") doesn't count as a real word.

If I was going to make resolutions, I might resolve to be a better husband. I'd never complain when my wife tells me to *do this* or *do that.* I would accept her "Honey do" lists with alacrity ("enthusiasm"), complete my assignments, and then sneak back to my recliner.

Maybe I should resolve to be a better reporter. I'd go out into the frigid cold, with tape recorder in hand, and see what I could come up with. But I'm a columnist – not a journalist. Besides that, I hate to commit myself into doing any real work.

I should resolve to read at least one good book per week. Waiting for the "made for TV" movie on a book doesn't count. You get a lot more out of reading the author's actual words than you get from hearing how Tom Cruise "interprets" those words for you.

I've come to realize that New Year's Resolutions can be bad for you. Lying to yourself about what you plan to do is worse than the underlying vice you express concern over. And resolutions are often expressed in a *backwards* manner ... Saying you're "never gonna' cuss" or you're "not going to eat cookies" is an unrealistic and foolish thing to do. Psychologists know this for a fact. It's better to say what you're *going to do* than it is to say what you're **not** *going to do.*

Don't get caught into the trap of saying you're going *to try* to do something. It's okay to publicly state your resolutions – that holds you accountable – but if you're just going *to try*, then you might as well not bother. "Either you do it," a psychologist once told me, "or you *try* to do it. Which do you think is better?"

Pop psychology seems to be divided into three camps: (1) Thoughts, (2) Feelings, and (3) Actions. A lot of time you can't help how you feel about something. At this time of year, for example, many people are feeling depressed about their weight and slothful lifestyle. Feeling bad doesn't help, though. Think through the situation: What am I feeling? Why am I feeling this way? What can I do about it? Given this insight, you are empowered to do something. You can join an exercise class, eat better, etcetera – which proves that actions are better for you than thoughts or feelings.

I wish life was as simple as my columns make them out to be. That's why resolutions are over-rated. Be that as it may, I hope all of you have had a Merry Christmas, and I wish all of us a Happy and Peaceful New Year.

Winter Games

(2/24/2010)

Have you been watching the Winter Olympics? You should be. Not only is America doing well, but it's a showcase for what an athlete can accomplish through hard work and determination. They also show "Winter Games" that can make the long and cold winter months pass more quickly.

The only problem with the Olympics, though, is that the sports they represent are not something a *56 year old man* can realistically participate in. There's no way, for example, that I could carry my rifle on my back, cross-country ski around town, and shoot at things – as they do in the Biathalon. I'd be arrested. And we don't have any Luge tracks around town, so that sport is also out. I did try Curling once (in Fargo) but was hopelessly inept at that. Ice Hockey is a sport that some older guys play, but with my limited skating ability it would be suicide for me to mix it up with real hockey players. I did check out an official Ski Jump once, but got scared to death. I attempted to ski down the landing hill, and wound up taking a death-defying ride on my butt.

They should have a "Special Olympics" for people like me. I did survive 13 years as a hockey parent, after all, and should receive some recognition for only having been thrown out of one arena during that time. It's wasn't easy to sit idly by as "our kids" were getting hacked, tripped, and otherwise abused. It was also a major accomplishment to drive to a Missoula hockey tournament one weekend and a Grand Forks tournament the following weekend. That was over 2000 miles and 30 hours of driving to get my kids to their hockey events. "Hockey Parent Dedication" of that degree should be recognized.

Ice Fishing also deserves recognition. Who in their right mind goes out into freezing cold weather, drills holes in the ice, and watches the circular hole to see if anything might happen? It's like watching Polish TV. You're ruled ineligible if you have a warming house, by the way. I've done this sport, and find it exhilarating.

Lutefisk Dinners are also popular at this time of year – and there should be an award given to the person who can eat the most of this lye-treated fish (without holding their nose) and tell novices how good it is. Norwegians usually win this award.

Sidewalk Snow Shoveling should also be recognized. Many people are in the running for the award this year. My neighbor gets my vote. He "snowblows" his and surrounding walks on a consistent basis. Everyone should have a neighbor like this. I hereby award him a gold medal for altruism.

Smiling in the face of bitter cold, helping someone get their car going, and doing other "small acts of kindness" can do a world of good – especially during winter weather like we've had. Acts of charity like these are what make winter in these parts tolerable. They are what make "northern people" special. The subzero weather might be numbing our ability to think clearly (from mass brain freeze) but does seem to be bringing out the best in people.

Valentine's Day

(2/10/2010)

Legends are sometimes born and sustained for the flimsiest of reasons. Such is the case with Valentine's Day, and the man (or men) behind the legend – Saint Valentine.

Valentinus (meaning "containing valor") was once a common name. And there was a Roman priest in the 3rd century that has traditionally become known as St. Valentine. This priest was arrested for marrying Christian couples at a time when all young men were supposed to remain single (and ready to serve in the Roman army) and when all Christian practices were outlawed. His biggest "crime," however, was trying to convert the emperor of the day, Claudius the Second, into Christianity. He was rewarded for his good deeds by being beaten with a club, stoned, and then beheaded.

It is also said that Valentine, the 3rd century priest, performed a miracle: he restored the sight to the daughter of his jailer. And he is said to have written a farewell letter to her on the night before he was martyred that was signed "from your Valentine." But the legends of Valentine, the saint of romantic love, were mostly "created" in 14th century England, and it is not known how authentic they are. For that reason, the Catholic Church took St. Valentine's Day off their "official church calendar" in 1969.

To compound the Valentine legend, there have also been other saintly Valentines in history: there was a Bishop Valentine from Raeta (a northern province of the Roman Empire) who died in 450, a fifth-century priest and hermit named Valentine, a Spanish hermit who died about 715, a "Valentine Berrio Ochoa" who was martyred in 1861, and a "Valentine Juanzarias Gomez" who was martyred in 1936.

As has been common throughout all of Christian history, the tradition of celebrating "St. Valentine's Day" in mid-February was an attempt to replace an existing pagan holiday with a day that has religious significance. The origins of Christmas and Easter are similar. There isn't much evidence, however, that the person (or persons) named "Valentine" did anything to promote romantic love between couples.

There have been several churches and hospitals dedicated to St. Valentine. The remains of the "lesser St. Valentine," the 5th century Bishop, now reside in Dublin, Ireland. They are carried in a solemn procession every year, and a Mass is dedicated to all people who are in love.

History is a funny thing. While it might be easy to criticize the sketchy origins of "St. Valentine's Day," it's hard to criticize the notion that "Romantic

Love" is basically a good thing. Psychologists say that all married people are initially drawn to each other by a mysterious biochemical (sexual? pheromonal?) attraction to their future mate. And without this magical elixir there is little reason to work through the rough spots in a person's marriage. As couples age their *romantic love* is usually replaced by *adult love*. But don't knock the "glue" that got them together in the first place.

For over two hundred years friends and lovers have exchanged *valentines* on February 14th. These are short little messages and cards (sometimes heart-shaped) that convey the message that your relationship with someone is valued. In South America they call this day "La dia del amor y la amistad" which is a poetic way of saying "Love and Friendship Day." Who can find fault with that? Whether you think the practice is silly or not, you should – if you value relationship in your life – send out a few valentines this coming week. (Information from Wikipedia.com and Catholic.org)

First Anniversary, 1984

Promises, Promises

(9/16/2008)

Last week I wrote my wife an intimate love letter. I advised her to read it privately. She gave it back to me – with some parts deleted, and words added to other areas. She edited my love letter! She thought I was going to publish it in the paper, and wanted to make sure I got it right. Such is the life and concerns of being married to "Dr. Dirt."

I had to convince my wife to move here. She is a North Dakota girl, and was reluctant to leave our home in Fargo. I had completed my residency training (medical apprenticeship) in Fargo, though, and knew it was time for me to go out and "put into practice" what I had learned. I wanted to go to a small town. That is where my triple certification (Internal Medicine, Family Practice and Geriatrics) would do the most good. I wanted to move to Sidney because the hospital was well-equipped, the medical staff was excellent, and there was a great need for physicians (like me) who wanted to work hard and practice medicine that would be truly challenging.

My medical practice was busy from the very first day. It was gratifying to be able to help people with a variety of problems. The clinic was particularly busy. I put a lot of thought into how I wanted my clinic to run. I wanted to be able to take care of "sick people" as well as provide top-notch preventive care. My wife was my first office nurse. She didn't share my enthusiasm for details. I always wanted her to "try harder" around the clinic. Although she didn't always do things the way I wanted, patients loved her – even while I was noticing her minor deficiencies. More than one patient told me to "be nice" to her. And over the years it has been my deficiencies, not hers, that have received the most attention. And so it should be. I am a flawed human being. My wife isn't perfect either, but that's not the point.

Living in eastern Montana has both advantages and disadvantages. Although it didn't work out for my wife and I to work together, other aspects of our life together went well. My wife and I had tried to have babies in Fargo, but it never happened. Someone must have put fertility pills in the local water supply, it seems, because we were able to have three quick babies after arriving here. It took "a leap of faith" for us to move here, and it seems like God rewarded us (with three wonderful sons) for coming here.

Being a small town doctor was very demanding. I was certainly busy, but wasn't getting rich. I was, after all, a "cognitive care" physician. Unlike surgeons, I didn't have very many *procedures* to bill for: it was my time, and my time alone, that generated revenue. Despite that limitation, I loved what

I did. And as time went by, I came to appreciate "the small things" in my life as a small town doctor.

The same thing happened in my personal life. It is the "small stuff" that matters most. Helping around the house is appreciated more than a fancy present. Experts say that "washing dishes" is the best foreplay, by the way. My wife is good at some things, and I'm good at others. We need to acknowledge each other's gifts, and try to get them to mesh. By ourselves we will always fail, though. We need to remember that Marriage is a Sacrament, and we should keep Christ at the center of our relationship.

On our first wedding anniversary, I gave Shelley a globe – and promised to give her the world. It was a joke, of course; but often we enter marriage with expectations that are impossible to fulfill. Couples subtly re-negotiate their marital vows. Romantic love may fade, but adult love can take its place. Husband and wife can become best friends. But every now and then it doesn't hurt to rekindle the romantic flames, remember why you got married in the first place, go on a date, and make a few wild promises on what you hope to do for your special lady (or special man) in the future. In that spirit, here are some of the promises I have made to my wife recently:

Mow the grass – at least every few weeks. Wash the dishes – a lot. Make the bed – occasionally. Get her a big TV – sometime this year. Take her to Europe – someday. Find a way to pay for the kids' college. Be nice – as much as my personality allows.

And that's what has been happening in the Kessler household lately. I know that your lives are also filled with "small stuff" that is both interesting and significant. I hope that once a week you will let me into your homes, peruse my "Dr. Dirt" column, and agree or disagree with what I have to say. Have a nice week. Make a few promises to your sweetie – even if you can't keep them all.

Easter

(4/7/2010)

Thanks to all the readers who have given me words of encouragement lately. It is hard for a novice writer to know if he is reaching his audience, and I regard any feedback as good news. At least I know I'm getting read. And in our society people are much more likely to criticize than they are to say "good job." This attitude may be because we've just come through a long hard winter. Perhaps it is time for us to give up our negative ways.

I get tired of hearing negative comments about everything. I'm tired of hearing how bad our President is, how terrible the economy is, how depressing the weather is, and so on, and so forth. "Death and taxes," the saying goes, "are the only things we can count on." Unfortunately, my friends, the list of potentially bad things is a lot longer than that. As a retired doctor, I can guarantee that you will eventually have to deal with things like arthritis, high blood pressure, heart disease, cancer, and loss of cognitive function. And let's not forget about "those other" life issues: financial insecurity, loneliness, dusty furniture, dirty dishes, etc. Negative stuff can easily dominate our thoughts, and it seems to be dominating many of our end-of-winter conversations.

Buddhism says that life is difficult. If you accept this noble truth, then life becomes less difficult. Hinduism says that if you screwed up your last life then you may have come back as a dog – or worse. Atheism says you should be skeptical about everything – even the hand you hold in front of your face.

Christianity offers a more hopeful message: We are all sinners but are saved if we accept Jesus Christ as our personal savior. He died for our sins, was buried, and was resurrected from the dead. Christ is the Son of God and the promised Messiah. Christians consider the resurrection to be the cornerstone of their faith, and the most important event in human history. It's the reason why two billion Christians celebrated Easter this past weekend.

Last week a local church leader visited with me at the grass dump. He enjoys my "Dr. Dirt" columns, he said, and particularly likes it when I discuss my "spiritual journey." We don't have to believe exactly the same thing to be Christians, he added. And I agreed with him. Whether we believe Christians need to live a good life – or do so an offshoot of our beliefs – is a point that is debated by theologians, but it should not divide us. The Great Schism and the Protestant Reformation divided Christians into different rooms, it seems, but we all live in the same house.

I hope all of you had a nice Easter weekend. The cool nights and gradually warmer days help us to shake off the cobwebs of our winter doldrums. And

April showers, as you know, will lead to May flowers. It's no coincidence that Easter is celebrated during this season of rebirth … Just when we have had all the inclement weather and "bad stuff" that we can tolerate there arises in each of us a glimmer of hope, and a realization that all of life is reborn in the springtime. And so I challenge each of you to witness this miracle, be a part of it, and give thanks to our good Lord for making this possible.

Yard Sailing

(6/23/2010)

You have to get up pretty early in the morning to go sailing with Judy Reid and Linda Mann – yard sailing, that is. They share a passion for going to garage sales, and spend almost every summer weekend visiting yard sales in the Sidney area. I joined them at 6:30 a.m. last Friday for the sake of learning about their hobby, and now appreciate a bit of what their passion is about.

"I like finding undiscovered treasures," says Linda Mann. She looks forward to the weekly routine of reviewing newspaper garage sale listings, planning weekend rounds, and visiting with other folks who also enjoy *yard sailing* – as some people call it.

"I just love it," says Judy Reid, referring to her garage sale routine. She has been *making the rounds* for about 15 years, has recruited several friends to join her, and is regarded by some (my wife, among others) as Sidney's "queen of garage sales."

There are 10-15 garage sales in Sidney each summer weekend. There were 118 ads for garage/yard sales in Saturday's Billings Gazette. But nobody knows how many of these yard sales there really are. Transactions are made on a cash basis. That's the main reason, I think, why national statistics are not available on the topic.

Judy and Linda tell me that clothing, books, decorative items, glassware and linens are the most commonly offered sale items. Antiques, furniture, toys, tools, and sporting goods are also available. "Miscellaneous" is another big garage sale category, and Judy has been amazed how often she is able to find specific things that she is looking for.

"I don't need anything," Judy says. "I do like to buy gift items, though." She also likes the idea of "going green" with the purchase of items that *should* be reused – like kids' clothing, silk flowers, etc.

Judy took me for a tour of her home, and proudly displayed many decorative knickknacks, antiques, and furniture items that she has bought at garage sales. Linda also has a collection of many garage sale bargains – including essentially new items that people received as gifts, but never had a use for.

"I found some never used 'plant watering tubes' recently – ones that were advertised on TV for $20 – and only paid $3 for them. Deals like this happen all the time," she says. I can verify that there are some great deals at these sales. During my "yard sailing" excursion with the girls, for example, I picked up a picnic basket (complete with plates and silverware), two classic books, and a coffee pot for only $6.

At "YardSaleQueen.com" there is a 13 page article entitled "Having a Successful Yard Sale." That article advises people to carefully plan for their garage sales, know what you want to part with, have prices on all the items, advertise, advertise some more, display your goods in a nice manner, have "teaser" items to bring people in, have adequate change on hand, and make sure you post an "All Sales Are Final" sign at the checkout. Most of this advice is obvious. Some of their other advice is a bit curious: Avoid being rude to your customers, don't expect everybody to be easy to deal with, and don't assume that yard sales are fun … That advice implies that there is "a dark side" to garage sales. My local experts, however, are not aware of these "negative issues" in the Sidney area.

Judy and Linda enjoy their garage sale hobby. They usually don't need what they buy at these sales – and sometimes sell these same items at their own garage sales. They don't sell things to make a huge profit. They participate in garage sales for the fun of it. They enjoy the camaraderie of visiting with other "yard sailors". That's what I think local garage sales are all about. It seems like an innocent hobby to me, worth checking out, and a nice way to spend a summer day.

Old as Dirt

(8/15/2007)

Because my wife is a few years younger than me, I have been accused of "robbing the cradle." When I woke up this morning, however, I discovered that I was in bed with an *old* woman. How did this happen? My wife turns 50 years old this week. But if she's that old, that makes me *really old*. I remember when we were just kids. Where has the time gone?

I think it is ironic that Artificial Intelligence (computer stuff), Play-Doh (kid stuff), and Shelley (my wife) were all "invented" fifty years ago. Computers can now do all our thinking so that we can play more. Being alive at this time in history has other advantages as well. We don't have to worry about food, water, or shelter. We have air conditioning to help us through the sweltering heat of the summer. We have heated homes to warm us on the coldest of winter days. Most of us live well into our eighties – compared to an average lifespan of 47 in 1900. Turning 50 is something we celebrate, and joke about; but is not usually associated with "end of life" concerns.

My dad never made it to 50. He died at age 49 of a heart attack. Even though I have enjoyed good health, I used to think that I was going to mysteriously drop dead on my 49th birthday. I don't run marathons anymore, but can still dig more holes per hour than the 18 year-olds who work for me. My dad smoked 4 packs of cigarettes per day, a habit he picked up in his youth. Since I don't smoke or drink, I can reasonably expect to live a few more years. It's all a crap shoot, though. I could be run over by a truck tomorrow.

My wife is 50, but has the spirit of a teenager. Most days she looks 15 years younger than her age. She isn't too old to act silly, and loves to help people celebrate their special occasions. And she does way too many volunteer activities. It must be a sign of my age, but I worry about her when she over-extends herself. I tell her to "slow down" in the same way my mother used to tell me to do the same.

We all need to slow down. Our days on this earth are numbered – no matter who we are, or how healthy we are. Whatever difficulties we encounter, it's important to be grateful for the things we have. Wise people even appreciate their difficulties, because they provide more opportunity for personal growth than does comfort or success. And we should never be reluctant to tell the important people in our life that we love them. You never know when you could lose that chance … forever.

It's true. With the passage of time, my wife and I are becoming forgetful. Being forgetful has its advantages, though. My wife used to get mad at me for leaving the toilet seat up; now she can't remember that it bothers her. And your secrets are always safe with us – because we can't remember your name, let alone what you have told us. We can watch the same movie night after night without getting bored, because we can't remember how it turns out. We have three sons and a dog. I often mix up their names, which irritates my dog to no end. Sometimes it seems like we're new parents, because we're getting to know our children (and each other) in a new way every day.

If you run into Shelley, my wife, make sure you wish her a happy birthday. Tell her she looks pretty good – for an old woman! And don't forget to tell your wife (or husband) the same.

Dog Days

(9/1/2009)

Since I'm not a *real journalist*, I get to write about topics that you don't find in other newspapers. One example is my dog, who I write about on a regular basis. My dog, Oscar, is now eleven years old, and is lazy as ever.

Everybody should have a dog like Oscar. He sleeps in my bedroom closet every night; and that's also his hideout if there is a vacuum cleaner in use, thunder, or other scary noise. During the daytime he sleeps on the family room couch, sometimes pointing all four of his legs to the sky, and dreams that he is a champion squirrel chaser. At least that's what I think he is dreaming about. He gets frustrated in his outdoor squirrel chasing, but in his dreams his legs churn and he makes triumphant dog snarl noises.

Saying that dogs have human characteristics is an example of *anthropomorphism*. Pet owners do this all the time. In that spirit, Oscar thinks he is king of our household, and we are his servants. He only occasionally gets up to greet visitors. He rarely barks. He just looks at the door when he wants to relieve himself, which can be a problem if you're not paying attention to him. Oscar expects to be noticed, though, and he pushes his snout under my hand when he wants to be petted. He eats and drinks, of course. But that's it. That's all there is to his life.

Oscar's lifestyle is the epitome of laziness and lassitude. And maybe you are feeling some of that "end of summer" lethargy as well. We are, in case you haven't thought about, at the tail end of the Dog Days of 2009. *Dog Days*, by the way, are defined as "the hot, sultry part of the summer between early July and early September." It's also regarded as a period of stagnation, inactivity and indolence. (Dictionary.com)

The tradition of Dog Days dates back to when *Sirius*, the Dog Star, rose at the same time as the sun. The Romans sacrificed a brown dog at the beginning of the Dog Days to appease the rage of Sirius. The Dog Days were believed to be an evil time "when the seas boiled, wine turned sour, dogs grew mad, and all creatures became languid … causing to man burning fevers, hysterics, and [frantic behavior]." (Wikipedia.com) In the modern era, though, the Dog Days are regarded more as a time to placidly lay around, a time when you can get away with putting off work – while you patiently wait for nicer weather.

This summer the weather hasn't been too bad. But we did have a handful of sweltering 90 degree days. That heat was hard on outdoor workers. I can vouch for that. Pushing 300 wheelbarrows of rock on a recent job was not easy. And people wanting a nice lawn had to do some extra watering. Your air conditioner also had to work harder this summer. Not everything, however, can be measured in degrees, wheelbarrows, gallons, or hours of productivity. Oscar, for example, can never be accused of being overly productive. If he could talk, though, he might say he has been busy teaching me how to be a better dog owner. He might also argue that Dog Days, in his opinion, are not really coming to an end – but last 365 days a year.

Summer's End

(8/25/2009)

"Are you looking forward to school?" I asked my son.

"Yes and no," he replied. "Right now it feels like I'm in *Limbo*, halfway between the carefree days of summer and the long school year ahead."

The innocence of youth, I thought … Limbo, by the way, is not official church theology; it's a place that St. Augustine (and other scholars) thought might be the alternative afterlife for babies who didn't get baptized before they died. It was an unfair situation: they hadn't sinned, so shouldn't to go to Hell; but hadn't been "cleansed," so couldn't go to Heaven. Nobody liked the concept, but even Moses had to wait "in the bosom of Abraham" before he could be saved.

Halfway here. Halfway there. That's how it is with all of us. My sons are good examples: they're home now, working, trying to make some money; but next week they'll be back in school. They're not kids anymore. They're becoming adults. They're halfway to where they're going.

Summer is that time of the year when the days are long, the weather is hot, and people spend as much time outdoors as possible. Winter is the opposite. Experts say the parade of seasons is due to whether the earth is tilting toward the sun, or away from the sun. Maybe human behavior is the same. Whether we are extroverted or shy, brave or cowardly, friendly or mean – may all depend on if we are tilting toward the light, or away.

We're just a few weeks away from September 22, which is the "Autumn Equinox," or halfway point, when the days and nights are the same length, when the sun is at the equator, when we're truly "in between" the extremes of the summer and winter. Gone are the 90 degree days of July. The "Dog Days" of August will also soon fade from memory. Now comes autumn: when leaves get painted many colors, when winter's chill creeps into the air, when farmers get harvest for their efforts, and when Thanksgiving reminds us all to be grateful.

Many people have trouble enjoying the weather as it is. In July we wanted cooler weather. In January we'll be longing for that same summer heat. It's the way we are. Never happy, I guess, always wanting something other than what we have. Autumn is that "in between" time, though, when we can enjoy short-sleeve-shirt warmth in the daytime along with naturally cool nights. We can turn off both the air conditioner and the heater. We get to experience the best of both weather extremes within the course of a single day.

So as your family says their good-byes, and the house quiets down, it's time – once again – to accept the fact that life is always changing. Lest the changes slip by without noticing them, however, pay attention to "mile markers" along the way. The next event will be Labor Day, which is what America regards as the ceremonial end to summer. Summer's end is not such a bad thing. Autumn, which many people regard as the nicest season, is on the way.

Roller Coaster Year

(3/24/2009)

It seems like the world, on both an individual and collective basis, has been on a roller coaster ride lately. I'm sure you know what I mean. The media has scared the bejesus out of us with news of the nation's subprime mortgage problem, falling real estate values, and global credit crisis. The stock market has dropped from 14,000 in 2007 to 6,500 on 3/9/09. Most "401K" pension plans are now "201K" plans. Needless to say, consumer confidence has suffered – and nobody knows if we have seen the worst of it.

Another example of our national "roller coaster ride" is in what we pay for gasoline. In February of 2008, my son and I paid $4.67 per gallon of gas in California. Twelve months later, my wife and I paid $1.46 per gallon of gas in Cheyenne, Wyoming. That's an incredible swing! And the price of a barrel of oil has gone from $147 on 7/11/08 to $34 on 12/21/08. What's going on? This chaotic swing affects whether or not it is profitable to drill for domestic oil – and the recent downturn has caused oil companies to lay off workers in our area.

The Organization of Petroleum Exporting Countries (OPEC) has been manipulating us for years. The price of oil doesn't go up and down by chance, you know. OPEC toys with us: they pull our strings back and forth as if we were a colossal puppet. And our relationship with China is similar: we desperately need them to buy our treasury bills – in order to fund our excesses. We now find ourselves in the strange position of being dependent on the whims of *other* economies.

Our national deficit will skyrocket from $162 billion in 2007 to $1.6 trillion in 2009. Nobody knows what the long term consequences of this will be – but it can't be good! Our national debt is now at 11 trillion dollars. Each American's share of this is $38,000, which is on top of each family's average non-mortgage debt of $19,000. This degree of borrowing can't go on forever. Borrowing excessively is, after all, what caused the economic recession in the first place. Let's hope the recovery begins soon; and hope that our income minus spending mismatch can be controlled before our country collapses.

We are told that if the economy doesn't do us in, then "Global Warming" will – but we had a record amount of snowfall this past winter. Other issues are also out of our control. The western part of Montana has decided that our local oil tax revenue should be "distributed fairly" around the state. That, in addition to falling population and business closures, threatens the long-term stability of our school system and local economy.

Perhaps the "roller coaster ride" affected you in other ways. The economy, politics and weather are irrelevant if you don't have your health, a loving family, and a few good friends. And I'm sad to say that more of my "old patients" died this past year. I regarded them as friends. Anyone you visit with over a period of many years, learn the intimate details of their life, and care for is a friend of the highest order. Your personal losses are also significant … But death, in some circumstances, can be regarded as a welcome respite for those who have been suffering.

Sometimes we feel like we're going to die – but don't. The roller coaster goes down, and then it goes up. If our train stays on track, though, the ups and downs of life should balance themselves out. Just hang on! I hope next year isn't quite so bumpy. If it's any remorse, I'm on the same roller coaster train … If you're up, then so am I. If you're down, you know where I'm at. And once a week my "Dr. Dirt" column will be with you – to help sort things out.

Section 2:
Pets & Plants

Oscar

(7/11/2007)

I have a dog – did you know I had a dog? When we picked him up our family had, as they say, "the pick of the litter." I tested the puppies for their agility and intelligence. The kids chose the puppy that couldn't find the hidden treat, but was the cutest. I wanted to name him Kirby, after the baseball player. The rest of the family decided that "Oscar" would be his name.

Oscar's mom was a great hunting dog. His half-sister was legendary for her good nose. Oscar can find doggy treats if you hold them in front of him, but doesn't know what you're talking about when you tell him to find the treat a few feet away. He's also gun-shy, and hides under the pickup truck when he sees a shotgun. His father's genes corrupted him. Just because he's not a hunting dog doesn't mean we don't appreciate him, though. He remains cuddly, and is the best 80 pound lap dog I know of.

If you read this article, please don't take advantages of Oscar's weaknesses. He likes to hear his name, and is friendly when one or two people approach him in a non-threatening manner. If you're a burglar, you need to be careful: you might trip over his sleeping body on your way to our treasures. (They're kept in a locked safe, so don't bother.) He also might lick you to death. He won't bite you unless you crowd him. Oscar is not much of a watch dog, you see, but he is generally a nice quiet companion. He doesn't even bark when he needs to relieve himself. He does go ballistic, however, when someone drives by in a motorcycle.

Don't mess with the "dark side" of Oscar's personality. Years ago he was run over by an ATV, badly dented their fender, suffered a bruised thigh, and was left with a paralyzed tail. Oscar was unable to lift his tail out of the way when he pooped, and stunk up our house. You could stomp on his tail without him even noticing. Being the gifted surgeon that I am, I cut off his tail. We no longer have the poopy tail problem. Insensitive people make fun of Oscar's nubbin, though. I can live with that.

Please don't feed my overweight dog. He turns up his nose to dog food as it is, and you'll aggravate his sweet tooth if you give in to his begging. Oscar thinks he's a person, you see, and expects "people food" at least three times a day. He especially likes ice cream and cookies, just like me. We're trying to break him of his junk food habit. My wife says I am the main culprit in giving Oscar inappropriate food.

Pets can have a beneficial effect on a person's health. If you take your dog for a walk, the exercise is as good for you as it is for the dog. I rarely have that experience, however. When I'm done with my landscaping duties, I'm too tired to walk my dog. Taking care of a dog also teaches kids how to be responsible. That is another benefit we have yet to experience. But we have trained Oscar to be a good house dog. He'll wag his nubbin of a tail and lick you in the face even if you have had a bad day. Pets are good at giving their owners unconditional love, and Oscar provides me with that on a daily basis. All he wants is a little bit of attention. Petting him makes him smile like a circus clown. His happiness is contagious, and reminds me that all of life can be broken down into a simple message: everybody wants a little love. Yes, it's true ... I love my dog, and he loves me. For all his shortcomings, I wouldn't trade Oscar for any dog in the world.

Oscar, 1998

A Dog's Life

(ca. 1974)

I don't believe in reincarnation, but I sometimes wonder what it would be like to come back as a dog. It might not be too bad. Imagine the conversations I could have with myself:

"Man, this place is noisy! Can't a guy get any sleep around here? Alarms go off; people run aimlessly around; everyone is in a hurry. And where are they going? To work, to school, to meetings … They must be crazy to spend their lives like this! Just plain crazy!

"It's hard to sleep with all this noise. And I do need my sleep. I get 12 hours of sleep each night – plus four or five naps during the day. But I do expect my master to wake me for meals. Breakfast is especially important. And lately the meal service has been terrible. Master runs off somewhere each morning, and he forgets to feed me. The nerve of him! I get hunger pangs if I don't get fed every 3 hours. And that 'mature dog formula' he bought is way too healthy. It's a good thing the boys secretly give me table scraps.

"I like going for walks with Master. He talks to me as we walk along – halfway expecting me to respond. It would be stupid for me to say anything, though. I'm not going to reveal myself. It's much more fun to have him *guess* what's on my mind.

"'You sure pee a lot,' he says. Doesn't he know I'm marking my territory? I need to let the ladies know I'm still available. 'You don't pee for 12 hours when you're sleeping,' he says, 'and then you pee 12 times on a 15 minute walk. What's the deal?' It's obvious he doesn't know how a dog's bladder works. He doesn't know about my other abilities, either. And I'm *not* going to tell him.

"He thinks I'm an obedient but stupid dog. When he says 'Sit,' what do I do? I sit, of course. What's the big deal? I like sitting. But when he says 'Fetch,' what do you think I do? I sit, of course. Why should I chase after that stinky old ball, anyway?

"Master prides himself on having *Free Will*. He thinks, since I'm just a dog, that I'm only capable of following my instincts and doing simple programmed behavior. Yeah, right. If I wanted, I could get a job as an airport security dog – sniffing people's bags for drugs and bombs, you know. I'd much rather sniff dog and people crotches, though. But only those private parts that *I choose* to sniff. Free Will indeed! He's the one who has to work every day. And he thinks he's the higher species.

"Enough talk. Please don't tell my Master what goes on behind my blank

44

stare, drooling tongue, and wagging tail. I like this gig. I don't want to mess it up."

"Come on, Oscar," Master says. "Let's go for a walk."

"'Woof, woof,' I say with enthusiasm. I've got him trained to put a leash on me before we go on these walks. That way I don't have to chase cats or squirrels anymore – as I did in my youth. I'm too old for that nonsense. You see, I've got my Master on a leash as much as he thinks he's got one on me. I like this slower pace. It's a dog's life, I realize, but somebody's got to do it."

Travels with Oscar

(11/18/2009)

In 1960, John Steinbeck, a Nobel- and Pulitzer-prize winning American author, went on a car trip with Charley, his beloved dog. He wrote a book on the experience. Steinbeck is best known for *Grapes of Wrath* and *Of Mice and Men* , but his "dog book" (*Travels with Charley*) was also well received. In 1976, I took a graduate-level course on Steinbeck (just me and the professor), read just about everything the author has ever written, and found *Travels with Charley* to be a strange departure from Steinbeck's usual polished writing style.

According to the book, Steinbeck and his dog go on a zigzag trip across America; they visit with many people; and Steinbeck records not only the details of his trip but also his thoughts along the way. Steinbeck was disappointed that Americans were more interested in sports than they were in the Vietnam War – and other issues of the day. Although Steinbeck was a Democrat, he did not want to be regarded as supporting any political viewpoint. He did support the troops, however, and thought the U.S. soldiers were fighting a noble cause. (*Bloom's Biocritiques*, 2003.)

When my dog (Oscar) and I travel, we don't talk politics. It's a waste of time. Politics is just one person trying to convince another person that their opinions are better. Or so it seems. Oscar and I are not into that kind of thinking. We simply enjoy each other's company. And Oscar was ecstatic to be included in my travel plans last week – when I headed down to St. Paul MN to help my mom celebrate her 89th birthday.

Oscar likes to sit on the passenger seat, next to me, and look out the windshield. Every now and then he looks over at me, smiles, and licks me with gratitude. We listen to the radio together, eat junk food, and act like kids. And sometimes we just turn off the radio, get real quiet, and listen to the road noise.

During one of those quiet times, I looked over at him: "Oscar," I said, "how is it that you're always so happy?" We're about the same age – after correcting for dog years, that is – but he seems to be so much wiser than I am. He has learned to accept the circumstances of his life better than anyone I have ever known. That, I presume, is the secret to his happiness.

Shortly after writing *Travels with Charley*, Steinbeck began having a series of heart attacks and strokes. He died in 1968. He had a very successful career as an author, and continues to be held in the highest regard. His writing is usually about *the common man*, and he is best known for defending the poor and downtrodden. He sometimes grew tired of people and society, though, and needed to be alone to get grounded. And sometimes he just wanted to be with his dog – in order to get in touch with his feelings about life, about relationships, and about America.

Oscar and I feel the same way about things. It can be difficult to deal with people, for example, who always want "more of this and more of that." Great books point out that the simple things are the most important; they warn that distorted values will destroy our soul, destroy relationships, and jeopardize the very roots of our society. Oscar has taught me that acceptance and love are more important than politics and materialism.

Peas & Pearls

(5/9/2007)

From riding around town, it is apparent that many homeowners are getting outside and working on their yards. Good for you! There's just something about working on your home and yard that Americans have always enjoyed. According to Wikipedia.com, about 70% of people in the United States live in their own home. We have the world's highest rate of home ownership. Despite some headaches associated with being a homeowner, we usually regard working on our homes as a labor of love.

While there are established guidelines on many landscaping topics (optimal lawn mowing technique, how to grow tomatoes, common plant diseases, how to pick shrubs that grow well in this zone, etcetera), there's also a lot of wisdom in what "regular people" have to say on these subjects. "People doctors" need to know what patients are feeling in order to know what treatment to prescribe. In the same way, "Dr. Dirt" wants to know if you have any pearls of wisdom on growing peas and other topics.

I have heard some good gardening advice in my lifetime. My dad told me that one man's weed is another man's flower. If you regard your Hosta as a nuisance, for example, maybe someone else can use them as ground cover in their troublesome shady areas. My English teacher taught me that no matter how hard you try, you're never gonna get rid of all your weeds – and she wasn't referring to vegetation. Two famous local gardeners have also spoken out on the subject. In order to have an efficient garden, Joe Halvorsen says that spacing is as important as timing. And Santos Carranza says the best way to have a happy garden is to "just do whatever your wife wants." All of you, I suspect, have similar "words of wisdom." Please call or email "Dr. Dirt" with your comments.

Get the Brown Out

(5/23/2007)

Some people think landscaping is a boring subject. Even the colors seem banal. Greens and browns, browns and greens. Yes, it's true: dirt is brown and plants are green. A green pigment, chlorophyll, is part of the plant's biochemical machinery that converts sunlight into food – so green is good. Brown is a good color for dirt – but not a good color for your plants. When the hospital nurses yell "Code Brown," however, they are talking about smell, not color – but that's another subject … This article is about ways "to get the brown out" of your plants, which is something people ask me about every day.

A lot of times the brown represents inappropriate trimming. Overgrown evergreens and shrubs will have brown on the inside because sunlight can't get to these areas. A good friend of mine recently spent $60 on chemicals to treat his brown evergreens – when he really just needed a three-year plan to prune his overgrown evergreens.

I see brown arborvitae evergreens all the time. My research says that the number one cause of arborvitae browning is inadequate watering. Excess watering also causes browning, however. Watering should leave the soil moist. Stagnant water implies clay soil that doesn't allow drainage. Winter kill, the drying effect of wind, acidic dog urine, road salt, fungal disease, and iron deficiency are other causes of browning in arborvitae. While browning can occur in other varieties of evergreens (juniper, spruce, pine, etcetera) as well, it seems like arborvitae are more susceptible to this problem than other evergreens. Newer cultivars of arborvitae are reportedly less likely to have this problem.

In the forests, arborvitae can grow very tall, and are referred to as White Cedars. For landscaping purposes, arborvitaes are pyramidal or global in shape. Despite what you may have heard, it is important to keep these trees trimmed to a manageable size. Once established, arborvitaes are quite hardy. They are an inexpensive and popular landscaping choice. If you look, you'll notice that almost every homeowner has a few arborvitaes in their yard.

Many mugho pines around town have an aphid infestation called "Pine Scale Disease." Other evergreens and shade trees can have a similar problem. Disease is another cause of evergreen browning. A Bayer product, available at Johnson's (formerly Danielson's) Hardware Store, can treat this problem; but the treatment takes time and is expensive. Show Ben Larson, County Extension Agent, a branch of your tree for advice on this problem.

Another way to "get the brown out" of your landscaping is to buy plants that have some color variety. Teri Kraft, co-owner of the Garden Center, recommends Dwarf Sand Cherry, Diablo Ninebark, and various Spirea species as hardy varieties that will add color to your yard. Visit Teri or her staff at their location across from the Moose Lodge in downtown Sidney. They have a large stock of healthy trees, shrubs, evergreens, and flowers to choose from.

Love of Yard

(5/30/2007)

Everybody wants the world to be a happier and healthier place. I have an outrageous statement to make in this regard: if people have love for, and take care of, *their own yard* – then the world would be a better place.

There are many forms of love, as C.S. Lewis so eloquently discusses in his book, *The Four Loves*. (I will paraphrase him throughout this article.) The "love of yard" I speak of is a feeling somewhere between patriotism and affection. A healthy love for your yard does not mean you want your neighbor's yard to face hardship, despite what some "political animals" claim. And you shouldn't love children "only if they're good." Likewise, you should love your yard (and your neighbor's) even if it isn't the fairest on the block. It's not competition. I love my yard (neighborhood, city, state, church, and country) even if it has a few blemishes.

Love of yard is certainly different than romantic love. In all honesty, I love my dog more than my lawn – that's why I put up with the bare spots he leaves all over the place. And if a person ever mistreats an animal, then I don't trust them to treat their fellow man in a civil manner. Affection for animals is a good thing. Nursing Homes have discovered that having pets around makes for happier and healthier living. In the same way, affection and care for your yard is not only good exercise, but leads to peace of mind.

Love will make you want to do the right thing for your home and yard. But don't get upset if your petunias don't look as nice in your flower garden as they do in the greenhouse. Don't let "curb appeal" become your god – otherwise it becomes a demon. The "love of yard" I speak of is not supposed to be that intense. Don't fight any *Holy Wars* if your neighborhood doesn't look the way you want it to. Learn from nature and adapt to things they way they are.

I hope you and your loved ones have had a peaceful Memorial Day weekend. We should all be grateful for the sacrifices that have been made for us and our country. Working in the yard is often part of the holiday routine. Try to enjoy this activity … Who knows? Maybe if we love our yard (and neighborhood) then the world will be a better place to live in.

Dog Spots

(4/28/2009)

It's pretty easy to identify who has a dog these days. Their lawns, like mine, look like a pepperoni pizza. They have a variety of brown and dark green spots on them. This is from "deposits" of urine and feces your dog has left in your yard over the course of the long winter. Experts say these spots are due to the Nitrogen in a dog's waste products.

Nitrogen is what you get when dietary protein is processed by the liver and excreted in the urine and stool. Nitrogen is usually regarded as a good thing, but if it is deposited in excess amounts it will kill grass. If only my dog would pee "a little bit here, and a little bit there" then I would get a "fertilizer effect" from his droppings. Nitrogen, in fact, is the major ingredient of lawn fertilizer.

Female dogs (and lazy male dogs, like mine) dump all their urine in one spot, which causes the grass to die. Sometimes these spots are brown in the middle and super-green on the outside, where the nitrogen concentration is lower, and even beneficial.

Most homeowners don't want grass with scattered brown and dark green spots. So what can you do about this problem? If you are super compulsive, you can follow your dog around (when he goes out to pee) and water down areas where he has urinated. Solid deposits release their chemicals more slowly, but should be picked up in a timely manner – especially if they are made in public parks or someone else's property (like my boulevard).

Dog spots, and other bare spots, give you an opportunity to practice your landscaping skills. You should rake out the dead grass, apply a grass seed mixture, and then cover the seed with a thin layer of soil or straw. I have read (in "plant answers. tamu. edu") that fescue and ryegrass are less likely to develop dog spots than Kentucky bluegrass. If the bare spots are more extensive, you might even want to sod the areas. And to keep the problem from repeating itself (as it does every year in our yard) you should try to get your dog to use specific "dog dumping" areas.

Grass seed is appropriate for small lawn repair projects, but sod, in my opinion, is better if you need ground cover of larger areas. The "up front" costs of seed and sod (a dime versus a quarter per square foot) doesn't tell the whole story. Sod is quicker, thicker, and weed-free. Regardless of what you choose, you will need to prepare the site and then plan on doing 3 weeks of intensive watering. If you have parts of your yard that get a lot of foot traffic or lack sunlight, then consider using an alternative ground cover – such as a rock or bark garden.

Dog spots are just one of the yard problems that you will face time and time again. If you love your dog, like I do, then you'll put up with them. Life has a lot of issues like that. If you can calmly handle the "dog spot" issues in your life, then you can deal with any problem you might encounter

Dog Yard, 2009

Dog Yard, 2010

The Long Goodbye

(9/25/2007)

The American elm (*Ulmus americana*) tree once stood as a graceful sentinel on almost every street and town square across our nation. The trees were easy to plant, grew rapidly, gave restful shade, and provided a beautiful boulevard canopy for many of our streets. I am sad to pronounce that this era is coming to an end. Dutch Elm Disease (DED) was accidentally brought to America in lumber received from the Netherlands in 1928. The disease rapidly spread from Ohio to eventually reach every metropolitan area in the country. Remote and isolated areas, like eastern Montana, were once spared; but now DED is spreading like a cancer through every neighborhood in town. The "Great American Elm Tree Story" has now become "The Long Goodbye."

DED is caused by a fungus (ascomycete microfungi infection) that has already destroyed over 99% of the elms in Great Britain, and threatens to do the same to our treasured American elms. The fungus is carried from tree to tree by elm bark beetles. The beetle burrows under the bark of elm trees to feed and find winter shelter. While the beetles feed, fungus (from the beetle's intestinal tract) is deposited, spreads through the tree's food- and water-conducting system, and eventually reaches the main trunk and roots. The disease causes blockage of "the blood supply" of the tree, causing death of extremities (similar to gangrene), and eventual death of the entire tree. To compound the problem, it may take 2 years of infection for a tree to show any signs of DED; and, by this time, the diseased tree might already be infecting an adjacent tree. Elms have been planted too closely together, their root systems have fused, and infection can be spread "by root graft." The disease can also be spread by storage of diseased elm firewood, use of contaminated chainsaws, and even by careless attempts to control DED.

Sidney, Montana, could once boast that it had avoided the ravages of this disease. Mayor Bret Smelser, who has been actively trying to help the city's trees for the last 15 years, was head of the "Tree Board" in the early 1990's; and helped develop the city's plan to deal with DED. Experience from other parts of the county showed that it was extremely important to have diseased trees cut down promptly and disposed of properly. Unfortunately, nobody seems to want the job of marking bad trees – they're not likely to win any popularity contests. And the city ordinance for removal of bad trees has not been enforced as vigorously as it should. Bad trees need to be removed! Leaving DED-infected trees in your neighborhood causes the spread of this awful disease.

Burton Barnes, University of Michigan Forestry Professor, said: "We have reduced the [longevity] of elms in nature from 200 years old to 30 years." Although elms seed prolifically and young elms spring up each year, DED prevents them from growing to maturity. We have already lost over 100 million American elms to DED, over 50% of our elm population, and it continues to kill over one million elms per year. The elm bark beetle, the carrier of this disease, is just one of many pests that have been accidentally brought to the US. In the early 20th century, Asian Chestnut Blight, another fungal infection, killed 3.5 billion American chestnut (*Castanea dentata*) trees, making these historic trees an endangered species. Another dangerous pest is the Emerald Ash Borer, first reported in 2002, which has already killed 20 million ash trees.

"We haven't learned our lesson very well — the lesson of invasive species," Professor Barnes said. "It's repeated over and over again."

Many people have sighed and given up on our fading American elm population. Not so John Hansel, who grew up in picturesque New Hampshire. He was sickened by what happened to the elm trees in his hometown. Before World War 2, his street had many beautiful elm trees; after he returned from the war, it was barren. He vowed to do something about the problem. Hansel launched a personal crusade against DED. In 1967, his 500-member organization renamed itself the Elm Research Institute (ERI). This is a non-profit organization that collects public grants and private donations in order to research DED. Their work led to the development of a preventive antifungal injection for American elms and the introduction of several DED-resistant elm varieties.

I too have been sickened by the ravages of DED. My wife and I were pleased to find a healthy stand of American elm trees in Central (now Memorial) Park on my job tour here in 1985. As we were lying down in the park, looking up at the trees, we decided to make Sidney our home. I thought Sidney's remote location would protect its elm trees. I was wrong.

In 1994, I became involved in Sidney's effort to do something about DED. Mayor Smelser, Fred Barkley, Chip Gifford, and I were the members of the city's first "Tree Board." We wanted to come up with a DED plan, institute a planting campaign (of trees resistant to DED), and get Sidney designated as a "Tree City." Part of the DED campaign was to inject important elm trees with the Elm Fungicide that was being used in other parts of the country. Fred Barkley, the county agent, worked out the details of this technique, and several entities (the city, the school system, Lonsdale church, and several interested citizens) started a local "Conscientious Injector" campaign.

The chemical that has been injected into many local American Elm trees is called "Lignasan" or, more descriptively, "Elm Fungicide." It is used to prevent the development of DED. The protocol for using this chemical was developed in 1975. The goal is to inject at-risk trees before they have significant disease (preferably less than 5% of DED signs). Elm Fungicide is environmentally safe. Holes are drilled (with a 5/16" bit) every 6 inches around the base of the tree; then 17 gallons of solution (1 gallon chemical and 16 gallons water) is injected under pressure, using an air compressor at 10–30 psi. Less solution is used for smaller trees. When the injection is done, the holes are plugged with grafting wax, and will heal without difficulty. This technique has been used annually on some trees for over 20 years with no visible damage. No trees have been lost to rot, but millions of untreated trees have been lost to DED. Since the 1975 EPA approval of Lignasan, over 100,000 American elms have been injected, with reported success rates of over 90%. This compares with losses of over 50% in untreated trees during the same period. A newer preventive fungicide, Arbotect, is said to be more effective. Lignasan has to be injected every year, while Arbotect may be used every 2-3 years. Once a tree has significant disease, however, nothing works. Injections are not used unless these trees have "great symbolic value" – in which case the diseased tree's lifespan may be prolonged for 5-10 years.

Under the county agent's tutelage, I started injecting trees in 1994. I formed "Kessler Landscaping" in 1994 in order to provide this service. The goal of my business was to inject as many elm trees as possible. During the next 3 years, my helpers and I injected 700 trees. Back then we charged $26 per tree. (This compared to a $90 fee that an out-of-town nursery was charging.) After consistently losing money on this venture, I closed down my tree injecting enterprise. By the end of the 1996 season, I was pleased to have injected many of the trees that I considered the most valuable: the trees at Central (Memorial) Park, Quilling's Park, Water Tower Park, Nutter Park, and the 4th St SE neighborhood. Many of these trees were injected 2–3 times. At risk trees need ongoing treatment, however.

For our efforts, Fred Barkley and I received 1995 "Outstanding Volunteer" awards from the Montana Community Forestry Program. In 2006, Sidney received one of two state community forestry awards. To date, the city has given away 1400 trees (of 20 different DED-resistant varieties) that have been planted at various locations around town.

After I retired from medicine (in 2005), I resurrected my landscaping business. Realizing there was a need for it, I resumed my elm injection business. My charge has been $40 per tree. My helpers and I have now injected a total of 850 trees. Despite everyone's efforts, some of the most valuable elm trees in town (for example, Central Park) appear to be on an irreversible downhill course from DED.

Elm tree injections require special equipment, training, attention to sterile technique, and a lot of time. It can take up to 8 hours to inject a single tree. The best time to inject is in the spring, but as long as the tree takes the chemical, it is useful. These injections are tedious but useful. With so few weapons in our arsenal against DED, I think we should inject American elms that have special value – at least until alternative trees have a chance to mature. The biggest problem of these injections is expecting them to work on trees that already have significant disease. The fungicide does not work on trees infected by root graft, which is always a more severe and rapidly progressive disease.

People who work with elms need to be aware of contamination problems. Injection equipment needs to be flushed and sterilized between each treatment. In a similar way, chainsaws (and other tools) should be sterilized with a 10% solution of household bleach or gas-line antifreeze (methanol) between each tree cutting. Avoid routine pruning of elm trees from April through August. And we are not allowed to keep elm firewood within the city limits – unless it has been debarked. If we are not compulsive about following these guidelines, we can aggravate the spread of DED throughout our city.

Insecticides can be used to inhibit the elm bark beetles (the disease vector) from lodging in the elm's bark. When I can get it, I have sprayed Dursban ™ on the trunks of elm trees. This should be early each fall. Regina, Saskatchewan, sprays 20,000 of their city trees with Dursban ™ each year. Digging a 5 foot deep trench around trees (to wall off a bad tree or protect a good tree) is another intervention, but this has rarely been done in Sidney.

Since many people have complained about the availability and cost of fungicide, Mayor Smelser has directed the City Parks Department to procure this chemical, and provides it "at no charge" to anyone who wants to inject elms. I used the city's chemical to inject 66 trees this summer. Let the Mayor and City Council know if you want them to continue or expand this program.

Many people say we can't cure DED – so why bother? I respond in this way: as a doctor, I knew we didn't have a "cure" for diabetes, but treated people so that they could live another 30 years, or so. My goal with elm trees is the same. At the very least, I don't want my elms to die a premature death.

An early sign of DED is yellowing of the upper leaves of an infected elm, especially if it's June through August, and is called "flagging." If this is less than 5% of the crown, there is hope … The diseased part of the tree should be pruned 5-10 feet below the yellowing, and the tree should be treated with systemic fungicide. Once you notice "flagging" in your elm tree, it is important to act fast! Notify your county agent and local arborist. Even with treatment, there is no guarantee that an infected tree can be saved – but surely it will die if you do nothing.

Homeowners never want to see their beloved trees cut down, and resent having to pay for these unanticipated expenses. The cost is greater if you allow other trees to get infected, and if you add in the cost of a city fees for not attending to the matter. The cost for cutting down an individual tree removed depends on the size of the tree and its proximity to other structures. When a homeowner receives a notice that he has a DED-infected tree, he has 14 days to remove the bad tree. If the tree isn't removed, the city is supposed to cut it down – and puts the bill on your property taxes.

In the late 1990's, Sidney was proudly able to say they had not lost "that many trees" to DED. That compared to over 2 thousand trees lost in Glendive. But that was then, and this is now. Nobody seems to know exactly how many elms have been lost locally to DED. Mayor Smelser thinks 1200 bad elms have already been cut down. Gale Pust, owner-operator of Valley Tree Service (488-8918), has cut 40 elms in 2007, and about 500 elms in the last 15 years. Pust cuts about 2/3rd of the bad elms in the area. Tip Top Tree Service (488-5555) is another tree cutting services in this area. With hundreds of DED-infected trees, both tree cutters will have a full workload for years to come.

Mayor Smelser has been actively promoting the planting of alternative trees. The city spends $2500 every year to purchase DED-resistant trees. Over 200 Liberty Elms have already been planted in the city parks and school areas. Other "safe" trees that the city has purchased include: Silver Maple, Honey Locust, Snow Crab, Hackberry, Burr Oak, Red Leaf White Birch, Blue Spruce, and Hackberry. These trees are given away to anyone who wants to plant them.

At one time, ash trees were also recommended – but now a terrible disease is killing those trees by the millions. This should be a lesson to all of us: We should not plant too many of one species, and should not plant the same type of tree too closely to other trees of the same species. Variety is truly the spice of life. Unfortunately, it will take many years to replace our American elm trees. Long-time Sidney resident, Earl Neff, summarized the situation this way: "We don't plant trees for ourselves; we plant them for the next generation to enjoy."

It's obvious that we're losing the battle with DED. It has truly been "The Long Goodbye" to our American elms. I don't like to give up without a fight, however. I want our remaining elms to last as long as they can. I also strongly support a planting program with alternative tree varieties. I would like our fine city to do everything it can to preserve its tree heritage.

Good Dirt

(6/6/2007)

Planting season is fast coming to an end. Farmers, who grow things for a living, put in their crop many weeks ago. Landscaping isn't life and death, so we amateur growers have a bit more leeway – but better be making our final selections if we want to have a successful growing season.

Success and failure is, of course, relative to what your goals are. If you don't care that much about the outcome, then don't worry about it. "Less than ideal" outcomes occur often enough, however, that we should try to learn from these. Rex Niles, a local farmer, reminds me that planting results are "only as good as Mother Nature allows, so accept things you can't control, and try to improve the things you can."

It's interesting how often things can be broken into three categories. There are three branches of government. Church people value Faith, Hope, and Charity. And landscapers need only three things for success: Sunlight, Water, and Soil.

Sunlight is obviously important. Some people make inappropriate plant selections. We live in zone 3, so if you buy something meant for zone 8, it will suffer winter kill. And some plants want full sun, while others tolerate shade.

Water is the next essential. Since we live in a semiarid region, don't expect green vegetation without some watering. A summary of techniques, called Xeriscaping (pronounced zera-scaping), has been developed that seek to use water resources efficiently. For example, choose plants that are drought resistant – like juniper, spirea, viburnum, daylily, sumac, and ash trees. Unless you're willing to water every day, you should avoid azaleas, hydrangeas, and most annuals. Consider converting some areas of your yard to water-free rock gardens. Aerate your lawn regularly, avoid cutting your grass too short, and don't use excessive amounts of fertilizer. You'll need more frequent watering if there is rapid run-off (from sandy soil or slopes) and less when there is poor drainage (from clay soil). Giving your lawn a good soaking twice weekly promotes healthier roots than if you water every day, and can lower your water bill by up to 50%.

"Poor dirt" is what I personally find to be the most frequent cause of plant failure. (Being "dirt poor" is another matter.) I believe we should regard "good dirt" as one of our most precious commodities. Although dirt is theoretically a renewable resource, it takes so long to make that the world has a topsoil deficiency. That's why no-till farming and other forms of erosion control are so important.

Topsoil is the approximately 6 inch layer of soil above the hardpan. It is darker in color than the other layers due to the presence of humus, or decayed organic matter. This is the "living" part of the soil, and is inhabited by bacteria, fungi, and earthworms. Plants generally concentrate their roots here, and obtain most of their nutrients from this layer. Below the topsoil is mineral-rich subsoil, and below this is partially weathered bedrock, which will eventually develop into subsoil. Topsoil quality varies from one location to another. It's incredible to realize that the world is already farming one-third of the Earth's land area, and almost all of the land worth or available for planting is already in farm usage.

In order to improve the quality of the dirt where your new tree, shrub, or evergreen will live, make sure you dig a hole that is 2-3 times larger than it needs to be. Loosened dirt around the new plant, without air pockets, will help it grow. Uniformly mix aged manure or quality topsoil with the native dirt, especially if the dirt is poor quality. The plant should be put in the hole at the proper level, neither too deep nor too shallow. If you are going to use weed barrier, use a breathable landscape fabric rather than suffocating plastic. A 2-inch top layer of compost or hardwood chips may be added around the plant (above the weed barrier, if present) to help retain moisture, and decrease watering requirements.

That's all there is to it! Count to three - Sun, Water, Dirt – and you'll have a healthy transplant before you know it.

Laying Sod, 2006

The Plant Psychologist

(ca. 1974)

"Chirp," said the bird.

"Tweet," said another.

"Brrring!" said the alarm clock.

"It's time to get up," said the woman to her husband. "You can't be late again. You'll jeopardize that precious job of yours."

The man, David Randon, hates getting up in the morning. He especially hates how his wife, Verna, reminds him every day that he has to get up. David is occasionally late for work, though. And he does love his job, so his procrastination is not avoidance behavior. He just has trouble getting up, and needs a few cups of coffee in the morning before he can carry on a conversation.

David Randon works at the University, and is highly regarded for the work he does there. He is reverently referred to as "Professor Randon, the best plant psychologist in the Upper Midwest." His pioneering research showed that plants are capable of complex emotional behavior. If you are nice to your plants, they grow better, produce more fruit, and will reciprocate positive (as well as negative) feelings to their care givers. Although his research findings have never been replicated, his book, *How to Get Along with Your Plants*, is a best-seller. The book has a flashy cover, promises that you too can get these results, and shows a picture of Professor Randon at his desk, quill pen in hand, with his famous quotation:

"Your houseplant can truly be your best friend."

Randon is an enthusiastic spokesman for plant psychology. "Plants have feelings," he proclaims; "but best of all – they only express their feelings in quiet ways, like when they drop a leaf out of season." Professor Randon really does love plants. He isn't too fond of people, though.

"What are you going to lecture about today?" asks Verna of her illustrious husband.

"Oh, you know how these kids are – they're interested in just about every aspect of plant psychology," he replies. "What are you going to talk about?"

The question is directed to Verna Random, who is an Associate Professor at the same University. She is also renowned in her field. At a recent symposium, she presented a paper stating the "houseplant and housewife" duo should be regarded as a holistic single unit. Her research shows that, approaching them in this manner, they will have a more fruitful relationship.

David and Verna live in a modest stucco rambler. There is a carved oak sign out front that proudly states this to be "Randon Manor." They don't have any children or pets. They have lots of plants, both inside and out, and their yard is one of the nicest in town. They both talk to their plants. They aren't crazy – just eccentric. They are fashionably agnostic, of course; but they do strongly believe in the tenets of their scientific field.

On a recent day off, David walked around his yard, admiring his plants, and gave them each a few words of encouragement. "Good morning, Mr. Mockorange," David says to one of his favorite bushes. "I want you to be the first to bloom this year," he said hopefully. But the bush doesn't look that healthy. Encouragement, figures David, overcomes many shortcomings. The elm tree doesn't look good either. David can't even look Mr. Elm in the eye, because it's dying, and he doesn't know what to say. The rhododendron was looking great, though; and this brought a smile to David's face.

"Oh, Rhoda," he said gaily, "do you know how happy you make me?"

But David's plant conversation is interrupted by a surly teenager, the paper boy, who points to the "Randon Manor" sign, and says: "You must be Mr. Manor. I'm collecting for the paper, and you're two months overdue."

"Randon is my name," says David.

"My name's Jim," says the young man, as he sticks out his dirty right hand – in a gesture of friendship.

"And my name's David," says Manor.

"Then my name's Goliath," says the boy, sarcastically. "Look, Mister, I don't care how many names you've got – I just want to be paid."

The boy looks the Professor in the eye. One is a boy, and the other is a man – but, in many ways, their roles are reversed. The man is awkward in many social settings; while the boy gets right to the point, and has an unshakeable command of the situation. "Another weirdo," the boy privately concludes.

Randon gave the boy some money. He doesn't know if it is the right amount or not. And then he goes back to talking with his plants.

"Oh, Celia," he says to his sensitivity plant, "at least you appreciate me." But Randon's breath irritates the plant, so it recoils away from him.

"Et tu, Celia?" Randon asks. Just then, a branch, from the dying elm tree, falls near Randon's feet. He startles, turns to look, and then steps on a barberry thorn. Another blow, he thinks to himself. He tries to run, trips on a suddenly appearing vine, and goes sprawling face-first to the ground. He rolls over, looks up at the sky, and examines the dying elm tree above him. The wind is blowing, and the branches look like black tentacles in the gray sky.

"My friends," he says aloud, "don't you like me anymore?"

His answer comes quickly. A gust of wind breaks off a dead limb above him, and the branch shoots down like an arrow into Randon's soft abdominal wall. The pain is excruciating. After one long yell, Randon tries to suck in a breath of air, but instead of air he gets a mouthful of leaves. He is unable to speak. He is unable to breathe. He dies a silent but painful death in his own front yard – surrounded by all his favorite plants. His plant friends, it seems, have had enough. They are sick and tired of hearing his "expert" opinions about what makes them tick.

Section 3:
Psychobabble

Eat Quiche

(12/18/2007)

When I was a boy, nobody talked about "sensitivity" like they do now. We heard that girls were made of "sugar and spice, and everything nice," and boys were made of "frogs and snails, and puppy-dogs' tails." With that in mind, it was okay for girls to be "mushy," but "sensitive" was the last thing a guy ever wanted to be.

Oh how things have changed! Now guys are not only encouraged to be sensitive – but it's also okay for them to admit that they don't know anything about cars, and to say they even like to read books. They still have to pretend to like football – even if they don't – which is a final vestige of what masculinity used to be about.

For years I had to hide the fact that I never learned how to throw a football. When I played catch I would lateral or punt the ball back to the one I was playing with. I also hid the fact that I knew how to play hopscotch – and even enjoyed it. That's what happens when you have six sisters, though. You get corrupted into doing "girly" things.

The Women's Liberation Movement (of the 1970s) gave women the freedom to do whatever their heart desired; it also liberated men from traditional masculine gender identities. Men no longer had to "love" sports. They could read books – if they so desired. And they could pursue careers that were once reserved for women – like nursing, for example.

Men realized that they can learn a lot from women. For one thing, women can chat about anything. We're deficient in this regard, but many men are now trying to be more conversant. In the right setting, men can even learn to talk about *feelings* as glibly as they talk about *football*. We don't have to be "tough guys" anymore. Chauvinism, it seems, is dead. Joke about it if you will, but "being sensitive" is in …

Bruce Feirstein jokes about this issue. In his 1982 book, *Real Men Don't Eat Quiche*, Feirstein talks about the reversal of society's gender expectations. His book was on the New York Times Best Seller list for 53 weeks, and sold over 1.6 million copies. It was a tongue-in-cheek look at our stereotypes about masculinity. He described a *quiche-eater* as a man who is effeminate or who lacked some traditional masculine feature. As the title indicates, there are some things that real men just don't do. As you'd expect, poking fun at this concept helped liberate men, and allowed them to be less chauvinistic.

Now we're at the opposite end of the spectrum. If you don't cry at weddings, for example, then you are criticized for being "insensitive." And

65

if you don't cry at funerals, you are regarded as "inhumane," and could be forced to get sensitivity training. It's now realized that *sensitivity* is an essential ingredient of being a normal human being. If you haven't learned *the sensitivity thing*, then someone in your life (your wife, boss, or local judge) may require that you get remedial training on the subject – available through Alcoholics Anonymous, church retreats, and related movements.

I'm okay with the idea of being *less masculine* than I used to be. I'm even willing to admit that I don't know anything about auto mechanics. I enjoy reading, and I've even started to enjoy eating quiche. But it's definitely an acquired taste. As a child I hated foods like this, but now I like them. And I'm not the only person who is that way. Things you'd never consider as a child are worth a second look as an adult. Being *tough* was okay when you were young. As you become a man, though, it's better to be sensitive.

For Men Only

(from CLM, 2005)

Have you ever wondered why women are the way they are? Despite what feminists say, there are very significant differences between men and women. These differences start either in the womb or in the Garden of Eden, depending on your religious persuasion, and the result is that the opposite sexes have – duh, *opposite* ways of interacting with the world. Sure there are little girls that are good at math, and there are even little boys who like to play with dolls, but these are the exceptions. Have you known any women that could have played on your high school football team? I suspect you have. Some women are strong as oxen. And some women can cuss like sailors. There are also men who are indisputably *pretty*. I know you don't want to admit it, but some men are prettier than any of the women you've ever gone out with. But I'm not talking about cross- dressing, homosexuality androgyny, or embryology here. I'm talking about middle-America *Mom and Pop* people. Men and women use a toilet in different ways, so too their psychosocial differences are significant.

Gender, genetic, and environmental variation make this world an interesting place. Women are different from men: not in all things, of course, but often enough to make this important in our day to day lives. Can we, as men, put this information to good use? I hope so; otherwise I wouldn't bother to write this. We need to know something about the opposite sex. I'm not a woman, so many would dismiss my opinions as invalid. But who else can you ask? A woman certainly isn't going to divulge her secrets, if she is even aware of them. Besides, I've been around women all my life: my mother is a woman; I have six sisters; I've been married for 27 years; and I've worked around women all my life. I am, for all intents and purposes, an *expert* on women – from a man's perspective, that is.

The experts say men think about sex *way* more often than women do. We could debate this point, and other known facts of anatomy and physiology, but I would rather not argue about scientific facts … Besides that, you probably learned everything you need to know about sex in middle school. Were you paying attention? Remember when all the girls were taller than you? They weren't just trying to embarrass you. Your female classmates were acquiring breasts, pubic hair, and child-rearing capacity. It might have taken you several years to notice, but they were becoming women. You were, of course, worried about with your acne, social inadequacies, and body odor. They were interested in relationships. They wanted to go out on dates. Chances are that you "didn't understand" what was going on, so most of your female classmates dated older guys.

Of course you didn't know what was going on! You were – and probably still are – just your average dumb guy! *Take it easy, buddy.* I'm on your side. We're all dumb guys, to some extent. For some of us, it's been all down hill since puberty. We just get dumber and dumber, relatively speaking, to the women in our lives. Those of you with daughters already know this fact. For those of you that are married, your wives may be hiding this information from you. Why else, do you suppose, did they marry an older guy – *I'm talking about you!* – have you buy life insurance, and want to go out to eat all the time? Did your wife ever ask you to work out at the gym? Wake up and smell the coffee. She isn't really "the weaker sex." Among other things, she is going to outlive you. Why do you think she collects all those travel brochures?

It is possible to wise up to these realities of life. You can live out the remaining years of your life in ignorant bliss, if that's what it is; or you can learn what it takes to co-exist with the women in your life. You might be dumb but you're not stupid, you know. Men consistently score better than women on college entrance exams. (Be careful, though; *someone* is changing the format of these tests so that women can outperform men.) Men are better at analyzing things. Men aren't as easily distracted as women are. Men are physically stronger than women. But all this doesn't matter if we don't recognize areas of life where women are more gifted than us: they integrate facts and feelings better; they get along better with others; and they have a secret power – it's called intuition. They don't care how a telephone works. All they care about is whether or not they can call their sister. They don't need to have a goal for all of their activities. They can carry on a conversation just for the fun of it. Keep this in mind the next time your wife wants to converse. Don't focus on what's being said – just pretend to listen, nod in agreement, and occasionally say: "Yes, dear."

Visiting with others without a need to manipulate or control is *sociable*. Women are definitely better than men in this regard. You're not a sissy if you master this art. In a similar way, brushing your teeth, combing your hair, applying deodorant, and using cologne once in a while won't kill you – and might make it easier for you to mingle. I don't always do these things. And smelling bad really isn't cool. When people turn up their nose to me, they are (I presume) just trying to preserve their olfactory nerve. And most people instinctively avoid other people and situations that don't smell right. Likewise, walking away from someone who isn't acting civilized is a matter of survival. If we want to do well in this civilized world, then we men should all try to smell good and act civilized.

Saying please and thank you is useful. Grunting your wants and needs might have worked in caveman days, but is positively anachronistic nowadays. Knowledge of the English language is also useful. And call people by their name. Dale Carnegie, in his book *How to Win Friends & Influence People*, says a person's name is "music to their ears." How do you feel if someone forgets your name? See what I mean? It doesn't win any friends if you call them by the wrong name, so at least pretend you remember in your forgetful moments. Knowing how to talk is one thing – but sometimes saying nothing is better than putting your foot in your mouth.

Women instinctively know these things. While prehistoric man was out hunting, his female counterpart was gathering crops, making coffee, and borrowing a cup of sugar from the neighbor. We may be good at killing things; but that ability doesn't help us in modern times. We have to unlearn our primitive aggressive tendencies. Women have lots of attributes that we men should emulate. Take the best of their world and integrate it into our world of watching football, golfing, and other activities that you certainly don't need to give up. As to the social graces, you can "fake it 'til you make it." You can pretend to be nice even if you aren't. We need to be interdependent with our neighbors if we want to get that cup of sugar, piece of pie, invitation to dinner, and fellowship of friends – things the female of our species have known for centuries.

Harold Emly Hunting With Kesslers, 2009

Communication

(1/29/2008)

I suspect married couples, even if they love each other, have occasional disagreements. Husbands might be spending too much time at the country club. And when they're home, they don't talk – so they might as well be gone. A wife might be spending too much time and money at the shopping mall. She's nicer to her girlfriends than she is to her husband. She complains about him. He complains about her. He calls her a nag. When tempers settle down, conversations like this occur:

"I'm sorry I called you a nag," he says to her.

"I'm sorry I complained about you," she says.

In order to cast some light on hypothetical problems like this, I dragged out my 15 year-old copy of *Men Are From Mars, Women Are From Venus*, by John Gray. Dr. Gray contrasts the communication patterns that men and women have. Scientific studies, he says, have found that women speak about six thousand words per day, while men speak about two thousand words per day. While women are adept at keeping conversations going, men often don't know what the conversation is even about.

As little girls women learn that talking is for entertainment as much as it is for gathering information. Women's conversations can jump from topics as diverse as the weather, new movies, recent tragedies, what Suzy wore to the office party, and why the dishwasher should be replaced. Husbands have trouble picking out the key points of these conversations – and are often accused of not listening.

Dr. Gray doesn't think women gossip. He says they converse a lot, though. He doesn't like to say wives nag. But they do have the bad habit of giving *unsolicited advice*. And men hate getting advice on things – even if they need it. Men try to *fix things*, even when their efforts do more harm than good. Women instinctively talk problems out. Men instinctively "go to their cave" if they are upset.

Many women have learned that the typical husband, after he has returned home from work, is not easy to talk with. In the husband's defense, the man has been slaying dragons all day, and isn't in the mood to talk. He needs to be by himself. He doesn't want to give a blow by blow account of how many widgets he sold, how many fires he fought, or what the boss said to the secretary at the water cooler.

Dr. Gray learned these things from questioning more than 25,000 participants (over a 7 year period) at his relationship seminars. Speaking metaphorically, he says men are from Mars. A long time ago they peered into their telescopes, and saw beautiful creatures living on the planet Venus. He's talking about women, of course. Man's passions were awakened. They invented space travel. They went on a mission to Venus. The Martians and Venusians fell in love. Back then, they loved their differences. When they moved to Earth, however, they argued about everything from "Who left the cap off the toothpaste?" to "Nobody helps me with the housework."

If they want things to improve, they need to communicate better. Martian man has to come out of his cave, converse a bit, help with the dishes, and take his wife to an occasional movie. He needs to listen to his wife without trying to fix her. And a Venusian woman needs to be nice to her husband. She should stop giving him unsolicited advice. Respect your man's desire to be competent. Don't give him advice on what road to take – even if you are lost. What's more important: getting there on time – or having a good relationship?

Scientific studies have shown that women use both sides of their brain when they walk into a room, meet people, and carry on conversations. They notice diverse things in the environment. They're good at integrating feelings and information. Men use smaller areas of their brain when talking, are more goal-oriented, and focus on whatever they're focusing on. Sometimes men miss the point. We're not really supposed to talk business at cocktail parties, you know. It's not interesting or sociable. It's impossible to say one perspective is better than the other. Men and women do seem to come from different planets. We're certainly different, and that's what makes life interesting.

Don't Call Me Momma

(5/11/2009)

Last year I wrote a Mother's Day article that drew more criticism than anything I've ever done. The article was based on the idea that my wife is "Not My Momma," and it's up to the kids – not me – to buy her gifts on Mother's Day. We actually did celebrate the occasion, but my wife and her friends found it repugnant that I would joke about such a thing. To make amends, I hereby make this public apology; and will now restate my position on this delicate matter:

***

I met a cute girl
with kisses like jelly
She turned out to be
My future wife Shelley

Of course we married
Wanted kids someday
But they did not come
Until we did pray

Then came the babies
Boy 1, Boy 2, then 3
And now we are 5
Mom, 3 sons, and me

They're taller than Mom
And smarter than Dad
So much like men
It's good, but also sad

We honor you now
For this is your day
Plant you some flowers
In the month of May

The boys know I'm Dad
And you're always Mom
But the boys and you
Get to dance at the Prom

You're not my Momma
As I've said before
And I thank the Lord
That you're not Al Gore

You're still my honey
With kisses like jelly
And I'm so glad
That you're my wife Shelley

***

This isn't much of a poem, but it's the best I've got. As much as I would like to be a poet, I realize it 'aint gonna happen … But I do thank my lucky stars that my sons have such a good mother. The Kessler Boys (father and sons) pray that your life continues to be blessed with happiness, good friends, and loving family.

Happy Mother's Day!

P.S. To the mothers in my audience, I hope that you have had a nice weekend. Being a mother is definitely the most important and most difficult job in our society. Being a mother also involves a serious commitment, but I suspect it is a labor of love. Sharing your child's precious baby smiles, tentative first steps, and childhood adventures no doubt exceeds "teenage rebellion" and other motherhood difficulties. Everyone has a mother, of course; and we all should have honored our mother this past weekend. If you missed the day, it's not too late to honor the person – whether it is through fond memories, kind words, or acts of kindness. There is no present, however, that a child can give that comes even close to what your mom has given to you.

Who's Your Daddy?

(6/24/2008)

Some of you celebrated Father's Day last weekend. In keeping with my desire to downplay these events, I told my family that I wanted to celebrate by staying home and barbecue hamburgers. Someone told my wife to say "you're not *my* poppa," and just ignore the event – but she would never do such a thing. Although she doesn't always agree with me, she does respect my role as father, and knows that the 4th Commandment says "Honor your mother *and* your father."

Since Father's Day is just another day, I did what I usually do: took out the garbage, washed the dishes, did some landscaping, and paid the bills. I also played baseball with my boys, which is something I used to do a lot. It's hard for me to play sports at my age, though. It is a "joyful pain" that I will someday miss. Playing and working with my boys has been some of the best times I've ever had.

Father's Day was officially declared a holiday in 1924, twelve years after Mother's Day received that recognition. Last year Americans spent $10 billion on Father's Day gifts, compared to $16 billion spent on Mother's Day. To illustrate, Americans spent $2.7 billion buying jewelry for Mother's Day presents. Since holiday gift-buying represents about 30% of jewelry stores' annual revenue, you can see why cheapskates like me need to support our economy by remembering these occasions.

While Father's Day is certainly not a *forgotten* holiday, it does seem to be less important than Mother's Day. Could it be that fathers are less important than mothers? Some people say that is the case. After all, a father's *donation* comes 9 months before the child is even born, and he doesn't *really need* to be present thereafter. Or does he? Compared to children with fathers, it has been reported that children from fatherless homes are 5 times more likely to be poor, 5 times more likely to commit suicide, 10 times more likely to develop chemical dependency, and 20 times more likely to end up in prison.

Adolescents in mother-only families are more likely to be sexually active, and girls from fatherless homes are three times as likely to be unwed teenage mothers. 90% of all homeless and runaway children are from fatherless homes. 71% of all high school dropouts come from fatherless homes. And boys from fatherless homes have a higher incidence of noninvolvement with their own children, so the cycle of *fatherlessness* can repeat itself.

Dr. James Dobson, from "Focus on the Family," writes extensively on the "fatherless home" problem. The statistics are not meant to denigrate or belittle mothers who are in a "single parent" situation. And many children from fatherless homes have been successful. Bill Clinton is one example. I myself, through the early death of my father, was rendered "fatherless" at the age of 14.

Half of all marriages now result in divorce. Remarriages and "unwed couple" living arrangements are common. Children are now being designated as "his, hers, and theirs." Identity problems are common. "Who's your *real* daddy?" certainly seems to be a common question in our society. No wonder "fatherhood" isn't held in high esteem. As "crappy fathers" are being blamed for many of the problems in our society, it is time to see what we can do to revive the vocation of fatherhood.

While "deadbeat dads" do deserve criticism, it is important to know that not all the financial, psychological, and spiritual problems in the world are the father's fault. That's using dad as the scapegoat. We must, as Aimee Colbert says (in her religious article, "God is not your father!") remember that our biologic father is a man before he is a dad. He's not perfect. He doesn't always say or do the right thing. Our earthly fathers should not be put on a pedestal – because they will surely fall short of our expectations.

Fathers need to "stick with" difficult family situations. They need to love their wife and help raise the kids – just like my dad did. He worked several jobs in order to put bread on the table. Even when he was tired (at the end of a long day) he would play catch with me. When Mom complained about money matters, Dad didn't say much in return. He knew he was doing the best that he could. Although he taught us all how to work – landscaping, janitorial work, etc – he also taught us there's more to being a good father than just making money.

Father's Day

(6/22/2009)

I didn't want to get out of bed on Sunday. I didn't want to spoil the mood. Surely my family would bring me breakfast in bed, I thought. It was *Father's Day*, after all; they wouldn't forget that!

My bladder couldn't take it anymore … I got out of bed, took care of business, and then went down to the kitchen. My wife was busy reading. The kids were still in bed. Coffee was on (thank God!) so I helped myself to a cup. But there was no fanfare, no drum roll, no crowd of well-wishers preparing to jump out and surprise me.

I dragged the kids out of bed, reminded them of church, and barely got them to the service on time. So what else is new … The priest reminded the congregation that it was Father's Day, so all the dads got some recognition; and afterwards we had a nice community meal.

To say that Father's Day *seems* less important than Mother's Day is an understatement. The Livemark ™ index, which tracks 150 internet shopping sites, notes that week-by-week shopping increases 16% in the seven days before Mother's Day, but drops by 3% in the week before Father's Day. The Hallmark company reports that 96% of Americans celebrate Mother's Days, while only 73% acknowledge Father's Day. And there are 150 million Mother's Day cards sent out, as compared to 102 million for Father's Day. This discrepancy *doesn't seem right* to me. Everybody, after all, has both a father and a mother – and both parents should be honored on their respective days.

According to Leigh Eric Schmidt, in his book *Consumer Rites: The Buying and Selling of American Holidays*, the very idea of having a holiday for fathers was once ridiculed. Many people thought the idea was a scam – just another way to support the greeting card industry. The recommendation to have a "Father's Day" was first proposed in 1908, was supported by Calvin Coolidge in 1924, and then was "studied" for many decades. It wasn't until 1966 that Father's Day became an official holiday – by proclamation of President Lyndon Johnson. Mother's Day, on the other hand, has been an official holiday since 1914.

Well, so much for "fun facts" about Father's Day … The Kessler family (minus one son) had an unpretentious meal together. Nobody wrote me any poems. I did get two cards, though. I also got a book, *Golf for Dummies*, from my sons. That's a book I need to read. I also spent the day doing *fatherly* duties: cleaning the gutters and painting the eaves on the house. I work on jobs like these when I'm not landscaping. Such is the life of a father: once his essential biologic contribution has been made, he trudges along, unnoticed and unrewarded, doing whatever he can to improve life for his family. Next year, though, I'm gonna drop a few hints … to see if I can get that Father's Day "breakfast in bed" I've been hoping for.

Father's Day, 2008

Changes

(8/29/2007)

The greatest temperature change in 24 hours occurred in Loma, Montana, on January 15, 1972. The temperature rose 103 degrees, from -54 F to +49 F. This is the world record for a 24 hour temperature change (as reported on the MontanaKids.com website.) I was a senior in high school back then, and suspect the weather in Minnesota was just as weird. In the last month, our local temperature seems to have changed almost as much. Our recent record highs are behind us. Now it feels like we need to prepare ourselves for another long winter.

The weather isn't the only thing that changes. In fact, the only thing in life that doesn't change is the inevitably of change itself. For most of us, the passage of time means a gradual process of losing things – our strength, bone density, memory, visual acuity, and so on, and so forth. It seems like the only thing we can look forward to is the inevitably of arthritis, cataracts, serious disease, and cognitive decline.

I'm having a hard time picturing myself as an octogenarian with an attitude. In my mind, I still see myself as a dashing young man, wearing bell bottoms or a leisure suit, and ready to conquer the world. Those old clothes still look good in my closet, but it's been years since I've been able to squeeze into them. My kids think I'm crazy when I tell them they were once in fashion. It's ego-deflating for me to realize that most young people just see me as a relic of the past.

I sent two of my sons off to college this past week. They think change is great. They are excited about college life, making new friends, and seeing what the world has to offer. Meanwhile, my wife and I are experiencing "Empty Nest Syndrome." I try to deal with my own sense of loss by reassuring myself that my boys are maturing into fine young men.

How are you coping with the changes in your life? I know you've had losses. I wish I had a few glib words of advice to help you through the painful changes you've had to endure. Chances are, in fact, that you've had at least as many good times as bad … Playing games as a kid, school days, your first car, falling in love, your wedding day, the birth of your children, watching them grow up, their marriages and having grandchild were no doubt "good things" in your life. It's important for us to remember these good times in order to balance out the not-so-good things that we've all had to endure.

Much has been written on the subject of change. In the 3rd chapter of Ecclesiastes (Bible, NIV) we are told that "there is a time for everything, and a season for every activity under heaven: a time to be born and a time to die ..." Just about everybody knows, and treasures, these words. Songwriters have expressed this subject in another way:

"And all the changes, keep on changing, and the good old days, they say they're gone. Only wise men, and some new born fools, say they know what's going on. But I sometimes think the difference is just in how I think and see; and the only changes going on – are going on in me." (by Harry Chapin in *Changes*)

Forgive me if I'm sounding melodramatic. Seeing my boys off to college has left me a little teary. Taking a nostalgic look at some of our photo albums, it seems like it was just a few days ago that they were born, a few hours ago that I was playing ball with them, and a few minutes ago that they graduated from high school. The second hand on my clock is ticking way too fast. If only I could slow it down. You know what I mean. Tick, tock. Tick, tock. And so on, and so forth.

Detours

(9/4/2007)

If you've done any traveling this summer, you have noticed a lot of highway construction. Perhaps you've had to take a detour or two. That's what happened to us when we took our kids to college last week. To compound the problem, I made a few wrong turns in the cities of their respective universities. Fending off criticism from my wife, I used J.R.R. Tolkien's words: "All those who wander are not lost, and all that's gold does not glitter." I love that quote, and use it often.

As I think about it, what would life be if we didn't occasionally get lost, and take a few detours? If my car hadn't broken down near Fargo, I might not have done my medical training there. If I didn't have to stop by the 4th floor at St. John's Hospital (in Fargo) I might not have met my future wife. If I hadn't gone to Williston ND for a medical rotation, I wouldn't have been interested in returning to this area to practice. After Williston made me a job offer, my wife and I took a side trip to Sidney – never realizing that we would, since 1985, be making this our home. If my workplace hadn't been mired down in politics, I might not have retired from Medicine, and then try my hand at writing. And so on, and so forth.

I'll bet you can think of a hundred "if-then" scenarios that have affected you and your family. Some are good, and some are bad. Scientists say these are random events in a world governed by the laws of chance. I think there are other forces at work. Some detours and coincidences seem like "minor miracles." Perhaps we are meant to get lost, stray off the main road, and have some unique experiences while finding our way back to a path we feel more comfortable with.

Dr. Scott Peck, in his best-selling book, *The Road Less Traveled*, says we need to directly face problems we encounter as an opportunity to learn and grow in maturity. And problems seem to occur at the worst possible time. Avoid procrastination. Take the time it takes to solve the problems we face. Detours (and other obstacles) force us to slow down, take a look around, see things as they are, and decide what our priorities are. Blaming others for our setbacks makes it more difficult to figure things out. Learn to become a safe and responsible driver. Using the road metaphor, it's better to get there late than to not get there at all.

The goal of a trip often has to be changed along the way. Once upon a time, for instance, I wanted to be the best doctor in the world: deliver babies from mountaintops, do life-saving operations, find a cure for cancer, and rescue heart patients from the jaws of death. I've had to modify my pipedreams. As a practicing physician, I had to be satisfied in knowing that I tried to get patients to avoid disease, diagnose problems at an early stage, and – once a problem developed – treat it appropriately. I didn't need to be the world's best doctor. I just wanted to do the next right thing.

But that was then, and this is now. When one door closes, another one opens. I've had to remember that these detours on the highway of life are inevitable. It's now time to slow down, enjoy the scenery, and make the best of things. And when you come to "a fork in the road," try to take the best possible alternative … then don't fret over your decision. In the words of Robert Frost: "Two roads diverged in a wood, and I took the one less traveled by, and that has made all the difference."

Good Person

(7/18/2007)

Are you a good person? Most of us think of ourselves as *good people*, but sometimes we think a little too highly of ourselves, and too little of our neighbor. You know what I mean. Liberals think Conservatives are morons, and vice versa. If only the other guy would do things my way, then the world would be a better place.

Thomas Aquinas, a 13th century theologian, said we all choose a life that *seems* to be good. Nobody really wants to be bad. In the simplest terms, if our behavior has been rewarded, then we are going to repeat that behavior. People with a healthy upbringing have been rewarded for doing the *right thing*. At first it took food, shelter, a hug, or some other positive consequence to reinforce a good action. Then the reward makes us want to do the good behavior again. And that, psychologists say, is how environment shapes personality.

Our genetic makeup also influences our personality. The age old question has been: What is more important – nature or nurture? If you are lucky enough to have *nice* parents, then chances are you are also nice. But can we really take credit for who we are? And isn't being good simply the result of good genes and good upbringing?

Most of us would deny that we *do good* only because of the rewards we receive. But don't you get a little bit irritated if you do something extra nice … and nobody notices? Being nice because of the rewards we receive is not a major accomplishment. Even criminals can behave – if it is in their best interest to do so. Children need immediate gratification for the things they do. As adults, we should be able to do the right thing for its own sake.

Richard Rohr, a priest and spokesman for the "Enneagram" movement, says we shouldn't be too quick to congratulate ourselves for our goodness. Our *apparent* goodness is simply doing what has always worked for us. It is what we have learned to do, and have been rewarded for. And none of us are as good as we think we are. For example, some people help others because they like the praise they get. (We still appreciate these helpers, of course.) And other people – be they leaders, comics, or skeptics – have learned how to interact with the world in a way that may be unique, but is generally in their own best interest. This variety of personalities makes the world go around. At the same time, nobody should get too much credit or blame for being the way they are. Our personality is so ingrained in us that we can't imagine being any other way.

Some might resent the notion that we're good only for the payoffs we receive. It sounds deceitful, but it's not. It's human nature. The truth is there's a bit of good in the worst of us, and there's some bad in the best of us. Most of us, despite our insecurities, are comfortable with who we are. It's almost impossible for us to look at the world in any other way. We regard whoever we are as the best kind of person to be. In most ways, it is. If God made you that way, then that's who you should be. It is a great paradox, however, that our greatest strength is also our greatest weakness. According to Richard Rohr, we become addicted to our gift – and it can become our sin.

If we want to *grow up*, we need to step outside of ourselves, see our strengths and weaknesses for what they are, and recognize that it's wrong to embrace our perspective too tightly. We need to be our own critic. We need to admit our mistakes and downplay our goodness. That's extremely hard to do. I hate, like most people, to admit that I've ever messed up. I'm like Lucy, of the Peanuts comic strip, who said: "I've never made a mistake in my life. Once I thought I did – but I was wrong."

Love to Hate

(8/12/2008)

Do you hate it when people disagree with you? Perhaps it's your wife, mother, boss, or business rival … It doesn't matter. Some comments (and some people) just evoke a negative response. If I say it's partly cloudy, someone will say it's partly sunny … Yet it's the same sky! Anyone can see that. If I had said "partly sunny" they certainly would have said "partly cloudy."

I accept responsibility for this. At one time I would have argued the point, but now I know what's going on. It's because I have, according to Richard Rohr, a "Type Eight" personality; and many people will inevitably take exception to what I've said or done. I'm naturally bossy, you see. I like to "take charge" of situations – not only times in need of leadership, and there have been plenty of those, but also during those times when a boss is neither wanted nor needed.

There are a lot of "Type Eight" people in the health care industry. They always know best. And sometimes they do. "Type Eight" people are also found in politics, commerce, church groups, and even your local neighborhood. They're everywhere! But it's not an epidemic … A 1991 study found that 17% of men, and 12% of women, are "Type Eight." These are people who "grab the bull by the horns" in order to solve problems. They can be pleasant, but are generally regarded as pushy. Some, like George W. Bush, are well-meaning but lack diplomacy. Some, like Jesse Jackson, like to defend "the little guy," and are not afraid to stand up to bullies. "Type Eighter's" are people you either love or hate. They are people that you love to hate – even when they're right.

I learned these things by studying the Enneagram. This is a spiritual direction program popularized by Richard Rohr, a Franciscan priest, who has written many books and given many workshops on the subject. His tape series, *The Enneagram: Naming Our Illusions*, explains the nine personality types from a spiritual rather than psychological perspective. This isn't just another self-help program. It is a heretofore "secret" knowledge that has been handed down (on an oral basis) by Jesuits, and other scholars, for centuries. Teaching this process helps bring about "spiritual conversion" for individuals who are brave enough to realize that their greatest weakness is the flip side of their greatest strength.

For example, medical doctors often take charge of situations. Sometimes they tell patients (and others) things they don't like to hear. Nurses usually help the doctor accomplish specific health care objectives. Hospital administrators meet the public (the media, etc.) and communicate what the goals of the hospital are. Chaplains meet with patients who are in need of compassionate care. Billing clerks and accountants attend to the finances of the hospital. Somebody else makes sure the hospital computers (and other machines) are working properly. "Rank and file" workers need to make sure everything else is running smoothly. Each worker is needed; and each personality type has advantages and disadvantages.

Telling you that certain professions attract certain personality types may sound like stereotyping. But that seems to be the way it seems to be. There is a lot of crossover in today's world, of course, but the fact remains that organizations run most smoothly when people like their jobs – and their personality is matched to what that job is expected to do.

Let Me Help You

(8/19/2008)

Do you hate it when people use psychology all the time? But we all do. It's just human nature. Richard Rohr, of Enneagram fame, points out that there is a little bit of good in the worst of us, and a little bit of bad in the best of us. The Enneagram, as you recall, is a spiritual discovery tool that explores how this can be so. It acknowledges and respects all personality types. No personality type is better than another.

Gut-centered people (Enneagram types 8, 9, and 1) are too quick to express their opinion. They direct their energy "over and against" obstacles they encounter. That's how I am. Head-centered people (types 5, 6, and 7) think too much, and their energy is "away from" issue involvement. Heart-centered people (types 2, 3, and 4) always worry what people think of them, and their energy is "toward" others. I am intrigued by how these heart-centered people are "tuned into" others – a social skill that I lack.

Some people are natural "Helpers." These "Type Two" people learned at an early age that their own needs are relatively unimportant, but if they help people in need – then they will be praised for their kindness. "Type Two" people are appreciated in our society, and are often found in the helping professions – health care, counseling, domestic services, volunteer activities, etc. Thank God we have these people.

The downside of being a "Type Two" is that they have suppressed their own needs. Although they don't admit it, they can be very "needy" people. They may subtly manipulate situations so that you continue to need them. They may be quite unhealthy. For example, a codependent wife will complain about her husband's excessive drinking, but still buys him beer. This type of behavior "enables" his alcoholism – and perpetuates the family sickness. And then the codependent wife (an unhealthy "Two") remains in control. She might say she wants her alcoholic husband to get healthy – but if he did, then she wouldn't feel needed.

There are many other examples of "Type Two" people. In the most benign form, they are the ones who always buy rolls and make coffee for the office. A more severe form is the doting mother who won't let her adult child grow up. A "Type Two" person can become "redeemed," though. They can acknowledge their own dark side. They can tend to their personal needs. They can help others without manipulation or expectation of praise. They can become saints, like Mother Teresa, who helped "the poorest of the poor" without expecting anything in return.

You can see that dedication to helping others is usually a good thing. While this personality trait is more often found in women, there are also men who are this way. But "Two's" often feel unappreciated and underpaid. They may feel unworthy of love – unless they are doing something that deserves acknowledgement and love in return. It's important to tell these people that you love them for who they are – and not just for what they do.

"Type Two" helping behavior can be "too much of a good thing." It can also be saintly. This is another way that the Enneagram teaches us about human nature. Stay tuned to future columns on this learning tool – and other lessons on what makes us tick.

Fr. Ned & Dr. Dirt, 2009

Trade Secrets

(8/26/2008)

"You shouldn't be telling people about the Enneagram," my priest friend said.

"Why?" I asked.

"You'll give away my trade secrets," he quipped.

All kidding aside, it is difficult to write about some subjects. The Enneagram, as you recall, is a tool that only spiritual gurus had access to until recently. It demonstrates that people are both good and bad – and different personality types face different challenges.

As I've discussed in recent articles, there are nine Enneagram personality types. People are generally *not happy* to find out what "number" they are. Like it or not, there are negatives (as well as positives) to your character. If you don't experience remorse when finding out your Enneagram type, then you probably don't have it right. While it may be fun to say that "So and so" is a certain number, the whole purpose of this tool is *self discovery*. So don't tell your neighbor that he's an "unredeemed Eight." He just might punch you in the nose.

My priest friend, by the way, is a classic "Seven." Although he deals with human suffering on a frequent basis, he has found a clever way of AVOIDING PAIN in life – he remains optimistic, tells jokes, and spreads JOY to others. He is full of idealism and tomfoolery. His enthusiasm for life is contagious. Many Irish priests, they say, are this way. They even throw parties when people die – celebrating that the dead person has moved on to a better place. This is typical of "Seven" people: they transform Pain into Joy.

Perhaps you have a "Seven" in your life. A healthy "Seven" can be fun to be around. They love to party. An unhealthy "Seven" can be *too happy*, though. As far as they're concerned, every day is their birthday. They want the "fun" to revolve around them every single day. But reality isn't always fun. That's when some "Seven's" try to make artificial fun – with excess joking, food, alcohol, travel, shopping, etc. A "Seven" doesn't mind being told they're joyful – unless they know this means they engage in avoidance behavior. They need to get grounded, slow down, and accept life as it is.

A major principle of the Enneagram is that you shouldn't sit in your compulsion. Once you know your type, you should move on … A "gut" person should move to his heart (become sensitive to others), a "heart" person should go to her head (explore objective truths), and a "head" person should go to his gut (accomplish something of value), and so on, and so forth.

Different Strokes

(4/21/2010)

There has been a controversy brewing in Sidney. It involves the recommendation to "non-renew" a young teacher's contract. This man is a native of Sidney. He was enticed to come back to town to teach band and choir. After just six months on the job he was promoted to chairman of the music department. He has been extremely popular with his students. Parents also like his easy-going style. He motivates students to do their best. Under his tutelage, music performances have been quite entertaining. Many students describe him as a "big brother" who always says "Hello." He relates to students on a personal level. His classes are described as educational and enjoyable.

There have been two school board meetings to listen to the public's opinion on the contract non-renewal issue. The meetings have been packed with students and parents alike. Many people have spoken on the young teacher's behalf. The recommendation to "non-renew" his contract came from school administration officials. While no one has publicly stated why there is opposition to the contract renewal (for "legal reasons," they say) it does *seem* that someone is concerned that the teacher isn't professional enough. He gets to know his students as friends instead of keeping detached from them. The implication is that teachers need to be detached in order to be professional.

I'm no expert on teaching methods, but I have had a lot of different teachers. I respected 99% of my teachers. I think education is one of the most important professions in our society, and I'm proud to say that two of my sons are pursuing a career in education. I have also read a little bit about teaching methods, and note that there are different ways to get the job done. There are, as they say, "different strokes for different folks."

Some teachers possess "expert knowledge" on a subject, and didactically impart their knowledge to their appreciative students. Some teachers rely on their "authoritarian role" to impress upon students the importance of getting assignments done on time, following orders, and avoiding classroom disruptions. Some teachers "delegate" learning tasks. They give assignments and expect the students to learn in an autonomous manner. Some teachers serve as "role models" and encourage students to emulate their skill in selected areas. Other teachers "facilitate" the acquisition of knowledge. Their personal involvement with students (through question-answer interactions, exploring of alternatives, etc) helps "give birth" to the student's capacity for independent thought. This is the "childbirth" model of learning: the teacher allows the student to labor through some of the learning process, gives help as needed, and allows the student to take credit for his own creation.

It should be obvious that most teachers rely on several of these techniques to get the job done. They don't strictly adhere to one technique or another – they just want their students to learn! Quality of education is more important than the quantity of students you move through the ranks. And the local school systems have always been about quality, I think; that's why I'm surprised that there is concern that this teacher's style is not "exactly like" what somebody thought it should be.

Missing Piece

(2/5/2008)

Have you ever lost something – and nearly gone crazy trying to remember where you put it? That happens to me all the time. My wife says it is me, and not her, that will be the first to move into the Alzheimer's Unit at the Nursing Home. She may be right … Last week, for example, I had an idea for a "Dr Dirt" column, but couldn't find the book I wanted to write about. The fact that my den is a mess contributed to the problem. In some ways, though, all of our lives are like my den – they are messier than we care to admit.

Ironically, the book I was missing is called *The Missing Piece*, by Shel Silverstein. I have loaned it out to dozens of people over the years, and wondered if someone had forgotten to return it. I was going nuts looking for it. Then a friend called asking for a favor. After helping him out, I returned home, and – guess what? I found my missing book. It was where I had previously looked. The answer to my search was right in front of me.

The book, *The Missing Piece*, looks like a children's book, but tells a profound story. It is the story of a person's search for completeness. "He" looks like a pie with a "missing piece." He goes rolling along – singing as he goes – in search of a piece that will fit into his empty space. His life, like yours, may be likened to a jigsaw puzzle. Some puzzles have many pieces, and look very difficult. Perhaps these puzzles are easier than they seem. The boy in *The Missing Piece* needs just one piece to be complete – but he doesn't know what it is. In his search, he takes time to talk to a worm, smell a flower, and race a beetle. He even lets a frog sit on his shoulder. He sings as he rolls along – even though he has to overcome a mountain, an ocean, rainfall, oppressive heat, and a snowstorm. Despite his challenges, he was not unhappy.

Eventually our hero finds "pieces" that he thinks will fill his emptiness. He swallows a few pieces, trying them on for size. He comes to realize that one piece after another is not a good fit. And when these pieces are "in him," he no longer rolls smoothly. With his mouth full of ill-fitting pieces, he can no longer "sing his song."

The book is a metaphor for our lives. We try to fill our emptiness with many things: excess food, fancy clothes, pretentious homes, alcohol, drugs, gambling, greed, extramarital affairs, etc. We try to fill our emptiness with many "things" that not only don't fit – but are unhealthy.

Our hero eventually realizes that it's okay to be less than perfect. It's okay to be longing for something to make us complete. We seem to be wired that way. And in this life we don't always get what we want. Even if our goals are worthy – love, wisdom, peace, etc. – there's always something missing. I, for one, can admit that I'm not a very good writer, a perfect husband, or a wise parent. Ask my family – they can give you a long list of my imperfections. Some of my landscaping holes aren't even round.

None of us will ever be perfect at anything. Perhaps what we search for isn't even of this world. Perhaps what we need is God. I'm no expert on the subject, but being incomplete seems to be inevitable. Having a "missing piece" is the way life is meant to be.

Wanderer

(9/2/2008)

We took our boys to college last week. I went west, and my wife went east. One kid is going to Missoula, and the other is going to Minnesota. In order to save a few bucks, I took the Greyhound back from Missoula. It really is an economical and enjoyable way to get around.

A young girl sat next to me in Missoula. We rode together to Glendive, and then she continued on to New York. She was pleasant, but wasn't all that happy about going home. She was searching for something she hadn't been able to find in her home town. Her father, a minister, "is working on his fourth wife." He is no longer a part of her life. She rejects him and his hypocritical ways. In recent months, she has been camping her way across the Western States – with an older man. But he had also let her down … It is curious that she sat next to me, an older man with gray hair and beard. Perhaps it says something about why she was wandering in the first place.

Her father paid for her ticket home. She had no other resources, though, so I bought her a few meals. She devoured her food – as if it had been a long time since her last meal. But she needed more than physical sustenance. She needed a father substitute and friend. She told me her story, and I told her mine. I had just dropped my son off at college. I told her that he was also twenty, and searching …

My new friend, as it turned out, dropped out of high school. She works factory jobs, and did get her GED. She has a real "thirst for knowledge," though, and carries a back pack full of books with her. She is smart. She tried to teach me a few things about astrology, and showed me her daily readings. I showed her a spirituality book I had with me. She doesn't believe in God, she said. After hearing about her childhood, I'm not surprised; but she was willing to listen. I told her God loves all of us – no matter what our past has been or what are flaws are. We prayed that our journeys would bring us safely home.

It's okay to wander, I told her. Everybody does – especially young people. Our children check out different colleges, churches, cities, and social companions. It's part of their journey. Parents try to help them out – these young adults of ours. We hope they find direction in their lives: a rock upon which to become grounded, a worthy mate, and a career they will enjoy. Some people find what they're looking for – but many don't. Some people are "riding the Greyhound bus" of life. And, as Harry Chapin (the singer and songwriter) puts it …

"Take the Greyhound. It's a dog of a way to get around. Take the Greyhound. It's a dog gone easy way to get you down."

And later in the song (*Greyhound*) Chapin adds …

"Stepping off this dirty bus, first time I understood: It's got to be the going, not the getting there that's good. That's a thought for keeping if I could. It's got to be the going, not the getting there that's good."

Everybody wants to find their way. I hope my friend does. I hope I do. Accepting life's imperfections makes the journey easier. And realizing that God is with us makes the trip worth taking.

Intolerance

(4/1/2008)

On my recent trip to California, I saw the "Tolerance Museum" in Los Angeles. Opened in 1993, it receives over 350,000 visitors per year. The museum's most talked-about exhibit is "The Holocaust Section," where visitors are taught about Hitler's slaughter of six million Jews during World War II. Hitler also persecuted Gypsies, Slavs, political dissenters, homosexuals, P.O.W.'s, the physically infirm, and the mentally ill.

Christendom has been accused of *doing nothing* to stop Hitler's persecution of the Jews. Some people accuse the Catholic Church of aiding the Nazis – through their *lack* of action. Lapide's 1967 book, *Three Popes and the Jews*, however, provides evidence that the Church was instrumental in saving 860,000 Jews from Nazi death camps.

Should individual Christians have done more to stop these atrocities? Absolutely! Most Christians acknowledge this. And some did stand up to the challenge. Oskar Schindler, born from Catholic parents in what is now Czechoslovakia, was an ambitious member of the Nazi party, but is credited with saving almost 1200 Jews – by employing them in his factories. Odoardo Focherini, a little known Catholic journalist in Italy, helped more than 100 Jews find hiding places – before being murdered by the Nazis. But more people should have stood up to Hitler's henchmen.

In recent years there has been a growth in the neo-Nazi movement. They claim the atrocity of the Holocaust is either a lie or is grossly exaggerated. Right-wing extremist groups have flourished world-wide, but are particularly noxious in "free speech" America. In addition to targeting Jews, neo-Nazi groups also target African Americans, Asian Americans, Latinos, Arab Americans, Native Americans, homosexuals, Catholics, and people who espouse political/religious opinions that disagree with their "pure American" ideologies.

Until recently, I haven't known that much about the "Intolerance Movement." When I came across a book entitled *Be Intolerant*, by Ryan Dobson, however, I felt compelled to research the topic. I read his book with great interest. I also did a Google search to see if "intolerance" is a virtue or a vice.

While his book has some merit, the title and parts of Ryan Dobson's *Be Intolerant* concern me. Believing that "there really is just one right way to do" things, as the author claims, puts people in the position of playing god. In Dobson's defense, he concisely reviews the major tenets of Christianity.

And readers are told to "transform [themselves] from the inside out." But you should, the author repeatedly says, confront people you think are sinning. The author (the son of evangelist James Dobson) proudly states that he frequently confronted sinners on his college campus – and, for his efforts, had the tires on his car "slashed at least ten times."

Puritanism has always flourished in America. For example, read Hawthorne's *Scarlet Letter* to see how adulterers were treated in the 16th century. But social and religious intolerance seems to be a growing problem. I personally don't think bombing an abortion clinic is a good way to express your "Pro-Life" views. And discrimination against Muslims makes us little better than Jihadists.

"Morally superior" attitudes led to 7,160 "Hate Crimes" in 2005. FBI statistics report that 55% of these incidents were triggered by religious bias and 13% were motivated by ethnicity/national origin bias. And the perpetrators of these crimes are mostly young people.

Ryan Dobson isn't a skinhead. But his book, which is recommended by many religious leaders, characterizes "intolerance" as an acceptable way of approaching "moral" issues. My concern is this: If it's okay to be "intolerant" of homosexuals and unmarried couples, then isn't it also okay to be "intolerant" of different ethnicities? Or those who go to a different church? Or those who don't vote the same way you do?

Our freedom of press allows Dobson's book as much as any other opinionated material – like my book or columns. But I like to see how things look from "the other guy's" perspective. For example, my son and I – although a bit hesitant – visited several ethnic neighborhoods while we were in LA. It was an enlightening experience to be the minority in these areas.

Many people have experienced discrimination. Encouraging "intolerance" will aggravate this societal problem. Certainly people of faith are encouraged to live by their principles. Telling others they are "sinners" is likely to backfire, though. Teaching by example does more good than preaching to others about "their sins."

Relativism

(4/22/2008)

As you probably know, Pope Benedict XVI visited America last week. A record crowd greeted him on the South Lawn of the White House. President Bush said that the Pope's visit was a reminder for Americans to "distinguish between simple right and wrong."

In 2005, the soon-to-be-elected Pope Benedict XVI coined the phrase "dictatorship of relativism." He said "we are moving towards a *dictatorship of relativism* which does not recognize anything as certain and which has as its highest goal one's own ego and one's own desires."

Morality, of course, deals with what is right and wrong. Jean-Paul Sartre, the famous 20th century French existentialistic, said that our moral positions are not absolute, but are subjective – which is the classic relativistic notion. What you believe is based on your personal experiences; and upon what your family, friends, and community tell you to believe. We adopt "societal values" in this way. And history shows us that these values have changed over time.

Pundits say our society no longer has worthy values. Morality has become a matter of individual opinion. You decide what's right for you, and I'll decide what's right for me. To put it another way: anything goes.

Judeo-Christian principles were once the basis for our civil law, but now our secular society doesn't know how to differentiate right from wrong. Our judicial system considers psychosocial factors, motivation, premeditation and emotional state before ruling on innocence or guilt. A "crime" is not a crime unless a judge and jury say it's so.

Paraphrasing Saint Paul (Eph 4:14), Pope Benedict XVI says we shouldn't be a society where we are "tossed back and forth by the waves, and blown here and there by every wind of teaching and by the cunning and craftiness of men in their deceitful scheming."

"Being an *adult*," the Pope says, "means having a faith which does not follow the waves of today's fashions or the latest novelties. A faith which is deeply rooted in friendship with Christ is adult and mature. It is this friendship which opens us up to all that is good and gives us the knowledge to judge true from false, and deceit from truth…

"Today, a particularly insidious obstacle to the task of education is the massive presence in our society [of relativism] … which, recognizing nothing as definitive, leaves as the ultimate criterion only the self with its desires. And under the semblance of freedom it becomes a prison for each one, for it separates people from one another, locking each person into his or her own ego."

Psychologists note that we are all born with a conscience. Children know the difference between "fair" and "unfair." We usually know when we have wronged others. We certainly know when we have been wronged. We act as though we expect others to know these standards. Even atheists want their rights protected. Nobody wants murderers, rapists, or other criminals to live in their neighborhood.

"The Golden Rule" and the "Ten Commandments" are *moral codes* worth adopting. But we no longer regard eating pork and sea creatures "that have no fins or scales" as sinful. (See Leviticus, chapter 11.) And while Solomon had "700 wives and 300 concubines" (1 Kings 11:3), polygamy is no longer tolerated. In most areas, though, the Bible provides consistent and practical moral guidelines.

"Christian Absolutism" believes that God is the ultimate authority, so "Moral Law" should be followed absolutely. But many have suffered in the name of Righteousness (e.g., Jews in the Holocaust, Blacks during Slavery, Muslim Genocide in Bosnia, etc.), so we should not be too quick to label our particular perspective as matching the will of God. Moral Relativism has gone too far the other way, though. It's time to use our God-given brains to become educated, listen to wise people, and analyze the merit (and fault) of different viewpoints. Reading the Bible is one way to learn what "God's Will" is for us. A truth-seeking mind will use this and other sources to learn these basic "Right versus Wrong" guidelines.

Do As I Say

(5/24/2008)

I am one of the worst golfers in Sidney. Ironically enough, my son is one of the best young golfers in the area. Last week I asked him if he has learned anything from me – about golf or anything else … There was an uncomfortable silence; then he tried to answer diplomatically.

"Dad, I have learned from you."

"How could that be?" I asked.

"Well," he said with reflection, "I try to do as you say – but not always as you do."

That was a left-handed compliment if I ever heard one; and it could also be my epitaph. It's true – especially in sports. I'm a lousy excuse for a golfer. I'm also weak in basketball and football. I can't skate worth a darn. I was a "good field no hit" baseball player. I was a good soccer goalie, though. I also had good running endurance (I completed 11 marathons) but wasn't very fast. And I had some success as a coach. But those days are long gone.

People used to think I was pretty smart. People aren't impressed by smart landscapers. They just want they lawn mowed. And when prospective clients see how many "dog spots" my own yard has, they don't care how smart I am. They want results. They might, in fact, disregard my landscaping advice altogether.

Why should my par-golfing son take advice from his double-bogeying father? For that matter, why should anyone take advice on anything – especially from someone who doesn't demonstrate proficiency at the activity in question? For example, should you listen to a cigarette-smoking doctor who is fat and lazy? Or listen to an accountant who can't balance his own books? Or trust a minister who doesn't follow the Ten Commandments? And should you take advice from a marriage counselor who has been through a messy divorce?

Is advice worth the proverbial paper it's written on? Should kids even listen to their parents anymore? Should we trust politicians and professionals who have disappointed us in the past – and don't demonstrate any more "expertise" than the average Joe? Perhaps we should all turn a deaf ear to the flood of "well-meaning advice" we hear every day.

Melody Beattie, in her classic book, *Codependent No More*, describes advice-giving as a prominent part of the *disease* of *codependency*. Yes I said disease. It is by far the most common addiction in our society. The desire to manipulate and control others usually arises as a response to being in a relationship where one partner is an alcoholic, and the other (a non-drinker) essentially *goes crazy* trying to control their partner's behavior.

Codependency is described as obsession with other peoples' lives. If you're codependent, you don't know what your own feelings are, but you are obsessed with what *the other guy* is doing and feeling. You always give advice. You believe other people "need" your help, and have the false notion that everything you do is done for unselfish reasons. While "helping others" may, in fact, be helpful – it also leads to subtle (and not so subtle) changes in the personalities of both the giver and the receiver.

Like so many other vices, I must also admit to having this one. Most health care providers are codependent. They enjoy giving advice, feeling helpful, and being thanked for their activities. Teachers, preachers, spouses, friends, neighbors, and even landscapers also like getting pats on the back. Unfortunately, the desire to help *excessively* can become *controlling*. Interfering with the lives of others can do more harm than good.

Giving advice, and interfering in other people's business, is a tendency that is rampant in our society. I should, for example, keep my mouth shut the next time I feel like giving my son advice on his golf game. He can figure this (and other things) out on his own. I should concentrate on my own golf swing. Too much advice is detrimental to his health – and mine.

Rational Animals

(5/25/2009)

Last week I attended, as my youngest son's guest, the annual banquet of the National Honor Society (NHS). A fine group of young men and women received recognition for their academic achievements. In our society, young people are much more likely to receive applause for athletic achievements – which is fine, I guess – but it's also good to reward their school work.

I never was in the NHS. I was a good student in high school, but I didn't really "hit my stride" until I got into college. I was a near 4.0 student in college, attended medical school, and so on. In a similar way, many people don't get motivated to reach their potential until later in life. And there are also many excellent professions that require "practical know how," rather than book smarts, to get the job done.

In college I wanted to get good grades. Most students do. Somewhere along the line, though, I realized that I actually enjoyed learning for the sake of learning. Math, Physics, Psychology, Literature and Philosophy – for some odd reason – became interesting to me. I'm not sure why. Maybe it was because I was surrounded by people who were also interested in these subjects. Or perhaps knowledge becomes its own reward.

My middle son has reached the point where he also seems interested in learning for its own sake. This past semester, for example, he had to do a term paper on a very complicated book, Alasdair MacIntyre's *Dependent Rational Animals: Why Human Beings Need the Virtues*. He was initially turned off by the book, but then he realized it contained some valuable information.

"Rational animals," MacIntyre says, are intelligent enough to communicate with each other, care for their disabled, and develop the "human" traits of cooperation and mutual protection. And it is our common experience of childhood *dependency* and *frailty* that teaches us (dolphins, gorillas, humans, etc.) that we need each another – for individual and group purposes – which has led to our acquisition of "virtues," and our ability to live as a society.

MacIntyre says the only way people acquire "practical wisdom" is by living life. You don't attain it from reading this or any other book. While MacIntyre does not specifically promote religion in this book, he does imply that there are religious lessons to be learned by studying science. My son wisely quoted the Bible to support the book's theme that "interdependency" among people is important. The Apostle Paul, for example, describes "the Body of Christ" as "a unit, though it is made up of many parts; and though all its parts are many, they form one body." (Bible, 1Cor12:12, NIV.) And no part of the body is less important than another. "There should be no division in the body, but that its parts should have equal concern for each other." (Bible, 1Cor12:25, NIV.)

I reviewed MacIntyre's book, and agree with its basic theme: "Self-knowledge" must come first, he says, followed by the realization that people need people. And I was pleased that my son recognized that secular knowledge and religious teachings can be compatible. Furthermore, he was allowed to quote the Bible in his term paper at a public university, which shows that some professors are open-minded.

Accepting our frailties and our dependencies, the author says, is the key to personal growth. And if you accept the idea that a hand is no greater than a foot (Bible, 1Cor12:15, NIV) then you can appreciate that it takes people from all walks of life coming together to form a community. Nobody is *better than* or *less than* anybody else, and we all need each other. Wisdom (from the Bible, from other books, and from life) has taught "society" about virtues, to care for its individual members, and to work for our common good.

Superman

(6/30/2010)

If Christopher Reeve were alive today, he might say starring in the "Superman" movies was his second best role. His greatest achievement, I think, was being himself – living life after his "Clark Kent" days were over, accepting his spinal cord injury with dignity, and serving as a spokesman for those with similar handicaps.

Wikipedia.com succinctly reviews his life: He was born into a wealthy family, received the best education, and decided (at the age of nine) that he wanted to be an actor. Some of his highbrow friends criticized him for acting in a TV soap opera, but he needed the money. Reeve was also in a play, lived on junk food, and collapsed – on the stage – from exhaustion in 1975. He worked hard, took many acting jobs, and eventually gained the admiration of colleagues and fans alike. At the tender age of 26 he got the role of his life. He became "Superman" in the 1978 blockbuster movie. He played the role again in three sequels.

The Superman role made Christopher Reeve a lot of money, and he became universally recognized; but he became type-cast, and this limited his ability to land other roles. He worked for next-to-nothing on jobs that attracted his interest, and proved he could successfully play other roles. Reeve also spoke out on political causes that he believed in. When the dictator of Chile threatened to execute 77 actors (who practiced freedom of speech) Reeve went there to lead a protest march. Fearing unfavorable media coverage, the dictator cancelled the planned execution.

When the "Superman" popularity faded, people said Christopher Reeve's career had "bottomed out." Reeve never looked at it that way. He starred in plays, built a sailboat, twice piloted a plane across the Atlantic, got married, and had a son. He became a serious equestrian. He said these were the happiest days of his life.

Being Superman has a downside. You are expected to be perfect, and expected to please all people at all times. Despite their popularity, I remember some people criticized the "Superman" movies as being too patriotic and overly chauvinistic. For crying out loud! Give them a break … They were, after all, just movies, based on a comic book, and they were meant to entertain.

Most people felt really bad when Christopher Reeve had his spinal cord injury. He had been riding horses for ten years, trained 5-6 days per week, and was felt to be a good equestrian. On May 5, 1995, on what was felt to be a routine jump, his horse suddenly stopped. Some say the horse was spooked by a rabbit. Reeve's body was thrown forward, and he landed on his head. His helmet protected his brain, but his upper spine was broken, which left Reeve paralyzed from the neck down. He became severely depressed. His friend, Robin Williams, cheered him up. Reeve was sent to Kessler Rehabilitation Center [no relation] in New Jersey. He felt deeply inspired by the patients and staff he met there. He worked very hard, and eventually was able to stay off his ventilator (breathing machine) for 30 minutes at a time.

After his injury, Reeve wrote two books, directed several projects, and made numerous media appearances. He was a spokesman for spinal cord injury patients. He created the "Christopher Reeve Foundation," which seeks to improve the quality of life for people with disabilities. Reeve was hopeful that he would walk again. He spoke out about the need to explore new treatment options, including stem cell research, to help people with spinal cord injuries.

It is terrible when people have to face a serious disease or sustain a disabling injury. Our community rightfully tries to reach out and support these people. I have great respect for people (patients and their families) who have been forced to deal with problems of this nature. Superman himself suffered from such an obstacle – and, with the help of his friends and family, tried to make the best of it. Let's hope than none of us has to go through a similar ordeal. But if we do, let's hope that we get the support that we need, and hope that we can summon a bit of superman-like courage to accept our problems.

Delay Gratification

(12/30/2008)

As we enter 2009, many people are worried about the future of our country. We are in the midst of the deepest recession since the Great Depression. Many people have lost their jobs. Our homes and savings have lost value, and there isn't great confidence that President-elect Obama will be able to rally friends and foes to effectively address these issues.

The world has always had problems. War, pestilence, poverty and natural disasters have scared us in the past – and seem to be scaring us even more now. The "gloom and doom" attitude took its toll on the Xmas shopping season, and dragged down our economy even more. The bad credit market seemed to have started this mess, and now people and businesses are having trouble borrowing money for anything. And one bad thing leads to another. If consumers are nervous, then they won't buy as much – which hurts retail businesses. If retailers suffer, then so do their suppliers. If businesses suffer, then so do their employees. And so on, and so forth.

The world economy is more interdependent than ever. While the recession is indeed a terrible thing, there may be an upside to it. The stock market will eventually recover. Stock prices are at multiyear lows. If I was smart, I'd buy up some of these bargains. The "Big Three" auto companies have needed restructuring for years, and now they're being forced to make changes – in exchange for government assistance. Our infrastructure (roads, highways, etc.) have also needed work, and under Obama's "economic stimulus plan" they will get some attention.

Switching from a national to an individual perspective, problems can also be "good" for you and me. In the opening words of his book, *The Road Less Traveled*, Dr. Scott Peck says: "Life is difficult. This is a great truth, one the greatest truths." Peck says that "life is a series of problems," and facing them brings about mental and spiritual maturity.

Peck's book is considered a classic. Like many great books, his genius is that he states truths we already know, but have not put into words. His appeal is widespread, and his book has sold over 10 million copies.

In order to achieve mental and spiritual maturity, Dr. Peck says we must face our problems – rather than avoid them. If you do try to avoid them, you will increase and prolong your suffering, and become "mentally ill" in the process. Dr. Peck, a psychiatrist, says that everyone tries "to a greater or lesser degree" to avoid problems and emotional suffering.

According to Dr. Peck, "discipline" is the healthy way of dealing with life's problems. As you know, discipline is also required if you plan to stick to your New Year's resolutions. But most resolutions are abandoned in a week or two. I can only imagine what Peck would have say about this ...

Peck defines discipline as "a system of techniques of dealing constructively with" pain, suffering, bad habits, and whatever else ails you. The four basic techniques of discipline are: delaying gratification, assumption of responsibility, dedication to the truth, and balance. All of these skills are important and useful in a person's quest for maturity.

"Delaying Gratification" is the focus of this week's discussion on discipline. It is an obviously important topic – especially during these economic times. *Not* delaying gratification is a major reason why we are in this economic mess in the first place. Instead of saving up for a rainy day, Americans have been using bad credit to get a new TV, an expensive vacation, or a house they really can't afford. Bad credit has been the catalyst of our economic recession. We should have been paying down debt, covering our essential expenses, and saving money for emergencies.

Delaying gratification is about more than just money. Young people should get a good education – instead of going for the "easy money" they might find in a temporary job. They need to study now in order to get a good grade (and a good job) in the future. Parents should spend time with their children, rather than only pursuing their personal interests. If you don't, your children may have abandonment issues, and more than their share of psychological problems.

From a medical perspective, patients should realize that quick (but short-lived) gratification of physical and psychological pursuits can lead to years of adverse consequences. Addicts of all kinds (alcohol, drugs, food, sex, anger, gambling, shopaholics, etc.) enjoy temporary relief of their addictive urges – and then later regret and remorse. In a corollary manner, if you don't tolerate some temporary discomfort now, you will not enjoy later successes. Smokers, for example, need to put up with "nicotine withdrawal" discomfort in order to have better health in the future. And "emotional hurts" need to be attended to in a timely way. If not, they can be like a wound that festers, infection sets in, and then can only get better with major surgery (i.e., psychotherapy).

Dr. Peck's comments on how we deal with problems are interesting and informative. Learning to delay gratification is the first step in developing the discipline we need to handle life's problems.

Accept Responsibility

(1/6/2009)

Everyone is blaming everybody else for the mess our country is in. It would be fun to point out, for example, that it was Bill Clinton who loosened the lending standards for Fannie Mae loans – but I won't do that. Critics could just as easily point out that George W. Bush didn't adequately fund the regulatory agencies that were supposed to monitor the lending agencies, the stock market, etc. And the failure of the American automobile industry is as much due to overpriced union labor as it is the industry fat cats.

Nobody wants to accept responsibility anymore. If you spill hot coffee on your lap, for instance, you can blame McDonald's for making the coffee too hot. Playing "the blame game" doesn't accomplish anything, though. Instead of going down that path, I'd like to discuss the process of "Accepting Responsibility," which Dr. Scott Peck writes about in his book, *The Road Less Traveled* (*RLT*). Peck says a person needs the tools of discipline (ability to delay ratification, assume responsibility, seek the truth, and balance) in order to achieve mental and spiritual maturity.

While no one has control over everything, it is important to know what problems we can influence. If you "accept responsibility" for something, then you can do something about it. Flagrant examples of *failure to accept responsibility* are the following: you gain weight because you say you can't get any exercise; you abuse alcohol because you say there's nothing else to do; you hate your job but don't do anything about it; you're going through a divorce – for the third time – because your wives have all been selfish; and so on, and so forth. Subtle examples of failure to accept responsibility are the following: you complain about global warming, but drive a gas-guzzling SUV; you don't like how the local school board is running things, but didn't vote in the last election; or you criticize national politics, but have never attended a local caucus meeting.

We all have at least some influence over the problems in our world. Blaming the "military- industrial establishment" for everything is a sure sign of immaturity. In the immortal words of Eldridge Cleaver, a 1960s black activist, "If you are not part of the solution, then you are part of the problem."

Of course there are things we have less control over than others. Thinking everything is *somebody else's* fault, though, is symptomatic of a "character disorder." The reverse of this – thinking everything is *your* fault – is "neurosis."

Many people are in one camp or the other. And some people are *neurotic* about some things and *character disordered* about others.

The picture is not quite as black and white as I (and Dr. Peck) have painted. Often we choose between "the lesser of two evils." Other times we choose between "the greater of two goods." Life is a series of personal choices, and some choices are more difficult than others.

Dr. Peck took the title of his book (*RLT*) from Robert Frost's poem, "The Road Not Taken." Frost's poem describes a person standing at a crossroads, facing a seemingly small and insignificant choice, but one that might change his life forever. After carefully evaluating both of his options, Frost chose the less traveled path. The poem states: "And I shall be telling this with a sigh. Somewhere ages and ages hence: Two roads diverged in a wood, and I – I took the one less traveled by, and that has made all the difference."

Dedication to Reality

(1/13/2009)

In these economic times, a lot of people would rather watch a movie, read a novel, or listen to a joke than hear how bad things really are ... I don't blame them. I am tempted to sleep for a couple of months while the stock market corrects itself. That, of course, would be "avoiding reality," which is something experts say we're not supposed to do.

This is my third and final article on Scott Peck's famous book, *The Road Less Traveled* (*RLT*). Dr. Peck, a psychiatrist, describes the four elements of discipline – delay of gratification, assumption of responsibility, dedication to reality, and balance – that a person needs to achieve mental and spiritual maturity. This week's article will discuss "dedication to reality" as it relates to personal growth.

As children, we form a "map of the world" that helps us negotiate our way through life. As we mature, our map is found to be wrong, and needs to be redrawn – according to the reality lessons we learn. If we don't redraw our maps, then we are forever stuck with our childish view of "reality." And no matter what your childhood was like, your childhood map needs redrawing.

If your parents didn't love you, then you learned that the world is a dangerous place – and you shouldn't trust people. If your parents loved you too much, and protected you from every danger, then you learned you should always get your way – which is not reality.

Changing our view of reality is almost always painful. Most people "revise their maps" on their own, but some need psychological help to make these adjustments. The best way to make these *reality adjustments* is by knowing you are loved regardless of your mistakes; and the ultimate source of love, according to Peck, "is Amazing Grace."

Dr. Peck summarizes his discussion of discipline by acknowledging that it can be "a demanding but also complex task, requiring both flexibility and judgment." For example, it can be difficult to know when to save for the future, and when to live for the moment. It can be difficult to know when to assume responsibility, and when the responsibility is not ours. And to *know reality* is also to know when to withhold the truth – specifically when thinking about confronting others with "truth" that is vindictive.

"Discipline itself must be disciplined," says Peck, with a process he calls "balancing." In order to reach higher levels of consciousness, we must set aside cultural biases, reject parental injunctions, and open ourselves up to new experiences and novel thoughts. We must not accept anybody else's version of truth or their "hand-me-down religion." We must "let go" of our old selves in order to "give birth" to our new and enlightened selves.

P.S. After completing *RLT*, many people complimented Dr. Peck for the way he communicated a Christian message under the guise of a *self help* book. His book is even recommended by some as a source of Christian insight. By Peck's own admission, though, he was a Zen Buddhist when he wrote the book. He did become a Christian several years after *RLT* was published, however.

Peck didn't think much of organized religion. He wrote: "I used to tell people only somewhat facetiously that the Catholic Church provided me with my living as a psychiatrist." But good therapists, says Peck, won't "throw out the baby with the bath water." Religion can be good or bad. Peck's complaint against organized religion is that it dogmatically tells people how they should pray, and what they should and should not believe – when it is healthier for them to seek the truth, and draw their own maps of the world.

Dr. Peck was a popular "spiritual growth" speaker for many years, but he often said and did things that were decidedly "un-Christian." He repeatedly says "our unconscious is God." Individuals, Peck writes, can evolve "to become as one with God." And Peck's behavior was not exemplary. He had many extra-marital affairs. The only thing that cured him of his infidelity, he admitted, was impotence.

Peck's comments on "Discipline" and "Love" are interesting and useful. His comments on "Growth and Religion" and "Grace" are also interesting – but controversial.

Love Weeds

(7/14/2009)

It was the summer of 1967, and I was looking for a summer job. My best friend was working at a tree farm owned and operated by Mr. Lueben (creator of the "Lueben Poplar Tree") and found out that there was a job opening. I was 13, and signed on for the job – which meant *weeding* for 8 hours a day and 5 days a week. It was a miserable job, but it was a good experience.

Mr. Lueben's tree farm was near a stream-fed bog in St. Paul, Minnesota, and was a great place to grow a wide variety of shade trees. Mr. Lueben was a strict boss. He wasn't exactly a slave driver, but he did want things to be done *exactly* his way. I'll bet everyone has had a boss (or parent, or spouse, or significant other) who is like that. *His way* was not necessarily bad, but it was *difficult*. Sound familiar? Dick Merry, my best friend, looked at the job as a survival test; and he was glad I signed on to *share the experience* with him. Dick was like that. He was three years older than me – and had a warped sense of humor.

Weeding the nursery meant skillfully using a hoe to loosen the weeds that inevitably took up lodging between the perfectly spaced rows of trees. I always thought the weeds had as much of a right to live as did the trees – but Mr. Lueben didn't agree. And the work meant sweating profusely in the hot and humid Minnesota weather, which I didn't mind, along with tolerating numerous mosquitoes, which I hated.

My friend had a devious sense of humor. He knew, for example, that Mr. Lueben got upset when his workers obsessed about time. Dick set me up. He told me to ask when lunch break was. When Mr. Lueben came around, I naively asked: "By the way, Mr. Leuben, what time is it?"

"Kessler," he said, "you think too much about the time. Get back to your weeding, and I'll let you know when it's time for lunch."

In his own way, Mr. Lueben was a wise man. He was also crazy. People obsess about the unpleasantness of life. There's always weeds, for example; and it's important to do the best we can to get rid of them. But since we're never gonna get rid of *all* the weeds in our life, it's also important to put up with them. And Mr. Lueben couldn't do that. As soon as we weeded his nursery – from one end to another – he'd have us start all over again. That was nuts, I thought. Why not give us a few days off, or have us work on something else. That wasn't how it was, though. So we weeded …

Nowadays, as a landscaper, I actually like weeds. My crew and I enjoy pulling them. Manually pulling them, and applying chemicals to them, is an okay thing to do. And we know they're going to come back (eventually) so weeds represent job security. Mosquitoes, on the other hand, are just a pest. Even though they are food for some insects, birds and fish, I have a hard time accepting them as a useful part of God's universe.

Obsessing about the minor problems in life is called *perfectionism*, and it's not a good thing. This *character defect* implies that we know best, and have a right to complain about the imperfections we see around us. It's like complaining about the speck in another person's eye when we don't notice the plank in our own eye. (Bible, Matt 7:3, NIV)

Perfectionism leads a person to always want things to be different – as if we really know what's best for everyone. Since things in this world are never going to be perfect, having this *character defect* is just going to make us unhappy "Acceptance," on the other hand, "is the answer to *all* my problems today. When I am disturbed, it is because I find ... some fact of my life unacceptable." And "nothing, absolutely nothing happens in God's world by mistake." (from the Big Book of *Alcoholics Anonymous*, p. 449.)

Weeds, and even mosquitoes, are not the worst things in life. I will try to accept them today – and accept the minor discomfort they cause me.

Queen for a Day

(7/21/2009)

Imagine what it would be like to be on top of the world – even if it was only for a day. That's what it was like when women were chosen to be "Queen for a Day" on the radio (1945-1957) and television (1956-1964 and 1969-1970) shows of the same name. The show was definitely a crowd pleaser. The 1970 version of the show ended in disgrace, however, when it was discovered that the "winners" were paid actresses chosen to win in advance. (Information from Wikipedia.com)

I think the whole concept of being "Queen" of the land is something of a scam. Even if you are hailed as being the most beautiful person in the kingdom, you aren't going to stay that way. You'll lose your figure – especially if you don't take care of yourself. You'll get older – as we all do – and your good looks will inevitably fade.

Being overly attractive in your youth is sometimes a setup for things to deteriorate. You're not always going to be the bell of every ball, you know. Consider the downside of being the woman every man wants. You date the most popular guy in high school, get voted homecoming queen, and get romantically involved at a young age. You get married in your teens and start having more children than you can manage. Before you know it you've got a family you didn't ask for, financial problems, and marital discord. Your dreams of being a movie star give way to the reality of being just another tired housewife.

In the words of *Scripts People Live*, a book on "Transactional Analysis" by Claude Steiner, your disappointments earn you a "ticket" to have a life disaster – your choice of a nervous breakdown or a divorce. But your "life script" is tainted from the very beginning. Thinking that you are "a princess" destines you to have one letdown after another. And so you go through one nasty divorce after another.

The years come and the years go. Fate smiles on you, though, and your latest husband *appreciates you* for who you are. Despite your faded glory, he still sees you as you once were. He sees you as his queen.

Your husband takes you out to dinner, helps you in and out of carriages, and treats you royally. He sees himself as *your knight in shining armor*, so he fetches everything you ask for. He not only helps you in and out of chairs, but also never lets you take an unassisted step. But your sedentary lifestyle aggravates your immobility. You gain weight and become even more sedentary.

Being "Queen for a Day" just isn't worth it. You look at yourself differently. You look at the world differently. You feel like you deserve to be Queen (or King) for more than just a day. This is called *entitlement*, and it is a dangerous thing. You'd be better off as a lowly ditch digger, who at least gets exercise with his shovel. Other *humble* professions also have advantages: barmaids learn how to listen, and waitresses know how to serve. Working – or, at least *staying active* – helps a person retain the ability to walk and talk. Thinking you are "special" is vanity at its worst; and "special treatment" isn't good for the giver or the receiver.

Survivalism

(7/28/2009)

Experts say the primitive part of our brain, the Limbic System, is the part that will never be bred out of us. No matter how smart we are, or how civilized society becomes, our behavior will always be driven by our instincts … Instincts are both good and bad. They are inborn patterns of behavior that promote self-preservation, sexual relations, and concern for our standing in society. The problem for modern man is that he needlessly obsesses about these matters.

Legend has it that prehistoric man had to battle *Saber Tooth Tigers* to survive, and modern man *still feels* like his "battles" are on the same scale. We have *fight versus flight* reactions to "enemies" that don't need to be fought nor run away from. In a similar way, we retain salt, binge on food, and store fat for "journeys into the wilderness" that are never made. Modern man is rarely deprived of food and essential nutrients, you know. And half of all Americans develop hypertension – for no good reason – a throwback to primitive times when even minor injuries could cause a significant drop in blood pressure. Medical students learn these *Physiology* lessons early in their schooling, and then spend the rest of their careers treating patients' overactive Neuroendocrine Systems.

Another part of our make-up that does more harm than good are so-called *Character Defects.* In recent weeks I have talked about some classic character defects – *Perfectionism* and *Entitlement.* This week I will add *Survivalism* to my list. I made up the word, so you're not going to find it in a dictionary. Traditionally, problems related to this are included under the *Seven Deadly Sins* – Anger, Pride, Greed, Envy, Lust, Sloth and Gluttony … I use the word *Survivalism* to point out that there seems to be a disturbed state of physiology (along with an unhealthy moral state) that leads people with these *sins* to think they *need more* than they really do.

People with *Road Rage*, for example, believe they have to get somewhere in a tremendous hurry – and it is okay to rage against drivers you are supposed to be sharing the road with. Experts say *Angry People* are afraid they're not going to get something they want (a job promotion) or are afraid they're going to lose something they have (the affection of a loved one). Their fears are out of proportion to reality. But anger is a *self-fulfilling prophecy*: if you're angry all the time, you do lose things you value, and you don't get things you want.

Sloth is extreme laziness; *Gluttony* is compulsive overeating; *Lust* is excessive and perverted sexuality; *Jealousy* is resentment of others; and *Envy* means compulsively wanting what other people have.

The greatest sin of all, though, is *Pride* – which is thinking too highly of oneself. "For pride, leading to self-justification, and always spurred by conscious or unconscious fears, is the basic breeder of most human difficulties ... Pride lures us into making demands upon ourselves or upon others which cannot be met without perverting or misusing our God-given instincts. When the satisfaction of our instincts for sex, security, and society become the sole object of our lives, then pride steps in to justify our excesses." (from AA's *12 Steps and 12 Traditions*, chapter 4)

Pundits say that people who seem prideful really have low self-esteem, but that doesn't matter. It's wrong to think that you are better than or less than anyone else ... The problem with all of these character defects is that we don't have the proper perspective on things, we don't know the difference between want and need, and we don't have faith that our needs will be met.

Section 4:
Medical Matters

Headaches

If my writing gives you a headache, think of what it does to my poor wife! She gets a migraine with each new embarrassing topic I discuss. Many of my "Dr. Dirt" columns have had to be censored. Some may show up in my next book, but most are not fit for human consumption.

Dr. Dirt isn't the only cause of headaches, though. Around 25 million Americans list headache as one of the main reasons why they go to the doctor. And while headaches have been classified as organic or functional, it is now recognized that all headaches have – to a greater or lesser extent – some degree of biophysical disturbance.

Organic headaches are those that are due to sinusitis, concussion, encephalitis, brain tumor, and similar problems. Sudden onset, trauma, fever, pain over the cheek bones, nasal drainage, headache at night, pain when bending forward, stiff neck, double vision, and difficulty concentrating are some clues that you may be dealing with one these more serious problems. Surveys have shown, by the way, that patients who go to the doctor for evaluation of headaches are almost always concerned that they might have something "really bad" going on – like a brain tumor. Fortunately, these problems are rare; and the doctor can rule out organic causes with a careful evaluation, and appropriate tests (CT scan, MRI scan, spinal tap, etc).

Migraine headaches are recurring episodes of moderate to severe headache accompanied by nausea, vomiting, sensitivity to bright light and loud noise, and a variety of other symptoms. These headaches usually affect one side of the head or the other, and are throbbing in nature. Up to a third of migraine sufferers also experience transient neurological symptoms before the attack: shooting lights, blind spots, strange smells, one-sided weakness, etc. The "pre-migraine" symptoms (called an "aura") have stroke-like characteristics, but then resolve with the onset of the migraine.

Research has shown that migraines run in families. Migraineurs have a number of biological abnormalities, and the attack itself is a complex inflammatory and vascular cascade of events. Sophisticated brain Xrays (like PET scans) have shown abnormalities that help with research, and someday may help with diagnosis and treatment in the general public.

Non-migraine headaches have frequently been labeled as "tension" headaches. Pain from tension headaches is mild, gets worse as the day goes on, and causes "band-like" discomfort to both sides of the head. These headaches are not preceded by an aura. Some of these patients do have migrainoid characteristics, though. Some tension headaches arise from "arthritis" in the neck or temporomandibular (TMJ) joint, and have been called "muscle contraction" headaches. Some tension headaches lead to secondary migraines, and are classified as "mixed headache" disorders.

There are other kinds of headaches. "Trigeminal Neuralgia" is a seizure-like irritation of the trigeminal nerve, which is the nerve that provides sensation to most of the face. "Temporal Arteritis" is inflammation to an artery in the forehead, but this inflammation can also affect other arteries – and puts patients (always older patients) at risk for blindness, stroke, and heart attack. This condition is easily ruled out with a simple blood test. Most other headaches do not have any specific blood or Xray abnormalities, though. The doctor makes the diagnosis on the basis of a careful history and exam. His job is to rule out more serious conditions.

Headaches are often precipitated by stress. Migraines may be precipitated by certain foods – like wine, cheese, caffeine (with or without), and food preservatives. Ironically, medications that are used to treat headaches can also cause withdrawal headaches; so getting shots or pills for the headache causes a vicious cycle of recurring migraines. This is especially true for narcotics, but may even occur with simple analgesics. Sleep difficulty is another leading cause of headaches. Headache patients often benefit from medications that have a sedative effect. And shift workers (people who go from day to night work) also have headaches. The best thing for headache sufferers to do is to get up and go to sleep at a reasonable time, take their prescribed meds, eat three meals a day, avoid troublesome foods, and avoid stress.

There are many available treatments for headaches. "Abortive" treatments are used to stop an attack. Examples of abortive meds are Acetaminophen, Ibuprofen, and Narcotics. The newer Triptan meds (like Imitrex) also abort migraines, and need to be taken as soon as possible after the onset of aura or throbbing headache. "Preventive" treatment is for people that have almost daily attacks – or 3 or more bad attacks per month. Antidepressants, Anti-inflammatory agents, Blood pressure meds, and Anticonvulsants can be used for this purpose. It is reported that 70 to 90% of patients are helped with these meds. As always, it is important to review specific treatment options with your doctor. What works for one person might not work for another. But don't lose hope! There is much that can be done to help the headache sufferer.

Back Pain

(8/4/2010)

Back pain is one of the most common health problems in our society. Some experts say it's because our spine was meant to be supported by four legs – not two. Ninety percent of people in our country experience some form of back pain sometime in their lifetime, and spine experts say that 36% of the time it is due to a "herniated disc" condition.

Our bony spine is composed of vertebrae that are separated by intervertebral discs. While the outside of these discs (the "annulus fibrosus") is tough, the inside (the so-called "nucleus pulposis") is soft and mushy, and is susceptible to acute and chronic stress injuries. Inappropriate lifting, excess body weight, and other stresses can cause the mushy part of the disc to be squeezed out of its normal position. This is what doctors mean when they say you have "a herniated disc." When this occurs it can cause pressure on the nerves exiting the spinal card. Pressure on these nerves causes back pain – which can radiate down the leg – and it can be associated with "red flag" complications: weakness, numbness, decreased reflexes, sexual dysfunction, and loss of bowel and bladder control.

There are many other causes of back pain. "Non-discogenic" back pain can be due to tears, strains and spasms of the muscles that surround the bony spine. Back pain can also be due to ligament strains, osteoarthritis, spinal deformities, osteoporotic fractures, and a variety of other conditions. Life-threatening causes of back pain can also occur – e.g., kidney infections, spinal infections, aneurysms and tumors.

When pain in the low back is associated with pain extending into the buttock and the back of the leg it is called "sciatica." It is called this because the pain follows the course of the sciatic nerve, and the pain is caused by herniated disc pressure at the L4-L5 and/or L5-S1 levels. This is the most common form of herniated disc disease. Ironically enough, though, many people have some degree of disc disease (on population CT studies) without having any significant pain or other problems. And there are some conditions (fat wallet syndrome, biker's butt pain, etc) that mimic "true sciatica." But these latter conditions are not caused by a herniated disc. If you have sudden onset of low back and leg pain, however, you are probably dealing with a herniated disc problem.

Many different kinds of treatment have been recommended for back pain and disc disease. Bed rest is sometimes recommended – but some studies have shown that patients who stay reasonably active do better than those who are put on bed rest. There is also disagreement as to what kind of bed back pain patients should use. A reasonably firm bed is usually preferred over an excessively soft one, however. Medications can help relieve the discomfort of sciatica. Tylenol, anti-inflammatory drugs, corticosteroids, narcotics, and muscle relaxants all can make the patient feel better – but do nothing to speed up the recovery of the back pain problem. In a similar way it has been shown that acupuncture, massage, ultrasound therapy, transcutaneous electrical nerve stimulation (TENS), and chiropractic manipulation can all provide temporary symptomatic relief of back pain – but have not been proven to speed up the recovery of discogenic back pain. The best way to recover from an episode of back pain, it seems, is the passage of time.

If your back pain does not improve in six weeks then it is appropriate to get an MRI of your spine – to see if there is a condition that might require surgery. If you have "red flag" problems (listed above) then you should get spine imaging sooner rather than later. Even if you have a documented herniated disc it is usually recommended that you try conservative treatment first (rest, medications, physical therapy, etc) before rushing into surgery. While many surgery patients do have prompt relief of their leg pain, studies have shown that their overall outcome (at 2 years of follow-up) is no better than those patients who are treated non-operatively. Your primary care doctor and spine specialist should work together when you have a herniated disc problem – and they should be able to agree on when surgery is "truly needed."

Back pain can be mild or severe, short-lived or chronic, a nuisance or completely disabling. Many different kinds of health care providers should be able to help you evaluate and treat this common condition.

Pain

(8/1/2007)

My "Dr. Dirt" columns regularly report on a variety of medical conditions. Last week I reported on how it is sometimes difficult to tell if new medical treatments are all that they are hyped to be. This week I'd like to continue with a related question: How can you get effective pain relief without getting duped?

There are over 200 different kinds of arthritis, and they all cause pain. Rheumatoid Arthritis is a serious disease that damages the joints but also affects the lungs and other body organs. This disease needs aggressive treatment by qualified professionals. Most arthritis is the more mundane variety, though. Degenerative Joint Disease ("Osteoarthritis") is what affects 75% of Americans. If you're like me, the most important symptom you have is PAIN. You want relief. You have heard a million ways to treat your condition. What is true, and what isn't?

Non-steroidal anti-inflammatory drugs (NSAID's) are medications that were once touted as being very safe and effective at relieving the pain associated with arthritis and related conditions. It has recently been reported that *all* of the NSAID's increase your chance of having a heart attack, especially if you have risk factors. For this reason, a once popular medication (Vioxx) has been taken off the market. But drugs like this cause fewer bleeding ulcers than alternative agents, so you have to balance the advantages and disadvantages of this type of therapy. This is not the first time (and certainly won't be the last time) that a "wonder drug" will gain widespread approval – only to have "post-market" analysis show the drug has unexpected side effects. And malpractice lawyers have been quick to capitalize on these perceived dangers.

Most NSAID's are still on the market, and are safe for most people to use. Ibuprofen, Naproxen, and Celebrex are well-known examples of these agents. After news came out about a possible link (with these drugs) to heart attacks, doctors became more conservative about their recommendations for pain relief. Acetaminophen (Tylenol) is once again the first choice for pain relief. When used correctly, it is safe and provides relief from mild pain. Muscle relaxants and physical therapy are also useful. A major review article showed that Low Back Pain gets better (in the majority of patients) with just about any treatment. Orthopedists, Internists, Family Practitioners, and Chiropractors all treat this condition effectively. Education, weight loss, joint protection, and reasonable exercise are also important ways to treat arthritis and back pain.

When treating pain, it is important to consider a patient's fears and expectations. In the same way that schoolchildren learn more if it is predicted they will, telling patients they are going to improve is therapeutic. "Self-fulfilling Prophecy" experiments prove that identically matched children tend to perform up to (or down to) the level of expectations they are exposed to. Telling a patient they are going to have less pain with a "sugar pill" has been scientifically shown to help about 70% of people. This is called "the placebo effect." The benefit may be psychological, or may be due to the body's intrinsic ability to heal itself, once the barriers to wellness are removed. (Placebos are never used for serious conditions, by the way.) In the same way, it is thought that much of the benefit that a patient gets from going to the doctor may be due to the "hands on effect" of a caring provider.

Many people believe that acupuncture, massage, magnets, prayer, and other interventions work better than traditional medications. Is it a placebo effect? Or is Glucosamine really helping my knee arthritis? Americans spend more than $30 billion of out-of-pocket money per year on non-traditional remedies. It's important to remember that if a treatment sounds too good to be true, it probably is. The National Institute of Health is studying these therapies, however, so we'll have a better idea of what works and what doesn't work in the future. Perhaps your insurance will pay for these options someday. In the meantime, it's important to be a well-informed consumer regarding treatment of your arthritis and related conditions.

More Pain

(1/15/2008)

I'm afraid 2008 isn't starting out too well. There have been way too many funerals. The collapse of the subprime lending market is causing serious problems to our economy. Many new homeowners are having trouble making their mortgage payments. The stock market is having its worst January ever. And the winter weather is chillier than we'd like, but lacks the blanket of snow that can beautify the landscape – and provide much needed ground moisture. On both a personal and public level, there's way too much pain and suffering going around.

Friedrich Nietzche, the great 19th century philosopher, said: "What does not kill me makes me stronger." Nietzche, who was chronically ill, thought that pain was a useful commodity. In America, though, pain is not regarded as a way to increase our strength, wisdom, empathy, and spirituality. Pain, in fact, is avoided like the plague. Ironically, Nietzche went completely insane (from neurosyphilis) at the age of 45, and died eleven years later.

Complete lack of pain is not a good thing either. When it occurs on a congenital basis, a rare phenomenon, children with this disorder do not practice risk-avoidance behavior; and the multiple injuries they sustain can be quite serious. Likewise, the deformities associated with Leprosy (Hansen's Disease) are mostly due to pain insensitivity – which leads to multiple untreated skin lesions. Diabetics also have decreased pain sensitivity. They can have sores on their feet that go un-noticed, get infected, and (along with poor circulation) lead to gangrene – which is the leading cause of amputation in our country.

Patients need to report their pain in order for doctors to figure out what is going on. Back and hip pain *usually* indicates problems with the back and hip, respectively. Headaches are *almost never* due to problems with the brain itself, however. The perception of pain is sometimes a complicated matter. There are "fast" and "slow" nerve pathways. Pain messages goes through a "gate" at the spinal cord level, and then on up to the brain. There are filters every step of the way. The pain message crosses from right to left, and vice versa. Knowledge of this system is important because different causes of pain need to be treated in different ways.

Sometimes a problem in one area is "referred" to another area: a heart patient may have neck pain, and a gallbladder patient may have shoulder pain. That's why doctors and patients need to pay attention to the characteristics of pain – rather than just always suppressing it with a pain pill. But pain from

125

a known (and difficult to treat) problem can cause continuing aggravation, high blood pressure, depression, and suicide.

Two weeks ago I broke a few ribs. The pain was so bad I didn't care if I lived or died. The pain was worse with movement and every breath I took. If I sneezed or coughed, I was gripped with pain and spasm that seemed intolerable. Medications and time gradually eased my suffering. I'm still not back to normal, but I can tell there is an end in sight.

Some types of pain don't seem like they'll ever end. And psychological pain (from the experience of loss) may be worse than physical pain – and may be accompanied by feelings of guilt, loneliness, and depression. There isn't any pill that cures this suffering. Antidepressant medications may help, but this type of suffering needs more than just pills. Time helps – but never in the time frame that we hope for. Prayers help. We need to give pain sufferers our understanding and support. Professional assistance is almost always indicated. If you can't identify with this problem, just hang around a bit. It is inevitable that you will experience "more pain" sometime in your life.

Attention Deficit Disorders

(10/30/2007)

The Attention-deficit disorders (ADD and ADHD) affect 3-5% of American children, and 2 million children in our country have one of these diagnoses. Is this because we are talking about a real biological disease – or have we stretched the definition of these disorders in order to put millions of children on drugs? I believe we are talking about real disease, but that these problems are over-diagnosed, and too many children are being put on potentially dangerous drugs.

The main characteristic of the Attention-deficit disorders is the inability to pay attention to the subject at hand. There may be associated hyperactivity. If there is inattention only, it's called ADD. If there is inattention with hyperactivity, it is called ADHD. Children with Attention-deficit disorders are easily distracted. They have difficulty completing their school work, and these problems usually get recognized during elementary school. That's when the diagnosis of ADD or ADHD is made. These children make careless mistakes, are disorganized, and get poor grades. It's not that these kids are dumb or lazy – they just can't focus on the work that needs to be done.

If there is associated hyperactivity (ADHD), the kids tend to fidget, squirm, and get up frequently. These children can't work quietly. They talk excessively. They may be overly aggressive, and get into more than their share of fights.

Children with an Attention-deficit disorder have a biological imbalance. They have low levels of neurotransmitters (Norepinephrine and Dopamine) in the Reticular Activating System, which is the part of the brain that regulates arousal, attention, and ability to ignore distractions. Neurotransmitters are the chemical messengers between one neuron and the next. The most popular way to treat this condition is by giving "Speed-like" drugs (Stimulants) that boost the body's Norepinephrine level. The main drug used is Ritalin, which is also called by its generic name, Methylphenidate. Nowadays there are also drugs that mimic the effect of Stimulants, and these agents are generally safer to use and equally effective.

Parents and teachers have been known to get frustrated with ADD/ADHD kids. They are more than willing to try drugs on these children. And the drugs work! That, my friends, is part of the problem. Whether a person has ADD or not, Ritalin (and related drugs), improves short-term school performance. But perhaps we haven't been maximizing our non-drug therapy for dealing with these school and behavior problems. I find it curious that North American doctors diagnose Attention-deficit disorders at three times the rate that British doctors do. I suspect the high percentage of U.S. children treated with drugs for these problems is due to the fact that we live in a drug-oriented and performance-obsessed society.

I am opposed to the indiscriminate use of Stimulant drugs for the Attention-deficit disorders. These are some of the very real problems that have been encountered with these drugs …

Drug Abuse and Misuse: Over 90% of American children with a diagnosis of ADD and ADHD are given a prescription for one or more of the Stimulants. Often there is poor monitoring of this therapy, and failure to recognize their potential side effects. And these drugs frequently fall into the wrong hands. Studies show that 8% of college students have obtained (and use) these drugs to improve their school performance. And 11% of college students use Stimulants, not for school, but to get high.

Paradoxical Drug Reactions: Depression is a common side effect to psychiatric drugs in children. Dangerous and/or suicidal behavior can also occur.

Growth Retardation: All children given Stimulants will have at least some growth retardation, which is thought to be reversible, providing the patient is able to periodically come off this type of medication.

Over-diagnosis & Misdiagnosis: England has a 1% prevalence of ADD and ADHD, compared to 3-5% rate in the U.S. and Canada. Not every disruptive child in England is given a diagnosis of an Attention-deficit disorder, as appears to be the case in North America. Many children with problems need a more definitive diagnosis – Depression, Learning Disability, Personality Disorder, Adjustment Reaction, etc. Calling all these kids "ADD" can lead to a worsening of their underlying problem, which may be aggravated by the inappropriate use of Stimulants.

Overdependence on Stimulants vs. Alternative Medications: There are a variety of other drugs that have demonstrated efficacy with the Attention-deficit disorders (and similar conditions) – like Desipramine, Bupropion, Effexor, Cymbalta, and other agents. Unfortunately, many American doctors go for the "quick fix" that Stimulants provide, which often fail to provide lasting benefit.

Overdependence on Drugs vs. Alternative Therapies: Improving parenting skills, teaching techniques, and study habits are other issues that need to be addressed in the Attention-deficit disorders. Cognitive and behavioral therapy should be used on virtually all of these children. With our overuse of drugs, however, these therapies are not even tried.

(The information in this report is from Medscape.com, a doctor's website, and the symposium they held on the Attention-deficit disorders in July of 2007.)

Abortion

(10/27/2008)

A young woman wrote a "letter to the editor" on the topic of abortion in our local newspaper recently, and expressed the viewpoint that women should be able to do whatever they want with their bodies. The letter argued that "a baby isn't yet alive with a beating heart until they are nearly born, not when it is a few stem cells grouped together." For this reason, it was argued, abortion really isn't any big deal – and pregnant women should be allowed to get an abortion whenever they want. I delivered nearly 200 babies in my early medical career, and feel compelled to comment on a few of the errors found in this kind of thinking …

A normal pregnancy lasts 40 weeks. The embryonic heart starts beating 22 days after conception, which is 5 weeks after the woman's last period. By 10 weeks, the obstetric practitioner can hear heart tones with a Doppler instrument, and by 20 weeks fetal heart tones can be heard with a regular stethoscope. Babies born prematurely (27 or more weeks) have a greater than 90% chance of surviving. Even at 24 weeks, babies have a 50% chance of survival. So to say that a "fetus" isn't viable unless it goes full term is grossly wrong.

Back in 1968 a *Psychology Today* article noted that "there's little difference between a newborn baby and a 32 week fetus. A new wave of research," the article continues, "suggests that the fetus can feel, dream, even enjoy *The Cat in the Hat*." An embryo responds to loud noises by 9 weeks and learns throughout pregnancy to respond differentially to the mother's voice. Birth, it seems, is an external event only. Janet DiPietro, a Johns Hopkins University psychologist, said that birth "is a trivial event in development. Nothing neurologically interesting happens."

There are many acceptable ways to deal with an "unwanted" pregnancy. That little burden living in your uterus could be a treasure to someone who is unable to have children. A friend of mine (name withheld upon request) was pregnant in her youth, and wrestled with what to do about her unplanned pregnancy. She chose to give the child up for adoption. In recent years, she was able (with the help of a Social Service Agency) to track down her 19 year old son. For whatever reason, it was the only child she was ever able to bring into this world. She enjoyed her brief visit with her long lost son. During their meeting, the boy, who was now a young man, made the following heart-wrenching statement:

"Thank you for not having an abortion."

As you can see, what we do does affect others. Abortion does not only affect the life of the mother. It belittles life, and prevents the miracle of a new birth from coming full circle.

Bedbugs

(3/3/2010)

"Goodnight, sleep tight, don't let the bedbugs bite."

We've all heard this rhyme hundreds of times. I now wish I had never even heard it. What was once a cute little rhyme has now become a sore reminder of the problems associated with a bona fide bedbug infestation.

I recently told you the story of how my middle son, Joel, moved into his first apartment. It was fun for him to look at apartments, decide on a place, and then go through the "moving in" process. Mom and Dad wanted to helped, of course. We didn't want to miss out on the fun. Joel also wanted someone to help pay for all the stuff he would need – a bed, a desk, miscellaneous knickknacks, etc. The experience of helping Joel kindled in me fond memories of my own first apartment.

Shortly after we returned home, we heard that Joel had developed a mysterious rash. The student health service wondered if he had been bitten by spiders. And "whatever it was" kept biting Joel every time he slept in that room. He developed insomnia. He had itching that distracted him from his schoolwork. He was frustrated and didn't know what to do.

Joel's neighbor then told him that there had been a massive infestation of bedbugs in the room he was sleeping in. Contaminated rugs were ripped out, and new hardwood floors were installed. Everything was made to look pretty, but hidden in the cracks and crevices of the apartment was a population of bedbugs that was quietly waiting for its next blood meal.

Bedbugs are like that. They are tiny little arthropods, measuring 4-7 mm in length, officially named *Cimex lenticularis*. They hatch from 1 mm white eggs, progress through five different larval stages, and usually live about 10 months. They need blood to progress from one larval stage to the next. And they are extremely resilient critters. In laboratory settings they can live up to 4 years and go without a blood meal for 550 days. They hide during the day and come out to feed at night. Each bedbug is capable of laying 6-10 eggs per week, and several hundred eggs in their lifetime. Females tend to cluster together, so there may as many as 500 eggs in one location.

Bedbugs have been around for at least 3500 years. Epidemic bedbug infestations have been noted throughout all of recorded human history. This has especially been a problem in overcrowded urban areas, but the distribution of infestations has been spreading. Nice as well as not-so-nice motels have recently had to deal with this issue.

According to Stefan Jaronski, USDA entomologist, bedbugs are "extremely difficult" to eradicate. DDT was once very effective at treating this infestation (with even a single application) but then resistance became an issue. DDT is no longer available. Insecticides ("Bedlam", etc.) are still the mainstay of treatment – but these have to be reapplied every 10-14 days in order to deal with bedbugs that have emerged from their dormant egg stage. Cyanide was once used to treat these pests, but can be lethal if improperly used. Heat and steam treatments have also had some success.

Non-chemical treatment of bedbugs is also important. For example, we had to throw out Joel's comforter, bed coverings, pillows and bedside rug. We did use insecticide on his brand new mattress, and are leaving it in a sealed bag for 60 days. This might also need to be discarded. His clothes were all washed (on one long day at the Laundromat) with 185 degree water.

Bedbugs suck blood, and there is concern that they might be able to transmit Hepatitis, AIDS, and other deadly diseases. That has never been documented, however. Bedbugs do cause "High Anxiety," however, and juries have occasionally given large rewards to plaintiffs who have had to deal with this problem. The old saying ("Don't let the bedbugs bite") remains as true today as it did centuries ago – and I hope it isn't something that you ever have to deal with.

Cough & Cold

(7/28/2010)

It won't be long before summer vacation is over and your kids are back in school. And that, my friends, will usher in another season of colds and coughs. Although I have written on this subject before (see my *Sidney Herald* article of 11/8/1987) there have been three recent medical articles on this subject that I would like to discuss with you.

A 10/7/2008 *WebMD Health News* release told parents not to use over-the-counter cough and cold drugs in kids under 4 years of age. The FDA ordered that infant preparations of these drugs be taken off the shelves altogether. And there was good reason to do so. It has never been shown that these products shorten the duration of colds, coughs, or ear infections. More importantly, however, is the fact that these drugs are often used inappropriately. About 7000 children go to the emergency room (ER) each year with overdoses of cold and cough remedies.

A 9/15/2008 report in *Clinical Infectious Diseases* noted that there are many adverse reactions to antibiotics. It was estimated that side effects from antibiotics leads to about 140,000 visits to U.S. emergency rooms each year. Dr. Daniel Budnitz, who led the study, made this comment: "This number is an important reminder for physicians and patients that antibiotics can have serious side effects and should only be taken when necessary." The study found that one-fifth of all drug-related ER visits are due to antibiotics. Penicillin and related antibiotics (such as amoxicillin) accounted for half of these ER visits. Keflex, Cipro, Septra and other antibiotics accounted for the rest. Dr. Budnitz said 78% of the adverse events in the study were allergic reactions, ranging from rash to anaphylaxis (swelling of the throat) and the remaining 22% were caused by errors and overdoses.

On 5/19/2010 it was reported (in the "British Medical Journal") that the overuse of antibiotics in general practice settings leads to "antibiotic resistance" that can last up to one year. This was an analysis of 24 other studies that found subsequent treatment of respiratory tract and urinary tract infections was more difficult in cases where antibiotics had been used in the preceding 12 months. According to Britain's Dr. Céire Costelloe, "some [of this] antimicrobial resistance may result from indiscriminate or poor use of antibiotics." As a consequence of using antibiotics when they are not really needed, infections are becoming more difficult to treat.

Doctors know that indiscriminate use of antibiotics and cold remedies can do more harm than good. Many doctors have a hard time saying "No" to patients who demand a prescription, however. Patients go to a lot of effort to get an appointment; they don't feel good; and they want "something" to show for their effort. They want a drug to make them feel better – even if what ails them (or their child) will get better on its own. Sometimes I told my patients that if their respiratory infection lingers on then an antibiotic might help, and they can fill the prescription in 3-4 days if it is still needed. I also was more likely to prescribe an antibiotic if the patient was elderly or had other medical problems.

Medicine still doesn't have a cure for the common cold. If you or your child don't have a fever, swollen glands, sinus headache, earache, or cough producing discolored sputum then the chances are what you have is a virus – and antibiotics aren't going to do any good. See your health care provider to make sure you're not dealing with something more serious, but don't always expect "a magic cure" for what ails you. Rest, fluids, and chicken noodle soup is still the best way to treat the common cold.

Normal Aging

(5/18/2009)

About 13% of our population is over 65 years of age. By the year 2030, it is estimated that it will be 22%, or 55 million Americans. "We're all getting older," the saying goes; and the implications of this are starting to hit home.

There are many age-related changes in our bodies. For example, it is "normal" to get thinning of our skin, loss of hair, "age spots," and loss of our skin's ability to protect us from heat and cold. Our lungs become less efficient. We get "short of breath" and are more susceptible to pneumonia.

As we age, blood pressure goes up, blood vessels stiffen, and heart size increases. The heart's ability to pump blood to our vital organs is usually maintained, however. Heart disease is common, but drugs and surgery are helpful. Our exercise tolerance and maximum heart rate decreases. As many as 30% of elderly people have a significant drop in their blood pressure when they stand up, which is called "postural hypotension." This causes unsteadiness, falls, and potential for serious injury. Many medications aggravate this problem. And falls are the leading cause of admittance to nursing homes.

The gut also changes with age. There is a decrease in saliva and digestive enzymes. The esophagus and stomach don't empty as well. The small and large intestine slow down, which may cause constipation; and some nutrients (like calcium) are not absorbed as well. Elderly people have mild "anemia," or low blood count, which may need evaluation. Although drug absorption is usually normal, older patients need lower doses of medications – because their liver and kidneys don't "get rid of" things as well. Drug side effects are very common in elderly patients, and account for as many as 1/3rd of all geriatric hospital admissions.

One third of eighty year old women will break their hip this year. It's from osteoporosis, "thinning of the bones," and everyone gets it. Most of us also get "wear and tear" arthritis, especially in the spine and weight-bearing joints. We may also become Diabetic, at least to some degree. Up to 1/3rd of 70 year-olds develop high blood sugars ("Glucose intolerance"). And we all lose muscle mass and have slowing of our reflexes.

"Experts" say Alzheimer's disease affects from 15 to 42% of those 85 and older, compared to 1% of 65 year-olds. "Small strokes" and other diseases may also cause cognitive decline, and these problems should be looked for if there is anything more than "benign forgetfulness." Drug therapy of Alzheimer's disease has only limited benefit, but research will improve our treatment options in the future. Depression affects about 10% of the elderly, occasionally mimics dementia, and is treatable.

The important thing to remember is that these problems *are not* a part of normal aging. If you're "bummed out" by what I've discussed in this article, then your brain still works, and life really is a heck of a lot better than it could be. It is also encouraging that 83% of those over 65 live in the community – and not in nursing homes. They live "normal" lives. They golf, play cards, take care of their home, go out for coffee, enjoy family, and do most of what they want to do. If they get sick, they have Medicare – which is "national health insurance" for the elderly. And if some doctor says "you're just getting old," tell them to take a hike … It is *never* acceptable to blame a person's medical problems on "old age."

Osteoporosis

(6/16/2010)

Some diseases are just not glamorous. That's how it is with osteoporosis. Even though 10 million Americans have this disease (8 million women and 2 million men) many people do not even know they have the problem. Furthermore, there are 44 million Americans who have low bone mass, or osteopenia – which can be regarded as a precursor to osteoporosis. In the public's failure to realize their "susceptibility" to osteoporosis, however, there lies an opportunity for doctors to treat this condition, and an opportunity for patients to be spared the ravages of this significant disease.

The defining characteristic of osteoporosis is reduced bone mass, making individuals susceptible to fractures of the hip, spine, and wrist. It has been estimated that osteoporosis accounts for more than 1.5 million fractures in the U.S. each year. These fractures can lead to significant problems – with hip fractures being the most disabling. More than 50% of patients who have had a fracture of the hip require nursing home care, and up to 20% die within one year of injury – of blood clots, pneumonia, and other complications of the bedridden state. Osteoporotic fractures also have substantial economic impact, with direct costs in the U.S. of $14 billion in 1995.

Bone mass increases throughout our early life, peaks around age 35, and then goes on a gradual decline thereafter. That's one reason why we should all consider ourselves to be at risk for osteoporosis. "Thinning of the bones" accelerates when our sex hormone production falls off: around age 50 for women and at a variable age for men. Other risk factors for osteoporosis include the following: cigarette smoking, excess alcohol use, poor diet, underweight condition, chronic illness, prolonged use of corticosteroid medication, use of excessive amounts of thyroid medication, and sedentary lifestyle. Caucasians and Asians have a greater risk of osteoporosis than other people. You can calculate your risk of osteoporosis by filling out the "National Osteoporosis Foundation" questionnaire on the subject. A periodic health care exam should also be able to assess your risk of osteoporosis. The other way to find out if you have "hidden" osteoporosis is by having a special X-ray (DEXA scan, et. al.) of your spine, hip, wrist or heel.

The most important thing to know about osteoporosis is that you should treat it before it leads to disabling fractures. You should get an adequate amount of calcium and vitamin D. And everyone with diagnosable osteoporosis should also get a prescription medication for their disease. Estrogen therapy used to be considered the best way to prevent osteoporosis in postmenopausal women.

Hormone therapy has been shown to improve bone mineral density and reduce fracture rates in women. Since publication of the *Women's Health Initiative* (WHI) in 2002, however, hormone therapy is no longer *routinely* used for long-term osteoporosis prevention. The WHI said there was an increased risk of heart attacks, breast cancer, and stroke among women receiving long-term estrogen and progesterone therapy. Short-term estrogen therapy is generally safe, however, and is still used to help women get through menopause.

In recent years the most commonly used osteoporosis medication is the bisphosphonate class of drugs. Bisphosphonates used in the U.S. include the oral medications Fosamax, Actonel, and Boniva as well as i.v. Reclast. Numerous studies have shown these medications to be effective at reducing fractures in patients with known osteoporosis. They are also widely used to prevent osteoporosis.

Second-line osteoporosis drugs are calcitonin (Miacalcin) and parathyroid hormone (Forteo). Other agents used are the selective estrogen-receptor modulator raloxifene (Evista) for women and injectable or transdermal testosterone for men.

All of these medications have their own specific side effects. The bisphosphonates can cause esophageal irritation and ulcers, and you need to stand or sit upright for 30-60 minutes after you take them. They can also cause drug interactions and problems with bone healing – particularly if you require dental surgery. Calcimar allergic side effects are common; and this drug can also cause nasal irritation or irritation at its injection site. Hormone side effects are discussed above. One of my biggest concerns about these medications, however, is their expense. These brand-name drugs typically cost about $80 per month (up to $900 per month for injectable Forteo) but generic Fosamax is now available for about $10 per month.

Some people have a hard time understanding why they need to take medicine to prevent a disease they don't even have. That's how it is with osteoporosis – and other diseases as well (heart disease, etc.) We have to listen to what scientists tell us about these things. Osteoporosis leads to one third of all 80-year old women having a hip fracture in any given year, after all; and that is certainly something that we should try to prevent.

Prostate Cancer

(9/23/2009)

September is "National Prostate Cancer Awareness Month." Although it is a relatively common problem, no disease is more *misunderstood* than prostate cancer.

A recent review article (*JAMA*, May 27, 2009) discussed this topic in a comprehensive and reasonable manner. They point out that prostate cancer was the 2nd most common cancer in the U.S. in 2008 (excluding skin cancer) with 186,000 new cases. However, in terms of cancer death, prostate cancer is "less lethal" than many other cancers. In 2008, prostate cancer ranked 5th in total annual deaths among all cancers. And the number of deaths from this disease has decreased from 35,000 in 1994 to 28,600 in 2008. This improvement is *probably* due to widespread use of PSA (prostate-specific antigen) blood testing – which helps identify patients with earlier stage cancer.

As men age, their PSA *usually* rises in a gradual manner. This is often due to "benign" enlargement of the prostate gland. Prostate cancer is extremely common, though. Autopsy studies (on men who died of non-prostate disease) found prostate cancer in 30% of men in their 50's and 80% of men in their 70's. An elevated PSA (or a PSA that has increased in a non-linear manner) *usually* requires evaluation. A needle biopsy can be done, and if it shows "aggressive" cancer, then treatment is *usually* indicated.

Radical prostatectomy is the "gold standard" treatment for prostate cancer. This surgery is technically demanding, however; and even in the best hands can be associated with complications – bleeding, loss of sexual function, loss of urine control, etc. Alternative treatments are: (1) External Beam Radiation, (2) Brachytherapy (radioactive seeds put directly into the prostate), and (3) Hormonal treatments (periodic Lupon shots). These alternative treatments can be given alone or in combination therapy; they have significant side effects; and up to 10% of patients who receive them have persistent or recurrent cancer.

There are *many things* that an individual with prostate cancer should consider. That's why it's extremely important to consult a urologist who is "balanced" in his approach to this disease. Most people with prostate cancer will not die of their cancer: they die of other causes. Death from prostate cancer (in the absence of treatment) generally occurs 10-20 years after diagnosis. That's why if you are in poor heart health, for example, you might not want to even bother with annual PSA testing. And if you do have an elevated PSA, "watchful waiting" is sometimes recommended. Since every treatment option (surgery, radiation, and hormones) has side effects, it is sometimes best to treat the prostate cancer only if it is causing symptoms.

As a practicing physician (from 1980-2005) I saw many instances where a man's PSA level caused concern. Some surgeons "cut first and ask questions later." Fortunately that is not the case here. Dr. Salem Shahin, a board-certified urologist serving Sidney and Williston, takes the time to explain what a patient should consider when they have an elevated PSA. While surgery is often the best thing to do, it's also true that there are situations when an elevated PSA should just be monitored – especially if the patient is not having any symptoms (related to prostate cancer) and if the treatment is likely to cause more problems than the underlying prostate disease.

Magic Bullet

(9/8/2010)

A "vitamin" is a small amount of a substance that is required for normal metabolism; if not present in a sufficient amount, it results in a specific disease process. "Nutraceutical" refers to any food substance that provides medical or health benefits. While there are many vitamin and nutraceutical products that do have some health benefits, Americans have become obsessed with the notion that there are "miracle" products that can be taken to enhance a person's health. We spent $27 billion on various health supplements in 2009. The FDA is allowed to remove these products if they are grossly unsafe – but rarely does so. And there is not any federal agency that certifies that these products do what they claim to do.

Many people have heard that some vitamins, if taken in adequate amounts, will prevent cancer. What they may not have heard is that reputable organizations have studied these claims, and failed to find any specific anti-cancer benefit. There was, in fact, an 18% increased lung cancer risk in people taking high-dose beta-carotene (vitamin A) in two large population studies. In a similar way, Folate (a B vitamin) caused an increased rate of colorectal cancer in a study done in China. No difference in stomach cancer was observed in a Chinese study with people taking vitamin C. While there was some anecdotal evidence that vitamin E and selenium might prevent prostate cancer, no such benefit was seen when it was formally investigated.

The last vitamin to be studied was vitamin D. Some people hoped that it would be useful for cancers of the colon, prostate and breast. Studies of vitamin D blood levels (done in the US, Europe and Asia) have not shown any cancer protective benefit, however; and high blood levels of vitamin D was associated with an increased risk of pancreatic cancer.

The story with hypertension and cardiovascular disease is a bit more encouraging. Correcting specific vitamin deficiencies has been found to lower blood pressure (BP) and reduce cardiovascular mortality. There are also a few nutraceuticals (garlic, fish oil, dark chocolate, flavonoids, etc) that have been found to have some benefit. But there is still no magic bullet. It was hoped that vitamin E, vitamin C, Folic Acid, and "antioxidant supplements" might be useful – but that has been disproven. Excess vitamin E actually increases BP and the risk of hemorrhagic stroke. Folic acid improves homocysteine levels (in a rare genetic condition) but has not been found to be useful in general patient settings. And a recent meta-analysis of 12,000 patients found that Calcium and vitamin D supplements caused a 30% *increased* risk of heart

141

attacks. When a person is already getting enough calcium in their diet, it may no longer be advisable to use these supplements.

There are many other situations where nutraceuticals were once thought to be useful – but formal studies have failed to show much, if any, desired effect. Calcium and vitamin D have only minimal osteoporosis benefit. Gingko biloba has not been shown to prevent Alzheimer's disease or stroke. Glucosamine, on the other hand, has been shown to provide some relief to people with severe arthritis. In most cases, though, the best source of "nutraceuticals" is a healthy diet, such as the following:

Eat more deep sea fish. Eat a high fiber diet (10-25 grams/day). Since it is hard to get enough fiber in an American diet, consider using a high-fiber cereal or a Psyllium fiber supplement. Use only olive oil or canola oil for cooking or on food. Eat fresh fruit and vegetables three times a day. The fresh fruit in your diet should have dark skins – since that is where flavonoids come from. Reduce the amount of red meat in your diet. Use whole grain products, as minimally processed as possible. Drink 2-4 oz of red wine or purple grape juice daily. Drink two cups of green tea daily. Use ½ cup of nuts daily – e.g., walnuts, pecans, almonds and peanuts.

Avoid any foods with partially hydrogenated anything in them (trans fats). Consider using Benecol or Smart Balance as a magarine/butter substitute. Avoid high fructose corn syrup (pop, etc). Avoid any highly processed or refined products, such as white bread.

This article may not contain "news" for many people. That's why I find it curious that Americans still spend so much money on dietary supplements. Their time and money would be better spent if they simply ate better and exercised more.

Sex Update

(2/17/2010)

It wasn't too long ago that the mere mention of "SEX" was considered taboo. Now we are bombarded with sexual themes in our TV shows, commercials, and mainstream magazines. "Super Bowl" ads exploit sex for commercial advantage. And the "Sports Illustrated" magazine relies on its annual "Swimsuit Issue" to generate ad revenue for the entire year.

The medical literature is also covering "sex topics" as it never has before. For many years doctors had to rely on outdated data from Drs. Kinsey (1948) and Masters and Johnson (1966). It was said that a man's peak sexuality occurred when he was 15-25 years of age, and a women's peak occurred at age 35. And the frequency of sexual activity was thought to decrease to "near zero" levels as people age. These decreases were thought to be "inevitable" because of age-related changes in human anatomy and physiology.

And then came Viagra … When this drug (also known as Sildenafil) became available in 1998, it finally gave doctors a medical therapy that worked. Viagra and its "PDE5 inhibitor" cousins, Cialis and Levitra, are very effective in treating Erectile Dysfunction (ED). Formerly called male impotence, ED is the persistent inability to achieve or maintain an adequate erection – which was the most common cause of decreasing sexual intercourse in older couples. These drugs are now widely used, and generated $3.5 billion of sales in 2007.

In "A Population-based [Sex] Survey" by Laumann, et al, from *Int J Impot Res*, 2009, it was discovered that over 70% of men and women in the 40-80 year range had engaged in sexual intercourse during the 12 months preceding these 2002 interviews. About 35% of men and 28% of women engaged in sexual intercourse regularly (that is, more than once a week).

Men reported early ejaculation and erectile difficulties as common sexual problems. Women reported lack of interest and lubrication difficulties as their most common sexual issues. It is noteworthy that most men and women in this survey reported continued sexual interest and activity as they aged, however – which is contrary to what was once thought to be the "asexual" nature of advancing age.

Of those people who were not sexually active, less than 25% of them had sought professional help for their sexual problems. Some cited embarrassment, the mistaken belief that asexuality was a part of advancing age, the belief that their problem was not serious, and the fact that doctors rarely ask them about sex. Nearly 60% of people think their doctors should ask them about their sex life, though.

Patients find it difficult to discuss sexual concerns with their doctor. It was not uncommon for patients to come into the office for an unrelated problem, and then – as I was leaving the exam room – for them to ask:

"Oh, by the way, Doc, what can you tell me about Viagra? Does it work? Is it safe?" These questions have to be addressed in the context of a person's individual situation. If you have a heart condition (and take Nitroglycerin products) then taking Viagra-like products can be dangerous. And if a man has ED, then their other medical problems need to be addressed: Is there evidence of a heart or circulation problem, diabetes, hypertension, smoking, or alcohol abuse? Women need a similar evaluation – with a special emphasis on their hormone status, lubrication, and relationship issues. And someday Viagra-like drugs may be prescribed for female sexual dysfunction.

Some experts (like my wife) say there is too much emphasis on sex in our society. On a cultural level, that is probably true. But medical science is recognizing that healthy aging and healthy sex go hand in hand. So don't be afraid to ask your health care provider if you have questions on these matters.

Obesity

(12/16/2009)

Did you know that over half of all medical expenditures are for diseases that are preventable? That's just one reason why it's idiotic for our nation to be enacting hastily conceived national health care reform. Why, for example, would anyone change their lifestyle when they "don't see" the connection between their medical health and their wallet?

It's easy to see the link between cigarette smoking and various diseases. Thank God the percentage of adults who smoke has gone down somewhat in recent years, but worldwide and young people smoking rates are still a huge concern. I'll discuss that topic at a later date. Today I will discuss a topic that nobody likes to talk about … Obesity.

Obesity is defined as a body mass index (BMI) of 30 or more. Google "BMI calculator" if you want to determine your exact BMI. Another way of looking at it is by saying that a 5'9" male is clinically obese if he weighs over 203lbs, and a 5'3" female is obese if she weighs over 169 lbs. Needless to say, I met the "obesity criterion" about 30 lbs ago. That's one reason why I have been remiss to discuss this topic.

The CDC says that more than one third of U.S. adults – more than 72 million Americans – and 16% of our children are clinically obese. Since 1980, the obesity rate has doubled for adults and tripled for children. Obesity does not discriminate: people of every age, sex, race, ethnicity, socioeconomic status, educational level and geographic region are affected by this disease. Colorado, in fact, is the only state in the country that has an obesity rate of less than 20% (their rate is 18.5%). And obesity is a major risk factor for cardiovascular disease, type 2 diabetes, high blood pressure, high cholesterol, sleep apnea, osteoarthritis, and certain types of cancer. In 2000, obesity-related health care costs totaled $117 billion, which is 27% of our total health care budget. It is amazing that insurance companies, including the government, will pay $50 to $100 thousand for each coronary artery bypass surgery done in this country, but won't pay for the preventive care that might help an obese person avoid this heart complication.

In 1989, a group of 12 patients urged me to start an obesity clinic for them in Sidney MT. These patients were on the older side, and all of them had diseases that are associated with morbid obesity. The design and implementation of the program was left to me. The hospital agreed to do the technical part of the program: a treadmill test, a pulmonary function test, blood work, and consultative services (with a dietitian and exercise specialist).

I was not able to get insurance company reimbursement for my "weight loss" services – but did bill them if they had associated medical conditions. My staff and I followed these patients every week for 3 months in my clinic … and longer if they were my "regular" patients. These patients named themselves "The Fat Clinic," and they helped support each other in their individual and collective weight loss goals. Some of these patients used a dietary supplement called "Medifast" to get "jump started" on their weight loss program. Others used traditional diets to lose weight, and two of them subsequently had gastric bypass surgery.

In order to better serve these patients, I joined the "Bariatrics Society" of physicians (ASBP) – which is a group that attempts to serve obese patients, research weight loss interventions, and point out fraud in the lucrative weight-loss industry. I told my "Fat Clinic" patients that the data on reaching weight loss goals is not encouraging. The short-term results, however, were nothing short of phenomenal. Many of these patients lost 50 to 60 lbs! But even a 5-10 lb weight loss can help diabetes and other problems. The longer these patients continued to come for follow-up visits, I noticed, the longer they maintained their goals. It's been twenty years since I took on that project, and most of those patients are no longer with us. The experience taught me (and these patients) that it is possible to lose weight, a multi-disciplinary approach is best, a variety of diets can work, and "mutual benefit self-help" group support is useful. I am also not opposed to obesity surgery – and for some people it can be a life-altering intervention.

So where do we go from here? Well, it will soon be time to make New Year's resolutions. It will soon be time to put holiday binging and snacking behind us. Hopefully this will be the year when truly revolutionary obesity interventions will become available – but don't count on it! Do not believe, as the saying goes, in anything that "sounds too good to be true – because it probably is." Listen only to true experts in the medical field of obesity and weight loss intervention. It is important, however, to make the effort to be as healthy as you can be. It will benefit you, your pocketbook, your family, and our society.

Health Care Reform

(10/28/2009)

Last month I wrote an article on "Health Care Reform" that appeared in the Sidney, Billings and Missoula newspapers. I received many favorable comments on the piece, but people said they wanted more information on the subject. Health Care Reform is an issue that everybody should have an opinion on. Insurance premiums have gone up 87% since 2000. If left unchecked, our nation's health care spending will double to $4 trillion in the next 10 years. (Hillary Clinton's campaign statement) While President Obama says it is essential that we act on health care reform this year, many people want Congress to stay out of the health care business. Eighty percent of people are happy with their current health care, and over half of Americans believe Congress is going to make the health care situation worse.

Many people don't realize that "the government" has been in the health care business for almost 45 years. Medicare, Medicaid, and other government programs paid for about 45% of health care in 2006. Furthermore, there are 47 million Americans who don't have any health insurance. When these patients get sick, they go to the Emergency Room, which is *the most expensive* form of health care around. Nobody gets out of the ER for less than $300. And many of these problems could be taken care of with a $30 office visit. For these reasons (and others) is not unreasonable that government should try to enact some kind of health care reform – but they have been going about it in the wrong manner.

The U.S. spends 16% of its Gross National Product (GNP) on health care – which is twice the amount that other industrialized nations spend on health care. It should be noted, however, that those countries get better *grades* than we do (from the World Health Organization) on the overall results of their health care. While it is possible that some of that greater expense of health care in the U.S. is due to its technological superiority over other countries, it is also likely that our doctors are overly concerned about getting sued, and order way more tests, expensive drugs, and unnecessary consultations than they need to. It is estimated that our country could save at least $100 billion per year if there weren't so many "Defensive Medicine" practices in our country.

Let me illustrate this point: A patient complained of dizziness, and it was demonstrated that his blood pressure was too low when he stood up. His doctor ordered a head CT scan, MRI scan, Cardiac Ultrasound and Brain Wave test to evaluate the problem. All he really needed was to have his blood pressure pills reduced. Unfortunately, however, many doctors order every "dizziness test" they can think of for a patient like this. I think the logical thing (lowering of the BP medication) should be done first, and consider doing those other tests later – if the patient is still having significant dizziness. These extra expenses are not doing anyone any favors. All they are doing is treating the doctor's paranoia that he might get sued. Everyone's insurance (and overall health care bill) goes up when the system has to absorb these costs on a regular basis – as is routinely the case in our country.

It's obvious that many doctors order way more tests than are necessary. They think that "if things go wrong" that having ordered every test imaginable will somehow protect them from a lawsuit. This is erroneous thinking. The laws of statistics tell us that at least 5% of the tests (probably 15% as "over-interpreted in real life) are going to show some insignificant finding – which will result in more tests being ordered, more "false positives" and more expense.

I believe that "the malpractice issue" is a major impediment to getting workable health care reform. Indicative of the problems is that the U.S. has over 50% of the world's trial lawyers – despite the fact that it only has 4.5% of the earth's population. (Data from Wikipedia.com) It is idiotic for liberal lawmakers to think they can represent both the "trial lawyers association" and our nation's health care needs. Hungry lawyers and ridiculously expensive litigation settlements will never allow the U.S. to have affordable health insurance. Congress should be enacting "Tort Reform" that allows injured patients to be fairly compensated – and discourages frivolous lawsuits and "defensive medicine" expenses.

Health care reform, as it has been proposed, will place a huge burden on our current system. And nobody really believes the President when he says health care reform isn't going to cost anything. Dick Morris (from DickMorris.com) says you can't provide more services to more people for less money without decreasing the quality of care provided. Furthermore, he predicts that many physicians will retire from medicine. They are already sick of government paperwork, and don't want to be squeezed into doing more work for less pay. Art Laffer, a guest economist on CNBC, puts it this way: "If you think Health Care is expensive now, just wait until you see what it costs when it is free." *Private pay* health insurance plans seem to have an inherent benefit over "public pay" options. It is important for patients to know what health care costs, and important for them to be "informed consumers" in the process. National Health Care, in Laffer's opinion, will drive a "wedge" between the health care consumer and the health care provider – and that is bound to further drive up health care costs. The old adage continues to ring true: There is "no such thing as a free lunch," and likewise there's no such thing as free health care.

President Obama insists that our health care system is broken – but it remains the envy of the world. There are certainly problems that need to be fixed: We need to take better care of uninsured and underinsured people. We need tort reform. It's erroneous to think that Congress should hastily push through health care reform, however, just so they can say they did it. A poorly designed overhaul of our health care system could certainly do more harm than good.

There are many things wrong with our current system ... People should take better care of themselves, of course, and primary care doctors should be "incentivized" to provide better preventive care. And many people need help paying for their medications – but they rarely need "the latest and greatest" new drug on the market. Most important of all, though, is our country's need to *honestly* discuss the "economic and ethical aspects" of health care. It's a sad fact, however, that the American public and our elected officials may not be ready to negotiate these issues.

Obamacare

(3/31/2010)

Last week President Barack Obama signed into law a historic healthcare reform package. The signing of this 2,562 page bill was dubbed "a monumental moment" similar to other historic signings: the Social Security Act of the 1930s and the Medicare Act of the 1960s. Many Democrats are calling this a huge victory, and many Republicans are calling it a disaster that ensures their candidates will prevail in this fall's elections.

As an Independent (by name and practice) I am not sure what this "great moment" really means. I find it curious that only 25% of Americans supported this bill in last month's CNN poll on the subject. But the juggernaut of "healthcare reform" could not be held back. While 80% of Americans have been content with their health care, the rest of the world wonders why the U.S. doesn't provide health insurance for all of its citizens. You can't argue with the fact that too many Americans are uninsured or underinsured. This bill will partially correct that problem. And "Right to Lifers" will be pleased to know that last minute deal-makers left funding for abortions out of this reform package … at least for now.

There is great concern that the government will bungle its role in the realignment of the healthcare industry. This reshaping of one-sixth of our nation's economy will take place over several years. Most of the bill's far-reaching changes don't occur until 2014.

One immediate consequence of this bill is that tanning salons will be subject to a 10% tax. Another immediate aspect of this bill is that Medicare recipients will be given a $250 rebate if their annual drug costs are over $2,830. This attempts to correct the so-called "doughnut hole" deficiency of the Medicare Part D medication plan.

I am pleased that the new program allows Medicare recipients to receive free preventive care (like cancer screening exams) without any copayments or deductibles. Private insurers will no longer be able to cancel policies of people who get sick. Insurers may not put lifetime limits on the dollar value of coverage. And children can remain on their parents' insurance policy up until their 26th birthday.

The number of people eligible for Medicaid will increase by 50%. This will help to insure many people who are at or near poverty income levels. But other uninsured people will eventually be fined ($95/yr in 2014 and $695/yr in 2016) if they don't have health insurance.

While Obamacare has many desirable features, there is concern that it will lead to increased "socialism" of our entitlement programs. Another huge concern is that someone has to pay for this $100 billion/yr program. Drug companies will have to pay a fee of $2.5 billion in 2014, and that amount increases to $4.2 billion in 2018. Insurance companies will have to pay a fee of $8 billion in 2014, and that amount increases to $14.3 billion in 2018. A 40% excise tax will also be placed on top insurance policies, which will start in 2018. The biggest source of funding, though, will come from shifting $500 billion (over 10 years) from Medicare to the new program.

Many people believe that mandating increased benefits will ultimately affect quality of patient care. Rationing of special services, limitations of choice, and other "Canadian Health Care" style changes may have to occur. Even without this legislation, physicians are scheduled to take a 21% cut in payments this fall. Saying Obamacare will save money implies to me that doctors are going to get "squeezed" into doing more services for less pay. Many doctors and clinics already refuse to accept Medicare assignment – and this could become a bigger problem in the future. And the reform package doesn't do anything to address our huge Medical Malpractice Problem.

I for one am glad that all the bickering over healthcare reform is now over. Or is it? Fourteen state attorneys general have already filed lawsuits saying the federal government is not allowed to legislate on healthcare matters – individual rights that they claim are inherently up to the states to decide on. One such suit says it illegal to force rationally uninsured individuals to subsidize older and less healthy citizens. Pundits say the battle on healthcare legislation may be over, but the fight has just begun.

Better Treatment

(6/10/2009)

Has your doctor ever told you to take your medicine, even though it could be *bad* for you? Perhaps he should. Some drugs that doctors use are later shown to have problems. Doctors aren't stupid, but our understanding of *how things are* has to be periodically refined. There are *good and bad ways* to treat certain conditions. And we are always trying to come up with *better* treatments.

"Hypertension" is an important example. It is sad that only 30% of the world's one billion hypertensive patients control their blood pressure (BP). Why so bad? There are many reasons ... In America, for example, doctors once ignored high BP unless it was *really high* (over 180/95), especially in the elderly, because treating it could cause side effects. But *not* treating this degree of hypertension is far worse than dealing with medication problems. The goal is to keep your BP under 140/90 – and even lower (130/80) if you have kidney disease or diabetes. With a bit of *tinkering*, your doctor should be able to find a way to control your BP without drug toxicity.

We have long known that treating hypertension reduces strokes, but some early studies (like the "MRFIT" Study) showed an increase in heart attacks with BP treatment. Doctors suspected it was the details of treatment that were wrong, and so the official treatment guidelines have been frequently revised.

There is, for example, a *class* of antihypertensive medication ("Beta Blockers") that is very helpful in "secondary prevention" – i.e., preventing problems in patients who have heart attacks and heart failure. They mostly work by lowering heart rate, and were also thought to be useful, until recently, in preventing problems in the first place – which is called "primary prevention" of disease.

Dr. Bangalore, et al, showed last year (in his review of 64,000 patients) that "a lower heart rate was associated with a greater risk of cardiovascular events and death for hypertensive patients." That was a big surprise. That's why these drugs are no longer used for "first line" treatment of hypertension.

In the USA, doctors can prescribe whatever BP pill they want. Let's hope they are keeping up with the medical literature, and have a treatment plan that is right for you. In Canada, doctors are told what meds to use. And maybe that's not such a bad thing ... A recent news release (from Canada) reported that a "single pill" that contains low doses of several medications, as opposed to the usual "multiple pill" options, resulted in improved BP control. Their so-called "STITCH" algorithm takes the guess work out of BP management. The USA, in future months, may adopt similar guidelines.

"High Cholesterol" is a similar problem. In the 1980's, many doctors didn't treat this unless the total cholesterol was over 300, even though the national goal was to get it under 260. We have known that cholesterol-lowering drugs are beneficial in established heart disease (for people with heart attacks or bypass surgery) but didn't know *for sure* that they were good *for everyone* until recently. A big "Primary Prevention" review (of 65,000 patients) put that question to rest. Death from cardiovascular "and other" causes was significantly decreased with medication. Doctors should now be trying to get everyone's cholesterol under 200, especially if you have "risk factors" and an unfavorable LDL/HDL ratio.

Patients who take "Statin" cholesterol-lowering drugs on a *regular* basis are 45% less likely to die than those who don't take their meds (under 10% of the time) as prescribed. And while cholesterol levels are important, *another* recent study shows it may be the "anti-inflammatory effect" of these "Statins" that is the important thing. Perhaps that is why Statins also reduce the risk of prostate cancer. Scientific studies (like these) help doctors to understand *cause and effect*, what works and what doesn't, and which treatments are "better" than others.

Hypertension

(8/25/2010)

Last summer I discussed "Better Treatment" for several common medical conditions. Hypertension, for example, can be treated in many different ways. New data keeps coming in, and "the latest guidelines" on this (and other) medical subjects keeps changing. At your request, I'll try to keep you up to date on these matters.

High blood pressure is defined as follows: (1) Optimal BP is under 120/80; (2) "pre-hypertension" is a BP in the 121-139/80-89 range; (3) stage 1 hypertension is BP in the 140-159/90-99 range; and (4) stage 2 hypertension is BP over 160/100. A BP over 130/80 is considered high in people with diabetes or kidney disease. "Systolic hypertension" is a normal lower (diastolic BP < 90) number but an elevated top (systolic BP >160) number, and is the predominant form of hypertension after age 50.

The following epidemiologic information has been noted: (1) Hypertension is extremely common – it affects about 29% of Americans; (2) one-third of people with hypertension don't know they have the disease; and (3) of those with treated hypertension, only about 53% have satisfactory control of the problem.

The following clinical data is also true: (1) Hypertension is associated with increased risk of death, heart attack, heart failure, kidney disease and stroke; (2) the greater the BP, the more likely you are to have one of these complications; (4) treatment of hypertension reduces the chance of these complications; and (4) while all hypertension medications lower BP, some specific drugs are recommended in certain situations.

American doctors are advised to follow a "Step Plan" in the treatment of hypertension. Dietary and non-drug treatment should always be recommended. If this doesn't work, then the first drug that should be tried is a low-dose thiazide diuretic. These low-cost drugs lower BP and prevent hypertension complications. If needed, a variety of other agents ("step two" drugs) may be used. Other countries are less regimented in their approach to hypertension, though, and combination therapy (i.e., two or more drugs in one pill) is often utilized. Doctors have found that several drugs are often needed to control a patient's BP.

Sometimes the best way to pick a hypertension drug for an individual patient is to look at what other problems they have. For example, certain drugs (ACE inhibitors and ARB agents) are particularly useful in diabetes and kidney disease, so these agents (Vasotec, Cozaar, etc) are used if the high BP patient has these problems.

What was said to be true at one time does not always stand the test of time. For example, beta blockers (e.g., Inderal) and short-acting calcium channel blockers (Diltiazem) were once thought to be particularly good at preventing first-time heart attacks ... but that is no longer felt to be the case. And beta blockers were once thought to be harmful in heart failure – but now have been found to be helpful. In a similar way, alpha antagonists (Cardura, etc) help both hypertension and prostate disease, but have not been shown to prevent heart attacks.

There are a few points I'd like to leave you with: (1) Every prescription is intended to do good, but may have unintended side effects; (2) it is important to avoid some side effects more than others – i.e., avoid drugs that can cause asthma when you have had asthma in the past; (3) treatment regimens can be "tailor made" to fit your unique circumstances; and (4) some BP pills have the potential to help more than one problem at the same time. Also note that you might be prescribed an expensive new drug because the drug company told your doctor that their drug is "superior" to another ... even when an older and cheaper drug might work just as well (or better) than the new one. Ask your doctor if any of these scenarios apply to you. And educate yourself on what "scientific knowledge" says about these topics.

Sodium

(5/5/2010)

Salt is in the news again. Salt restriction has been recommended since the 1970s, but Americans are remiss to follow voluntary guidelines – and indeed have increased their salt intake by nearly 50% in recent decades. We consume twice as much salt as is recommended. A recent article (by Bibbins-Domingo, et al, <u>NEJM</u>, 1/20/2010) pointed out that 100,000 lives could be saved each year if Americans reduced their salt intake by 3 grams per day.

We have long known that high salt diets lead to high blood pressure, which in turn leads to heart attacks, strokes and kidney disease. Modest salt reduction reduces BP by 5-7 mmHg. Many cases of mild hypertension can be treated by salt restriction alone. And "resistant" hypertension is often due to the patient not following the doctor's "low salt" recommendations.

When doctors speak of salt they are referring to sodium. Table salt is composed of sodium *and* chloride, so it's important to know which nutrient (salt or sodium) you are referring to – and it's important to read food labels carefully. For example, it is recommended that "non-hypertensive" people consume less than 3.7 grams of salt per day (2300 milligrams of sodium), and that people with hypertension consume only have half that much … So a typical hypertensive patient is advised to limit their salt to 1-2 grams per day, or 1200 milligrams per day of sodium. Modest reductions of this degree are achievable – especially if the salt reduction is done gradually.

Some people say they "need salt" in order to taste their food. Food processors, in fact, count on you "enjoying" their products more by artificially inflating the sodium content of their goods. And 80 percent of our salt intake now comes from the food processing industry. The FDA has overlooked this "sneaky salting" activity for years. Now several medical committees and public health agencies are calling on the FDA to mandate sodium reductions in our foodstuffs.

While salt does enhance the taste of food, our salt taste buds do adapt to the gradual reduction of salt content. National campaigns to reduce salt content have been successful in England, Finland and Japan. And hypertension-related disease and death rates have gone down. There are, in fact, only a few instances where "high salt" ingestion is needed – mostly in cases where people who work in hot weather need to avoid dehydration.

Many people think all they have to do to follow a "low salt" diet is to avoid using a salt shaker. That is unfortunately not true. Virtually every major player in the food industry has contributed to our national salt addiction, and that's why public policy action (through the FDA) is now being called for. Forty years of asking people and companies to voluntarily reduce salt intake has not worked. I have no doubt that some companies will now announce their intention to cut back on the sodium content of their products. Pepsi™ has in fact announced that they will reduce the salt content of their beverages by 25% by the year 2015. That's a good thing – but may be a case of "too little, too late." Don't be surprised if you hear more about this "Great Sodium Debate" in future months, and don't be surprised if your salt taste buds go through some re-conditioning.

Winter Doldrums

(1/27/2010)

"Another winter storm hit last night. My snow blower is broken – and it feels like my 'snow shoveling' back is on the verge of breaking as well. With all this snow, I hardly ever get out of the house. This weather is getting me down. Doc, I think I've got a bad case of *Winter Doldrums*. What should I do?"

Doctors need to be alert to these kinds of comments, especially during winters like this. Not only is it hard to get out and around in this weather, but "Seasonal Affective Disorder" can make these difficult times seem even worse.

Everybody experiences ups and downs, of course. When our "doldrums" make us feel overly depressed, though, it can interfere with our ability to function in everyday life. We then qualify as having an "Affective Disorder." The most common affective disorder is Major Depressive Disorder, which is also called Unipolar Depression. Another affective disorder is Bipolar Depression, which implies that the patient has extremes of both high and low mood. The official prevalence of these conditions is 12% and 2% of the population, respectively, but many experts believe that twice that many people are affected.

Drs. Ratey and Johnson, in their book *Shadow Syndromes*, note that many people have "bits and pieces" of diagnosable mental illness. "A shadow syndrome is an indistinct and seldom obvious form of a [more] severe disorder." The authors say that these problems occur because our body's neurotransmitters (chemical messengers) do not respond perfectly to the ebb and flow of environmental stress. Sometimes these syndromes are inherited; sometimes they occur as a result of environmental stress; and sometimes they are due to a combination of both inherited and environmental factors.

These Shadow Syndromes are very common. They usually don't have an "official" medical name. Examples of "lesser forms" of Depression, however, include the following: Dysthymic Disorder, Premenstrual Tension Syndrome, Prolonged Grief Reaction, Adjustment Reaction, Seasonal Affective Disorder, and so on, and so forth.

Experts say that these Shadow Syndromes respond to antidepressant medications, just like regular Depression. These medications are usually quite effective, and can be life-changing. All medications have the potential for side effects, however. And it is possible to treat these conditions without drugs. Regular exercise, exposure to daylight, and talk therapy can be useful. If you can't get outside – or don't want to in this cold – you can use a "Light Box" to prevent and/or treat Seasonal Affective Disorder.

One problem with these "Affective Disorders" is that they affect your *thinking* as much as they do your *feeling*. In his classic 1967 book, *Depression*, Dr. Aaron T. Beck was one of the first to suggest the importance of cognition (thinking) in what causes depression – and why it isn't always easy to treat. It's hard to come up with novel ideas on how to "get over" your depression if your thoughts are clouded. That's one reason why antidepressants are often needed to "bridge" a patient until they are able to make lifestyle changes.

So if you've been experiencing *Winter Doldrums* lately, realize that you're not alone. Maybe all you need to do is get some exercise – or ultraviolet light – to straighten things out. If not, you might need to visit your doctor, tell him what's going on, and see if there's anything that can be done to remedy the situation. Even if you don't have a full-blown Depression, you might benefit from treatment.

Third Opinion

(2/17/2009)

Your doctor says you have lung cancer, and schedules you for a leg amputation. "Hold on," you think; so you get a second opinion. The next doctor, an expert in holistic medicine, tells you "not to worry" about the cancer. All you need to do, she says is "eat healthy, take vitamins, and pray a lot." For obvious reasons, you feel uneasy. Nobody faults you for wanting "a third opinion."

Illustrations can be useful. You want your doctor to have an excellent knowledge of biology, which is "the science of life and living organisms." Your living body, you know, is comprised of organs and systems that function in predictable ways – and knowledge of how they work helps to figure out what to do when they are not working properly. He also should have a valid medical degree, be certified in his specialty (whether it is primary care or a subspecialty) and should do follow-up training and re-credentialing. And that is no small matter. As someone who is certified in three specialties (Internal Medicine, Family Practice, and Geriatrics) I know how much work it takes to stay up to date.

You want your doctor to know when to use medicine, and when to recommend surgery. It is also useful if he has some understanding of "holistic" medicine. This means that he realizes that what you are, as a person, is more than the sum of your parts. You are not only a kidney or a stomach. Your body systems do interact with each other, after all. Your doctor needs to remember that disease does not occur in a vacuum. He should not only take care of your medical needs, but also be concerned about your psychological and spiritual health. He should treat you like a person.

Some people believe we live only in a scientific world. We should only believe in what we can see or touch. If you can't measure it, then it doesn't exist. Any mention of philosophy or religion is counter-productive. "It's just witch craft," they say. Where medicine is concerned, it keeps people from getting the drugs and surgery they need.

Whether your doctor is a God-fearing person or not, medicine has learned that positive expectations and prayer can influence the outcome of treatment. Patients who believe they are "on the mend" follow treatment guidelines, do necessary rehabilitation, are happier, are easier to work with, and reach their full potential in ways that persistently negative patients ever will. While prayer has never been scientifically demonstrated to make documented cancers disappear, it has been shown to help patients in other ways. Anecdotally speaking, I have doctored a prayerful patient with metastatic colon cancer who lived eight years – when death within six month was the norm for his problem. And I have taken care of many heart and lung patients who lived many years longer than they were supposed to. Belief in the unseen (prayer and positive expectation) turns out to be more useful than previously thought.

When facing a serious problem in your life, don't accept a "scientifically-based" treatment only. And please don't settle for only a "spiritually-based" treatment, either. Man has a dualistic nature. Medical advances have helped people live longer – and so has indoor plumbing, a clean water supply, improved agricultural products, and a variety of public health measures. There will come a time in your life, however, that modern treatment will not be able to "fix" what ails you. When you have a disease that cannot be cured, you want your doctor to be honest with you, reduce your suffering, and be open to your non-medical needs. It's okay to have a "third opinion." It's okay to want the best of the scientific world *and* the spiritual world.

Section 5:
Politics & Religion

News or Opinion

(10/2/2007)

As a newspaper columnist, I have enjoyed the liberty of being able to write about a variety of topics. Even though I try to include a lot of "objective" material in my columns, I also constantly remind myself (and my readers) that my writing is mostly "subjective" in nature. More people in media should do this. They should reference their sources and never disguise their opinions as news.

Sometimes the media takes advantage of their position by disguising their political viewpoints as news. You know what I'm talking about. The media constantly portrayed President Gerald Ford as an uncoordinated idiot – even though he was the best athlete to ever hold the office. The media also loved to discuss how much President Richard Nixon perspired, and implied – from the very beginning of his career – that he was just a dirty politician. No wonder he said, in 1962, that "you won't have Nixon to kick around anymore." And the media also loved to make fun of George W. Bush, and made fun of him for making off the wall comments like this: "I have opinions of my own – strong opinions – but I don't always agree with them."

The media's ability to "color the news" is sometimes used in a responsible manner. During World War 2, for example, the media chose not to show President Franklin D. Roosevelt as handicapped, even though he was crippled with polio. They never filmed or photographed him in embarrassing situations – like when he needed to be lifted out of automobiles, or needed to be moved around by wheelchair. They didn't want him to appear "un-presidential" during the war. Likewise, the media was well aware of President Kennedy's womanizing, but his personal life was regarded as a taboo subject. My how things have changed ...

The ideal of keeping news separate from opinion may be impossible to meet. In medicine, for example, doctors are introduced to new drugs that the industry hopes will replace an existing treatment. The information that doctors receive about these products is supposed to be unbiased. And if "scientists" say one product is superior to another, then everybody starts using it.

Let me cite a specific example: In 1993, the "GUSTO" trial said Alteplase was markedly superior to Streptokinase. The new drug cost $2300 while the older drug cost $200. The investigators in that study were given "stock options" in payment for their services, and benefitted handsomely when this new drug started raking in the cash. The international medical community thought American doctors were crazy for recommending the more expensive drug – when the difference between the two drugs was minimal.

Most of us do not have training in Logic and Statistics, which are tools to analyze the significance, validity, and usefulness of new information. And what are journalists taught about scientific inquiry? I know they are taught to avoid all reference to themselves, but this gives the reader the impression that there is no opinion involved. Maybe this is a mistake. Maybe they should clearly state their political affiliations. Many studies, in fact, show that the majority of journalists have a strong liberal bias.

I hope I'm not being a hypocrite. On this subject, the Bible says: "If any one of you is without sin, let him be the first to throw a stone." (John 8:7) I too am a sinner, and readily admit that I am biased. I also like to see my name in print, so the things I write shouldn't be taken too seriously. That's the good thing about writing a column like this. I get to write about subjects that I'm interested in, and don't hide the fact that I have opinions on these matters. I never have, and never will, pretend to be a *real* journalist. If I do report a fact, I cite my reference. I think it should be recognized, however, that almost everything you encounter in the media has a strong element of opinion. Our perception of "the Truth" as it exists "out there" is often just a reflection of the truth that we hold in our hearts. Not only can't we see the world without bias, but we will never be able to see things as another person does. To paraphrase Henry David Thoreau: the greatest miracle is to look through the eyes of another. (FamousQuotes.com)

Can He Say That?

(7/1/2008)

"Do you think I'm fat and stupid?" I asked my wife.

"Well," she replied, "I don't think you're stupid."

Smile when you say that, I thought; otherwise it's not funny. Putdowns, intentional or unintentional, aren't much fun. But being the butt of jokes gets easier with age.

Self-deprecating humor is more amiable than jokes that target others. Here's my retort, for example: "Your forgetfulness is so bad that I can give you the same present over and over again – because each time it seems like new." Just kidding! See what I mean? It's not funny if the joke is made at someone else's expense.

Another Example: "What are the 3 most difficult years in a North Dakotan's life?" Answer: "Second grade." (from *The North Dakota Joke Book*, by Mike Dalton)

Some jokes are funny, and some aren't. There are places around the world where offensive jokes can even get you executed.

Unlike rehearsed jokes, some people just say funny things – without even trying. The best example is Yogi Berra, the "Baseball Hall of Fame" catcher and manager. Some classic "yogi-isms" include the following:

(1) "It ain't over till it's over." (2) "Baseball is 90% mental, and the other half is physical." (3) "When you come to a fork in the road, take it." (4) "Always go to other people's funerals, otherwise they won't come to yours." And, toward the end of his career, (5) "I never said half the things I really said." (brainyquote.com)

Words can also be used to say profound things. Classic examples are: (1) FDR (in 1933) telling us: "the only thing we have to fear is fear itself." (2) JFK (in 1961) saying: "ask not what your country can do for you; ask what you can do for your country." (3) Will Rogers saying: "be thankful we're not getting all the government we're paying for." (4) Walt Disney saying: "the way to get started is to quit talking and begin doing." (5) Lucy Van Pelt, from "Peanuts" by Charles M. Schulz, saying: "I never made a mistake in my life. I thought I did once, but I was wrong." And (6) Albert Einstein saying: "anyone who has never made a mistake has never tried anything new." (FamousQuotes.com)

Here are some other classics:

"Be who you are and say what you feel, because those who mind don't matter and those who matter don't mind." Dr. Seuss.

"Whoever exalts himself will be humbled, and whoever humbles himself will be exalted." Bible, Matthew 23:12.

"I do benefits for all religions. I'd hate to blow the hereafter on a technicality." Bob Hope. (FamousQuotes.com)

"Everybody is a little bit crazy – some more and some less. You're just a bit crazier than other people. When you accept this, you'll be less crazy – and 'normal' enough to go home." (from *Crazy Like Me: Memories and Musings of a Retired Small Town Doctor*)

Thank God that America allows writers to say funny, profound, and even stupid things. I hope that you, as citizens of this great country, also appreciate our many liberties and opportunities. With these words of wisdom and wit to ponder, I wish you and yours a happy 4th of July.

Hobglobin

(5/17/2008)

I have been criticized for writing about psychology, politics, and religion – which is taboo in most circles. My columns also wander from topic to topic in chaotic manner. Sometimes I am too sarcastic, which is also true. My last entry ("Not My Momma"), for example, was one that my wife "didn't appreciate." My attempt at humor was certainly not intended to criticize her. Only a crazy man would make anything other than flattering remarks about his wife. I guess she'll have to start proof-reading my articles again. I apologize if my words offended her or anyone else.

If you think everything is honky-dory, and are always happy, then I congratulate you on your consistency. But God didn't make me that way ... As you may know, I have Bipolar Disorder. Some days I am upbeat and optimistic. Other days I see the dark side of life. I didn't ask for this problem – I just have it, and try to make the best of it. Having this disease puts me in pretty good company, though, because Ted Turner, Tim Burton, Charley Pride, Mark Twain, Sylvia Plath, Winston Churchill, Teddy Roosevelt, Jane Pauley, Robin Williams, Jim Carey and Beethoven have had the same problem.

Mental illness is very common. According to the CDC, psychiatric disease affects 46% of people sometime in their lifetime; and 22% have at least one of these disorders in any given year. To break this down, Anxiety Disorders affect 29% of the population, Impulse Control Disorders 25%, Depression 21% and Substance Abuse 15%. There are also 2-4% of people with Bipolar Disorder and 1% with Schizophrenia. Situational "mental" problems (grief, stress, etc.) will strike everyone – at one time or another. Every family has been touched by mental illness. In the Dark Ages, affliction with psychiatric disease was labeled "demonic possession." In Modern Times, patient advocacy groups say "We are *not* bad, dumb, weak, evil or crazy people. We have a biochemical imbalance, and deserve the same respect that other diseases – like diabetes – routinely receive."

When I write about spiritual matters, I try to respect each person's right to go to the church or synagogue of their choice. A physician colleague once told me this: "Muslims recover from disease the same way that Christians do." And he's right. There is only minimal evidence that having "religion" improves longevity – and that is mostly in matters where attitude is important. Healthy living and positive attitude does help people recover from illness, you know.

It is wrong for one religion to think they are "superior" to other religions. And haven't all Christians, Jews and Muslims come from the same God of

Abraham? To say that your religion is "superior" to another's is tantamount to claiming that you have the mind of God. And C.S. Lewis, famous author and theologian, wrote this about divisions in the church: "Almost all the crimes which Christians have perpetrated against each other arise from … religion [being] confused with politics."

The Great Schism

(11/4/2008)

It's hard to believe this was ever an issue. The early church, however, didn't have the words to understand abstract concepts. The word "Trinity", for example, was a word that many scholars argued about. The Eastern Church couldn't grasp how "God the Father" could have a Son, and yet the two of them were the same entity. A council was assembled in Nicaea, in the Roman province of Bithynia (now a part of Turkey), in order to debate the issue. This was the first ecumenical council ever. It is referred to as "The First Council of Nicea", and started in the year 325.

The doctrine that Christians (Roman Catholics and Protestants) generally accept today is summarized in St. John's Gospel, who quotes Christ Himself: "I and the Father are one." (Bible, NIV, John 10:30) At that time, though, several Greek bishops disagreed. They thought that God the Father ("Reason") existed before God the Son ("The Word") and before God the Holy Spirit. God has always existed, they said, but there must have been a time when Christ didn't. They felt the entities of the Trinity were of "like substance" but not the "same substance."

In Nicaea, the "consubstantial theory" was formulated. The bishops in attendance were told to profess the "Nicene" creed, which is a summary of Christian beliefs. Those who said "but there was a time when Christ was not" or "they are of another substance" were condemned. All but 13 bishops agreed – and soon the number of dissenters was down to seven. Steps were taken to label the dissenters as "outcasts." Eventually the number of dissenters was down to three.

The main proponent of the "different substance" theory was Arius, a Greek bishop. One by one his supporters vanished. His views were labeled heresy, and he was banished. But Alexander, the patriarch of Egypt, supported Arius. And Constantine the Great – the Roman Emperor who brought persecution of Christians to an end – also voiced his support of Arius. And so Arius was forgiven. He was paraded around town. But the evening before Arius was to receive public Communion, he died suddenly. The church felt this was a judgment from heaven. Foul play may have caused his death. The passing of Arius, however, did not make Arian teachings go away.

The church held 14 councils between 341 and 360. The Rome-based church rejected the Arian philosophy, but the Eastern Churches clung to it. 94 Latin and 70 Greek bishops debated the issue, but could not come to terms. The Asiatics withdrew, and held a separate meeting in Philippopolis;

169

which led to the unfortunate schism (or splitting) of the Eastern and Western Churches.

The Greek (eastern) and Roman (western) churches worship the same God. In a similar way, people of Jewish, Christian and Muslim religions all worship the God of Abraham. Catholics and Protestants worship the same God. It's amazing to me that "semantics" has caused such deep divisions between these major religions – church communities that share a common ancestry.

The Schmitz Brothers

(10/14/2009)

"Who is the better looking brother?" I ask.

"He is," they say in unison – pointing at the other. It is indicative of their respect for one another, and their humility. It reflects their personalities. They are certainly not afraid to voice their opinions, but always do so in a polite manner. That is one of the impressions I got from interviewing Al and Fred Schmitz last week. And despite the fact that they both use a cane, and are getting up there in the years – 93 and 84, respectfully – they are intelligent, politically astute, and fun to visit with.

Their ancestors left Germany in the middle of the 19th century. Their grandparents homesteaded near Brockton. There were nine kids in their family. Al went to college in Missoula, got a degree in economics, and then ran the family farm. He and his wife Christine (now deceased) had 14 children of their own. Fred started his college training in Bozeman. He later went to the seminary – for seven years. After deciding the priesthood was not for him, he got a degree in physics from Gonzaga, and wound up working for NASA.

The Schmitz brothers have a great love for America. They don't want to see us give up our individual freedoms. They enjoy talking about politics, and describe themselves as "conservative." They think we need to get back to what made America great.

"The constitution," says Al, "gives *the government* the right to issue money – not *the banks*." As a result of this situation, the "big banks" have become way too powerful, and this is eroding our quality of life.

With monetary policy being dictated by a relatively small group of people, many people think there is a New World Order (NWO) that is secretly trying to establish a totalitarian one-world government. This is making individual countries obsolete. The demise of nations (in name or function) will take away the world's system of "checks and balances" on matters of international importance.

Al says our current government is dishonest. Power is secretly being transferred to powerful "front" organizations. This process is fast moving us toward a NWO that few people really understand. They cite as examples the Federal Reserve Bank, the International Monetary Fund, the United Nations, the World Bank, the World Health Organization, the European Union, and the World Trade Organization. Perhaps the next step will be the tearing down of borders between Mexico, Canada, and the United States (aka, NAFTA) – and the creation of a "North American" currency. In a similar way, Russia and China recently discussed having an "Eastern Asia" currency at a UN panel. Regionalism of this kind will increase in the future. As time goes on, the European Union, the Shanghai Cooperation Organization, and the G20 will become increasingly powerful. The question now is not whether global governance is coming, but rather how these regional powers will interact with one another.

In the past, NWO concern was mostly found in anti-government right wing and Christian fundamentalist subgroups. Some of these concerns are now shared by society as a whole. And some politicians are very adept at using emotionally charged issues to further their NWO agendas. These *demagogues* can lead a country down a path that it doesn't want to go. Fred Schmitz likened this situation to Adolf Hitler's persuasion of the German people (in the 1930's) to accept his agenda. The similarity "makes me tremble with fear," he says.

Al and Fred Schmitz are not fear mongers. Their ideas are thought-provoking, to say the least, and intended to get our country back on the right track. Al has written a number of articles on his theories. They were published (in the 1980's) by "The Billings Gazette" and "The Farmer's Union." He is also writing a book, entitled *Debt Money: The Burden of the People.* He has several recommendations for our current situation (listed below) that are "common horse sense that has just been presented wrong." I told Al that I am intrigued with his economic recommendations, but do not completely understand them. I do know that you could not meet two nicer men ("with a bundle of experience," says Al), and promised to present Al's theories in an entertaining and (hopefully) informative manner.

The Basics of Al's Plan:

Money is a tool for people to carry out transactions – to buy goods and services, etc. The founders of the Constitution wanted the issuance of money to be completely in the hands of the Congress. If Congress truly represents the people – and not the bankers – then they should be less likely to fall prey to bribery, dishonesty, etc. Our lending institutions have been lending money that they didn't really have. That is what caused of the recent "Global Debt Crisis." It doesn't make sense that we are now trying to borrow our way out of a problem that was caused by excessive borrowing.

Is it okay for to artificially create money? Al doesn't think so. It is causing the value of the dollar to fall. The value of your savings has also fallen. It would be better if the government issued the money – instead of the banks – because they have the full of faith of our nation's people, resources, and taxing authority to back it.

Congress should put the Federal Reserve Bank out of business. The government would then issue Treasury Notes to pay off all legal debts and support all ongoing government obligations (Military, Medicare, Social Security, etc.) This would be done in a "dollar for dollar" manner.

Since the days of Medici (a 12th century Italian banker) money has been printed that has no intrinsic value. These bankers have been making fortunes from lending money they don't have. We should give control of our money supply back to the people – instead of a small group of elitist New York and European bankers.

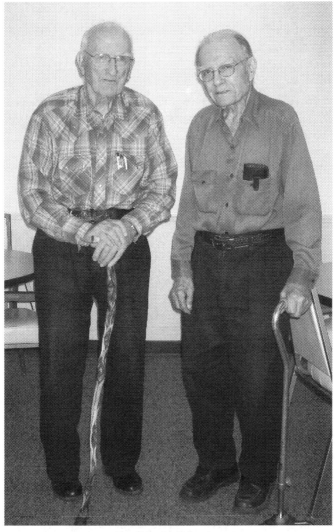

Fred & Al Schmitz

Originality

(11/11/2008)

I've got a problem. It's 10 p.m. on Sunday night, and I've got to get a completed article to the publisher by morning. I don't have time to interview anyone. I don't have time to do research. I'm in a bind … It's hard to come up with something original in such a short time.

Some experts say there's no such thing as an original thought. I disagree. While I have read highly regarded books that present only one or two quasi original ideas, I always appreciate the nuances of a different author's perspective. Hearing the same idea expressed in a different way can make it easier to understand.

Lack of originality is a real problem. My wife, for example, has told the same story about a dozen times in the past week. (Details withheld to protect the innocent.) At first it was a little bit funny. Lately I could almost strangle her for repeating the story. As a loving husband, I'd never do such a thing … so I've suffered through her word-for-word retelling of this not-that-funny story. It's the same thing with my articles. I ask her to read the 1st, 2nd, and 3rd rewrites of my weekly columns. I can see the boredom in her eyes. That's how it is with married couples: we tolerate each other's banality for the sake of maintaining peace and harmony.

The science of originality is interesting, though. We live in the Milky Way Galaxy, which is one of 10 billion galaxies in the universe. Our sun is but one out of 200 billion stars in our galaxy. The earth is the third planet out of nine that revolves around the sun. It is felt that there are only a handful of planets in the entire universe that have "earthlike" potential to support life. The earth itself is 4.5 billion years old. Creatures with humanoid DNA have been around for 200, 000 years. There are currently 6.7 billion people (*Homo sapiens*) on our planet earth. Each human being has 20,500 genes, variously located on 46 chromosomes. Chromosomes may contain up to 100 million nucleotide pairs, which form the double helical macromolecule we refer to as DNA. The majesty of the DNA code is that no two people (except monozygotic twins) are the same. Even twins go through epigenetic (after conception) and environmental changes that ensure they develop different phenotypes – i.e., have different personalities. This system makes each one of us a truly "original" creation. That, I think, is a miracle. There never has been, and never will be, a person just like you …

My comments on "originality" are not completely original. While I sometimes blur fact and fiction, I'm not kidding when I say you are unique.

These columns continue to be an experimental venture, a strange mixture of science and humanities, and I hope they don't bore you. I do appreciate the tips and feedback that some of you have given me, though, and will do my best to work your ideas into future columns.

Before I fall asleep, I better have my wife edit this column. She doesn't agree with everything I say. She is her own person. When she doesn't edit my columns, though, my writing has occasionally come across as noxious, or boring, or both … But tonight I will try not to be boring. I will try to be original. Tonight, if it's not too much trouble, I'm going to see if she will let me sleep on the left side of the bed.

Planet of the Apes

(3/10/2009)

It has been forty years since the first *Planet of the Apes* movie came out. As you probably know, this is the story of astronauts that got caught in a time warp, and came back to the earth in the year 3978. The movie script was written by Rod Serling, of Twilight Zone fame. It generated four sequels and two TV series, and enjoyed great critical and popular success.

When the astronauts landed, they did not know where they were. The environment looked earthlike, but society had gone through incredible changes. Human beings didn't speak, dressed like cavemen, and were on the low end of the primate totem pole. They were hunted down, forced to do slave labor, and used as guinea pigs in crude scientific experiments. Second lowest were gorillas. They were the hunters, soldiers and police. Then came chimpanzees, who were the smartest, but were "kept in their place" doing meaningless scientific research. At the top of the pecking order were the orangutans, who were the lawyers and the politicians.

The head ape, Dr. Zaius, felt his mission was to maintain the social order and guard their "sacred scriptures." Zaius kept secret the fact that humans once ruled the earth. Man had nearly destroyed the earth with his nuclear bombs and evil ways. Zaius warns that man is a "warlike creature who gives battle to everything around him, even himself."

A theme of the movie is that the apes must not learn they have descended from humans, who are the source of all evil. Although it is fiction, there are people like Dr. Zaius in today's world. In a manner that is oddly similar to Planet of the Apes, these people want to suppress discussion of how the world evolved. Like it or not, Charles Darwin's theory on "Natural Selection" and "Evolution of Species" explains things better than anything out there. Saying everything magically appeared some 5000 years ago is not consistent with scientific observations.

Science is a self-correcting process. If a theory is shown to be false, it is thrown out. Philosophy and Religion should be willing to do the same. For example, the church once insisted that the earth is the center of the universe. When Copernicus, the 16th century astronomer, proposed that the earth revolves around the sun – and not the other way around – his theories were felt to be "contrary to the sense and authority of Holy Scripture." His followers were told they would be excommunicated if they did not abandon this thinking. We now know, of course, that Copernicus was right. We also now realize that his theory in no way threatens the integrity of Holy Scripture.

The earth is 4.5 billion years old. The Bible, the inspired word of God, was written from approximately 2000 B.C. to 200 A.D. Why doesn't the Bible discuss dinosaurs, germs, atoms, continental drift, the Baja Peninsula Meteorite, global ice ages, and other major earth happenings? Because it was never intended to be a scientific text, that's why ... But the Bible itself says there are "many other signs Jesus performed in the presence of the disciples, which are not written in this book." (John 20:30) This does not sound like a prohibition of other books to me. "And there are also many other things which Jesus [God] did, which if they were written in detail, I suppose that even the world itself would not contain the books that would be written." (John 21:25)

Is it really important whether the world was created in six days or six hundred millennia? Isn't it possible that the Genesis account is metaphor? Like so many other symbols and parables in the Bible, isn't it more likely that the essence of "the Genesis account" is not about creation of man's body, but about the creation of man's *soul*. It makes so much more sense this way ... That, in effect, is what Pope John Paul II has said. He also said (in a carefully worded address on October 23, 1996) that it's time to recognize "the theory of evolution as more than a hypothesis." This theory has been (the Pope went on to say) "progressively accepted by researchers, following a series of discoveries in various fields of knowledge. The convergence, neither sought nor fabricated, of the results of work that was conducted independently is in itself a significant argument in favor of this theory."

I am encouraged that some people have an open mind on these matters. And the Catholic Church, which messed up on the Copernicus issue, wants to get it right this time. Pertaining to this issue, Pope Leo XIII said: "truth cannot contradict truth." The Pope went on to say, in so many words, that evolution is certainly not a contradiction to the central message of the Bible. While scientists might chuckle at my attempt to be diplomatic on this issue, this column is not directed at them, but at those who say evolution is not compatible with Christianity. I respectfully disagree. No matter what you say about science, the world itself is proof of God's majesty ... and I believe we need knowledge of both God's word *and* His creation.

Dow 10,000

(10/21/2009)

If you live on the planet earth, then you've heard that the Dow Jones Industrial Average (DJIA) climbed over 10,000 last week. The DJIA first closed over 10K in 1999, peaked at 14K in 2007, and then went on a long decline. The Dow was still over 10K last October, but then plummeted to below 7K in March of this year. But it's just a number, you say, so who cares?

Like it or not, "the Dow" does impact your life. If you own anything (stocks, mutual funds, the house you live in, etc.) then the "market value" of those assets goes up and down, and they generally do so in proportion to the Dow. And the principal on your 30 year home mortgage is supposed to go down – providing you are making payments – but it does so in a painfully slow manner. You can easily get "under water" when the value of your home is less than the amount you owe on it.

When the value of your assets goes down, and your debts pile up, then many bad things can happen. Your credit rating falls. You can't get your wife a car loan or your kids a school loan. You might even have trouble paying your monthly bills. You can't get your kids all the "cool stuff" they want for Christmas. Your boss feels the same way. He is less likely to give you a raise (or hire new employees) if the overall economy is in the tank. It's just the way it is, they say. One bad thing leads to another. And the "bad thing" that starts the downspin is a low Dow number – or so it seems.

Some numbers are more important than others. Turning 50 was a milestone. It was just a day, I realize, but it was the day that I had to admit that "the road ahead" is shorter than "the road behind." And some people get nervous when Friday the 13th rolls around. SEVEN is a lucky number for many, but some husbands get "the itch" when they've been married seven years – so some numbers can be both good and bad.

Numbers are used to measure things. There are 12 months in a year. I have two legs and my dog has four. Even at his advanced age (84 in raw dog years) he can run twice as fast as me – and he's not the least bit jealous that my IQ "number" is higher than his. Numbers can also be used to describe and predict human behavior, mostly because we regard some numbers as special. For example, it was significant when my wife and I had our 25th wedding anniversary last year and it will be significant when my son turns 21 in seven weeks. But 21 and 50 (among others) are *just numbers* – and the only reason they are significant is because we say they are.

When the Dow was under 7K just 7 months ago, many said we were "in another Great Depression." Now that it is over 10K, those *same experts* say we are in full recovery. Such is the case with numbers. They can make us feel good; they can make us feel bad; and they can influence our behavior. Now that the Dow is up, experts say more people are going to buy cars, go on vacation, invest in the stock market, and get kids the stuff they really want. We're happy for the kids, of course, but we should be grateful to the number that makes gift-giving possible. Tell the kids to thank Dow, and all his derivatives, for the good things He has done; and we pray his number behaves for the shopping season ahead.

Politics

(6/3/2008)

I meet a lot of people in my landscaping business. Last week a client complimented me on a poem and article I wrote that my wife hated – so I felt reassured that I'm not a total failure. I then learned that this new friend was a staunch Barack Obama supporter. I also noted that both Obama and Hillary Clinton visited our fine state last week. Montana's 25 electoral votes (for the Democratic Convention in August) have become important in this hotly contested race. It is a rare event for a sparsely populated state like Montana to get so much political attention.

This new friend is a lifelong liberal Democrat. Although I often adopt the conservative viewpoint, I found that her views and mine meshed in several areas. I thought about what this might mean … Could it be that I'm a closet liberal? As a young man growing up in Minnesota, I was inundated with the Democratic Party perspective. My family still won't *even consider* voting Republican. When I first moved to Montana, I was exposed to "The Conservative" point of view.

Differences in political opinion should never lead to bloodshed. Although I plan to vote for John McCain, it might not matter that much which political machine wins the election. That's a pragmatist viewpoint. In my youth, I was more of an idealist. In fact, I worshipped the ground that Hubert Horatio Humphrey walked on. He was "The Happy Warrior" Democratic Senator from Minnesota, Lyndon Johnson's Vice-President, and narrowly lost (to Richard Nixon) in his bid to become President. Montanans might have the same affection for Mike Mansfield, who was your four-term Democratic Senator, and served a record 15 years as Senate Majority Leader.

I met Humphrey twice. Once when he was stumping for votes at the State Fair, where I was working as a fry cook; and another time when I ran into him at a late night convenience store – where HHH and his secret service agents were purchasing beer and munchies.

I once attended a George McGovern rally. Another time I waited two hours to have Jimmy Carter sign one of his books for me. I tried to support Carter – even as his unrealistic dreams were going down the drain. I also voted for Walter Mondale, another Democratic Senator from Minnesota and former Vice-President who wanted to be president. Since then, I've voted Republican … So you see I'm not the right wing conservative that people have made me out to be. I do hate it, though, when liberals badmouth our conservative presidents. My brother-in-law's remarks have been particularly offensive. I'd like to take him over my knee for his "anti-Republican" remarks. Since he's 6'8" tall, that's not likely to happen.

A well-known local priest, Fr. Ned Shinnick, chastises me for supporting George Bush (1st and 2nd), but I remind him that *real* Americans stand by their presidents – for better, for worse, for richer, for poorer, in sickness or in health, to love and to cherish 'till the next election do us part. For example, I didn't vote for Ronald Reagan the first time around, but the moral majority (i.e., my wife) convinced me I'd "go to heck" if I didn't support him in his re-election bid. Besides that, she threatened to negate my vote if I "voted for the other guy." Implied negation of other areas also influenced me. Politics and marriage, it seems, have become wed together in ways the Constitution never intended.

In order to avoid getting any more "Dear Jerome" letters thanking me, in advance, for supporting the party favorite – I'm officially labeling myself "Independent." That has a nice ring to it. I also hope the months ahead will include some level-headed discussion of candidate public service records, voting records, national security, etc. Regardless of what most of us want, this could be another nasty presidential campaign. Before we let that happen, think of "the other party's candidate" as a prospective in-law: you might not like him (or her) but you might have to live with him – for the next four years, anyway.

Natural Gas

(3/4/2008)

Experts say we are in the midst of an Economic Recession. The subprime mortgage crisis hasn't helped. Another cause (of our country's economic woes) is our continuing over-dependence on Middle Eastern oil. A barrel of oil now costs $100. Gasoline is over $3 per gallon. Our country is held ransom by oil-rich countries, and many of their radical leaders would like nothing better than to see our country go down the toilet.

This is, once again, the political season for recommending "alternative energy" sources. We've been down this road before. Many promises are made. In the past, though, we've seen little action. Solar Energy tax incentives come and go like the wind. And most "Wind Power" comes from the politicians themselves, and not from wind generators. Maybe this time will be different. We'll see.

Agricultural production of Ethanol looks good on paper, but is not economically feasible unless the government (i.e., your tax dollars) pays over one dollar per gallon to make Gasohol competitively priced. Diverting farmland to the fuel business leads to higher food prices. Corn-based ethanol also increases greenhouse gas emissions. A better choice is to convert natural ("cellulosic") vegetation into ethanol. Trees and grass are used for this. Even garbage (another form of "biomass") can be converted into useful energy. This reduces greenhouse gases and alleviates the burden placed on our landfills.

It's been said that Montana has enough coal to meet our country's energy needs for 200 years. Coal runs electricity power plants, and also can be converted into liquid fuels. Governor Schweitzer has trumped the idea of increasing our use of coal. Some critics have said he is grandstanding. I heard his presentation on CNBC, and it sounded good to me. Unfortunately, nobody wants a strip mine in their backyard. And Global Warming alarmists are opposed to this technology. They say carbon-based emissions have greatly increased the planet's temperature. The average temperature *has* gone up by *one degree* in the last 100 years. Ironically enough, though, it is the Greenhouse Effect that allowed us to emerge from the last ice age; and makes life on this planet possible.

Fossil Fuels provide 86% of the world's energy needs. Experts say we should reduce this percentage – so that we don't aggravate the carbon dioxide emission problem. Nuclear power sounds like a good alternative to me. It already provides about 20% of our country's electricity needs. Because of public resistance, however, there hasn't been a nuclear reactor built in this country in over 30 years. A proposed plant (in North Carolina) is being "choked to death" by public criticism. And this plant wouldn't come on line until 2016. No wonder experts go crazy trying to meet our energy needs.

So where does that leave us? I think it's time to harness all the "hot air" and "natural gas" that naysayers have been spewing into the atmosphere. This is an opportunity to use their negative energy in a positive manner. And since the presidential campaign is heating up, we should convert their rhetoric into something useful.

I am, of course, talking about flatulence. Everyone makes gas, but some people are copious producers of this commodity. We shouldn't politely ignore them anymore. Our large intestine has millions of bacteria that transforms food residue into methane. Collecting this gas in small tanks is technically feasible. Some people (particularly those who consume more than their share of foodstuffs) produce more gas, and should therefore carry larger tanks. It's the responsible thing to do. They should give in proportion to what they have received.

Think of it ... The next "Earth Day" could celebrate an intervention that would accomplish two things: remove odiferous gas from the air we breathe, and fuel our energy needs. Politicians produce a lot of hot air and natural gas. Their B.S. will finally accomplish something. Your contribution could even be tax-deductible. And your dog and kids will finally have a good reason for smiling when they pass gas – they would, in effect, be saving the planet earth.

Highway Robbery

(6/17/2008)

If you haven't noticed, it now costs $4 per gallon to fuel your car, minivan or pickup. The people who deliver our goods and services are also paying through the nose. It's Highway Robbery. When I was in high school, gasoline was 30 cents per gallon. And gasoline costs $7 per gallon in London, Paris, and Hong Kong. What's next? And what can we do about it?

They say the meteoric rise in the price of a barrel of oil (from $90 to $135 in recent months) is primarily due to increasing demand – from countries like India and China. The economies of these countries have been growing by leaps and bounds. The world supply of oil (about 88 million barrels/day) has been stable – but demand has increased. And good old-fashioned greed has undoubtedly fueled some of the recent oil speculation. Something's gotta' give. But don't panic! It isn't happening overnight, but our peak oil days are behind us.

In 1956, M. King Hubbert, an oil geologist working for Shell, predicted that oil production for the continental U.S. would peak between 1965 and 1970. His predictions were silenced. As it turns out, the U.S. lower 48 oil production did peak in 1971. He also developed the "Hubbert Curve" analysis of what happens to oil production on both a local and global basis.

Global oil discovery peaked in the late 1960s. Since the mid-1980s, oil companies have been finding less oil than we have been consuming. Of the 65 largest oil-producing regions, 54 of them have passed their peak oil production, and are now in decline, including the USA (1971), Indonesia (1997), Australia (2000), the North Sea (2001), and Mexico (2004). According to EnergyBulletin.net, from which much of this information was obtained, the public should *not* regard optimistic reports from OPEC, USGS, or oil companies as reliable. Some people say that if dramatic action isn't taken *now*, the world could face Armageddon-type meltdown.

Both *Supply* and *Demand* sides of this issue need to be addressed. Like it or not, more expensive gasoline makes us less likely to go on summer car trips. We're also more likely to car pool and/or use mass transit. And higher-priced fuel certainly gives us incentive to develop energy alternatives. Wind farms, solar energy, more nuclear energy, and energy-efficient automobiles are needed. Corn-based ethanol is not a long-term solution. Biomass-powered production of electricity is a good idea. Hybrid cars are okay. Hydrogen fuel-cell cars will eventually be feasible, but the energy and infrastructure for this option needs to come from somewhere.

It seems ironic that just a few years ago protestors were saying "No Blood For Oil" in their opposition to the March 2003 invasion of Iraq. Now we need, more than ever, to get Iraqi oil back online. We need stabilization of this region. No matter what, though, it is a sad state of affairs that the U.S. imports 11 million barrels of oil per day (about 60% of our consumption) from many unstable geopolitical regions.

Robert Redford, actor-activist, recommends a grass roots campaign that encourages every person to take an interest in energy matters. We need to demand that our government and industry "seize the opportunity" we have to take corrective action. We need to "kick the oil habit" and launch a movement for real solutions and a better future.

Some people in this area might not mind the current "oil crisis." Unlike past boons, we now have the technology (like "horizontal drilling") to recover the vast reserves in our "Bakken Oil Reserve." Enthusiasts say this contains 10 times more oil than Alaska's North Slope. As long as oil remains over $100 a barrel, extraction will be profitable.

No matter what, oil is a finite, non-renewable resource. Although it has fueled tremendous global economic growth over the last century and a half, our peak oil days are behind us. As demand has continued to grow, but production leveled off, our days of cheap oil are forever gone. If we don't make drastic changes, we'll feel (over and over again) like victims of Highway Robbery.

The Big Bailout

(10/1/2008)

"My name is Bob. My wife's name is Buffy. Dr. Dirt asked me to give you an illustration [semi-fictional] of what our country's economic turmoil is all about, and why some experts think 'a really big bailout' is needed to fix the mess that we are now in."

"Ten years ago, Buffy and I got married. We wanted to move from our apartment to a house. I wanted to buy a 'fixer upper.' Buffy wanted a dream house. She said 'bigger is better.' As it turned out, we wound up buying more house than we could really afford."

Many young people go through this process. They are told that owning is better than renting. The U.S. government has given homeowners $62 billion of tax benefits since 1995, which is a strong endorsement of home ownership. Studies have shown, however, that about half of all homeowners would have saved money by renting comparable housing. Among other things, renters preserve the ability to move with their jobs – without the transaction costs of buying and selling a house. Homeowners also use excess energy, defer tax money from worthy social programs, and don't get adequate diversification of their savings.

The rate of home ownership in the U.S. is 69%. That has increased from 62% in 1960. Comparable rates are 69, 55, and 42% for England, France, and Germany. Minorities in the U.S. also want their share of the "American Dream," so their rate of home ownership has increased from 48% in 1993 to 59% in 2005.

"Buffy and I didn't know much about finances. We barely qualified for a 'Fannie Mae' home loan. Our mortgage payment [principal and interest] was 28% of our combined incomes. But nobody told us there would be other homeowner expenses – like maintenance, repairs, insurance, improvements, etc. The 'true cost' of our home ownership has been 40% of our income. That hasn't left much money for restaurants, vacations, health care, children, savings, etc." And that's what young couples all over the country have learned.

"Fannie Mae" is the nickname for the Federal National Mortgage loan program. This program was formed way back in 1938, as part of FDR's "New Deal." Fannie Mae and its brother program, "Freddie Mac" (created in 1970), buy loans that local banks make to prospective homeowners. This has given U.S. citizens great credit flexibility. In order to give disadvantaged people an even better chance to buy a home, the lending requirements for these loans were relaxed in the 1990's. These GSE's (Government Sponsored Entities) own or guarantee about half of our country's $12 trillion worth of mortgages.

Borrowers who don't qualify for the best loans have turned to the "subprime" mortgage market – which has higher interest rates and less favorable payback schedules. Since 2007, however, a significant number of people who hold these "subprime" loans have not been making their payments on time. Foreclosure on these mortgages has led to a glut of houses on the market – which brings down the value of all homes.

"When Buffy and I were looking for a house, everybody said that real estate is a good investment. Some said that the value of our house would always go up, so we could refinance later – if we needed to." That thinking has led many borrowers into taking out suspect loans. They assumed the appreciated value of their homes would allow them to get better financing later. Other borrowers didn't even know what they were getting into.

When the value of homes was increasing by 6% per year (from 1978 – 2003), refinancing wasn't a problem. But after the boom, came the bust. The value of the asset (your house) could no longer cover the amount of your loan, so financing options disappeared. In recent years, home values have been decreasing. The nationwide average went down by 6% last year. Some homes have depreciated even more. So it's not surprising that some homeowners have been walking away from their commitments. Banks and financial institutions have been left holding homes and mortgages they didn't want.

Home prices declined further as foreclosures added to the already bloated inventory of houses for sale. Lending standards have, of course, become stricter again. Depreciation in home prices has led to growing losses for Fannie Mae and other financial institutions. Despite the government's attempt to bolster confidence in these stocks, FNM has gone from $65 to $2 in one year. Other companies have gone bankrupt or been sold for a pittance. People who own these stocks in their retirement accounts have been decimated.

This subprime mortgage crisis has caused economic turmoil of historic proportions. Some experts say this could cause a "Great Depression" unless drastic measures are taken. The Treasury Secretary's recommendation for a $700 billion government rescue is both good and bad news. Experts say this money is needed to remove the bad debts that are clogging up the system. If nothing is done, it will be hard for everyone to get credit for anything. The problems of Wall Street, they say, are affecting Main Street.

It should be noted that more than 90% of homeowners are making their mortgage payments as scheduled. While talk of "the big bailout" temporarily boosted the stock market, many people are not happy with having to pay for another big government bailout program.

"I'm mad," says Bob, "that my tax dollars will be used to rescue people and institutions who didn't know that loans are supposed to be repaid. The bailout will also reward overpaid CEO's and federal oversight agencies for their incompetence."

Cash for Clunkers

(8/11/2009)

"If only life was that simple," the man said to his wife; "this 'Cash for Clunkers' deal the government has come up with sounds just too good to be true."

In case you haven't heard, the government now gives you a rebate (up to $4500 cash value) if you trade in your old car ("clunker") on the purchase of a new car – providing it gets at least 25% better mileage. This kind of program has been around Europe for several years, and has been here since May. In recent days, there has been a flood of news reports saying the program is "an overwhelming success."

The car companies love this program. Environmentalists also like it – but they haven't commented on whether disposing of the old cars (metal, rubber, and miscellaneous junk) is going to be a problem. Improved gas mileage, even if it is modest, might reduce "greenhouse gases." The car fix-it industry, on the other hand, will potentially lose business with this program. And other industries might feel like their concerns have been overlooked.

"Here we are incentivizing the purchase of cars, [and] we're taking money from our grandkids by adding to the national debt," Sen. Tom Coburn (R-Okla.) huffed. "Why not incentivize demand for boats? Or how about RVs?" (New York Daily News, 8/5/09)

"Why not?" asked my imaginary hero. "Why not get rid of all the *old stuff* in our country, give everybody a government check, and have them buy *new stuff*? Maybe I could get rid of my lumpy old couch, outdated stereo, and super-slow computer. And I don't get much mileage out of my 12 year-old dog. If I traded him in, I would have a better bird-hunting season." Then he added, with a wink: "My wife is also slowing down, you know …"

The man explained the "Cash for Clunkers" program to his wife. She just listened. And then he went out to mow the lawn. With his arthritis, though, he wasn't able to complete the job. So he went out for one of his *long* lunch breaks.

When the man came home, he noticed that his lawn was mowed. "How'd that happen?" he wondered. And his white picket fence was freshly painted – a job he has been putting off all summer.

"Maybe my wife and kids have finally decided to help me out," he said. "It's about time. At my age I can use all the help I can get."

The man walked into his house … It was spotless! Everybody seemed so happy. All his previously unfinished jobs were now completed. The TV was off (for a change) and the kids were quietly reading books. And his wife was smiling from ear to ear.

"What's going on here?" he asked.

"Well … I got to thinking about that 'Cash for Clunkers' deal you talked about, and was able to work something out."

"What do you mean?"

"Meet my *new husband*," she said with a smile; then she pointed to a neatly dressed, svelte, and handsome man who was quietly washing the dishes – a younger version of himself.

"I've taken your advice on the 'Cash for Clunkers' idea," she said. "Since you're getting old and inefficient, I decided to trade you in for a newer model …"

Thanksgiving

(11/8/2008)

As you all know, Thanksgiving will soon be upon us. But will you be thankful? I don't know about you, but the recent economic tsunami has got me worried. My retirement savings account, which supports my family, has lost 25% of its value. And nobody knows how long this recession will last. I can't remember the last time CNBC has had anything good to say ... There is so much negative talk that Thanksgiving may not be a happy occasion.

Polls say about 2/3's of Americans are "unhappy" with how things are. These are excerpts from a 2006 article by Craig Smith that seem relevant:

"So being the knuckle dragger I am, I started thinking: 'What are we so unhappy about?' Is it that we have electricity and running water 24 hours a day, 7 days a week? Is our unhappiness the result of having air conditioning in the summer and heating in the winter? Could it be that 95% of these unhappy folks have a job? Maybe it is the ability to walk into a grocery store at any time and see more food in moments than Darfur has seen in the last year?

"Maybe it is the ability to drive from the Pacific Ocean to the Atlantic Ocean without having to present identification papers as we move through each state? Or possibly the hundreds of clean and safe motels we would find along the way that can provide temporary shelter? I guess having thousands of restaurants with varying cuisine from around the world is just not good enough. Or could it be that when we wreck our car, emergency workers show up and provide services to help all and even send a helicopter to take you to the hospital ... [Or the fact that] 90% of teenagers own cell phones and computers. How about the complete religious, social and political freedoms we enjoy that are the envy of everyone in the world? Maybe that is what has 67% of you folks unhappy.

"Fact is we are the largest group of ungrateful, spoiled brats the world has ever seen. No wonder the world loves the U.S., yet has a great disdain for its citizens. They see us for what we are. The most blessed people in the world who do nothing but complain about what we don't have, and what we hate about the country instead of thanking the good Lord we live here.

"I know, I know. What about the president who took us into war and has no plan to get us out? The president who has a measly 31% approval rating? Is this the same president who guided the nation in the dark days after 9/11? Is this the president that cut taxes to bring an economy out of recession? Could this be the same guy who has been called every name in the book for succeeding in keeping all the spoiled ungrateful brats safe from terrorist attacks? [Is this] the commander in chief of an all volunteer army that is out there defending you and me? Did you hear how bad the President is on the news or talk show? Did this news affect you so much, make you so unhappy you couldn't take a look around for yourself and see all the good things and be glad ...

"So, why then is there the flat-out discontentment in the minds of 67% of Americans? Say what you want but I blame it on the media. If it bleeds it leads and they specialize in bad news. Everybody will watch a car crash with blood and guts. How many will watch kids selling lemonade at the corner? The media knows this and media outlets are for-profit corporations. They offer what sells ...

"Stop buying the negativism you are fed everyday by the media. Shut off the TV, burn Newsweek, and use the New York Times for the bottom of your birdcage. Then start being grateful for all we have as a country. There is exponentially more good than bad. We are among the most blessed peoples on Earth and should thank God several times a day or at least be thankful and appreciative. With hurricanes, tornados, fires out of control, mud slides, flooding, severe thunderstorms tearing up the country from one end to another, and with the threat of bird flu and terrorist attacks, are we sure this is a good time to take God out of the Pledge of Allegiance?"

This message has been circulating on the internet. It has been falsely attributed to Jay Leno or David Letterman, been discredited, and left to die in a pile of patriotic journalism that nobody considers. But it's no joke – our collective national negativism will kill us, if we let it. The economic downturn, for example, is as much about a loss of confidence as anything. And the media loves to play "the blame game" as to who caused the subprime mortgage meltdown, which led to a credit crisis, and so on, and so forth.

It's true: America has a lot of problems that need attention. But we've always had a lot of problems. President-elect Obama has ideas on how to fix things. We need to rally behind him, get the bureaucrats in Washington, D.C. to take a centrist position, and stop all the negativistic talk. This Thanksgiving is a good time for America to say "Thank you," remember that we've overcome obstacles in the past, and get back to doing what has made this nation great.

Freedom

(7/4/2007)

I hope all of you have a nice 4th of July holiday. My wife and I will be watching that great American pastime, baseball. As you may know, I have two sons on the Richland Patriots Legion baseball team. Five of the boys on the team also help me with my landscaping business. This year the team is doing quite well, and it's been fun to watch them. Come to Moose Park some evening, have a hot dog, and cheer the boys to victory.

Independence Day is a time when we should be grateful to be American. We're not perfect, but we are the country that saved the world from the tyranny of Fascism. After victory was gained in World War II, we treated our conquered foes (Germany, Japan, and Italy) with incredible kindness and support. We have also helped the people of Korea, Vietnam, Russia, China, Afghanistan, and Iraq with amazing grace and generosity.

It sickens me that many people, even our allies, shamelessly criticize our country and our people. Every week our country is blamed for another problem: destruction of the environment, unequal distribution of global wealth, uncaring government, and heavy-handed use of our military. Our troops are not supposed to be where they are, and are chastised for not being where they aren't. There is, of course, an element of truth to all of these comments. It's wrong, however, to criticize everything associated with our country and our government. America never claimed to be perfect. Even the song, "America the Beautiful," acknowledges our imperfections, and prays that "God mend [our] every flaw."

The great thing about our country is that if you don't like how things are, you can voice your complaints without fear of retribution. One bad thing, however, is that most people who complain never lift a finger to actually make undesirable situations better. You can give your time and talents to do volunteer work. If that's not possible, you can make monetary donations to support your favorite charity. As a matter of fact, Americans gave a record $295 billion in 2006 to support every cause from AIDS, the Arts, Cancer research, Hurricane Katrina recovery, and Asian tsunami victims. Americans gave at a rate (2.2% of the GDP) which is twice the rate of the next most charitable country, Great Britain. France, a frequent critic of the USA, is 12th on the list – giving less than countries such as South Africa, Singapore, and Turkey.

Being American means you are free to speak your mind, free to improve yourself, and free to get a better job than your parents. Donald Rumsfield, former Defense Secretary, has made some interesting comments on freedom. After the downfall of Saddam Hussein, some Iraqi people engaged in looting and other crimes. The press was quick to blame the USA government for failed strategy. "Freedom's untidy," Rumsfield said, "and free people are free to make mistakes and commit crimes and do bad things. They're also free to live their lives and do wonderful things. And that's what's going to happen here."

Many people say America isn't the land of opportunity it used to be. Colin Powell, the first African-American Secretary of State, is deeply involved in the "character development" movement. He wants young people to quit complaining about perceived inequality, and make the best of the opportunities they do have. He has said: "Get mad, then get over it." Powell has also said: "There are no secrets to success. It is the result of preparation, hard work, and learning."

Countries that are unhappy with the USA are free to refuse our handouts, our technological leadership, and our military protection. Individuals may do the same. It's time to take note of what's right with America – instead of always being critical, and trying to knock it down. Among other liberties we enjoy, we're free to make our country a better place, and free to participate in the democratic process. And we have, more so than any other country, the freedom to determine our own destiny.

Global Warming

It was 36 degrees below zero in east Fairview last night – which is where I watched the Texas-Alabama game with friends. It's 29 below zero this morning. What's going on? I thought Global Warming was supposed to rescue us from all of this cold weather misery … Instead, it seems like we're entering a new Ice Age.

It doesn't take a genius to figure out that people who are warning us about Global Warming have a political agenda. But the last few winters have been colder than usual. And that is "proven" in a way that the original Global Warming scientists (Jones and Mann) were not when they, in 1999, first warned of "human causation factors" in world climate trends. Those two scientists were found to have fudged their own data – and their conclusions were not accepted by the United Nations and the National Academy of Sciences. It wasn't until Al Gore and other movie stars got hold of the warming idea that anyone listened to these doomsday prophesies.

The earth is one degree warmer than it was in 1880. That's a scientific fact. Some glaciers got smaller, and some got bigger. The earth has been going through changes of this type since the beginning of time. Significant warming periods also occurred one thousand, ten thousand, and 130 thousand years ago. We know this from studying human and fossil records. And those warmer spells occurred long before man could have had anything to do with it.

In the 1970s everyone was afraid of Global Cooling. Now there's money and reputations to be made by scaring people about Global Warming. The world was also supposed to come grinding to a halt at midnight on 12/31/1999 (because of Y2K computer glitches) but that scare fizzled without a whimper. And we didn't even get an apology from all the "experts" who told us to buy "special equipment" to get us through the night. The $20 trillion dollars that the world is now spending on energy research (in order to decrease CO_2 emissions) is not necessarily a bad thing, by the way, but we could do without the theatrics. In a similar vein, the world is supposed to come to an end in 2012 – because that's when Nostradamus and the Mayan calendar said it would – but at least Hollywood has had the decency to make a "fictional" movie about this subject.

I'm a lot more afraid of another Ice Age than I am of Global Warming. My metabolism slows to zero in the cold. I like the heat, and enjoy mowing lawns in the summer. I'd have more grass to mow if the temperature was a bit warmer. Besides that, I think women look better in bikinis than they do Eskimo parkas – at least some women, anyway.

It's more difficult to stay alive in cold weather than it is in warm weather. Car accidents, hypothermia, and cold-aggravation of many medical conditions can and should concern us. Human beings get complacent when it comes to assuming they can survive any and all weather conditions. We rely on heaters to warm us in the winter, and air conditioners to cool us in the summer. We get "disconnected" from the way things actually are. That's why a few extremes of weather are good for us: they remind us how fragile we really are.

Tell Al Gore to send some of his Global Warming my way. This winter's frigid weather has been a real problem: the family cars won't start in this subzero weather, I'm tired of shoveling snow, and delivering my newspapers really shouldn't be a matter of life and death. It was an Ice Age that killed off the dinosaurs, after all, and that's not a fate I want for me or anybody else.

Cold Car, 2010

Earth Day

(4/28/2010)

We didn't hear much about it, but last week was "Earth Week" and Thursday, April 22nd, was "Earth Day". This is the largest secular holiday in the world, and is observed by more than half a billion people every year. What did you do to honor the day?

The idea for Earth Day came from Fred Dalton, who was a strategist for the John F. Kennedy administration. Gaylord Nelson, a Democratic senator from Wisconsin, is given credit for advancing the idea, however; and he, along with Republican Representative "Pete" McCloskey, spearheaded the effort to make this a national holiday. The first official Earth Day was held on April 22nd of 1970. That first year some 20 million people honored the event. Now the day is celebrated in 175 countries around the world. The message to "take care of our planet Earth" is certainly not political; it's a theme that everyone can embrace.

I wish I could say I did something special on Earth Day. I drove our aging minivan to Billings, where I had a doctor's appointment, and also went shopping at Costco. I bought a ton of bottled water that day. Bottled water comes in handy for my landscaping work, but the plastic bottles are a terrible source of pollution. I also filled my gas tank with $2.75 per gallon gasoline. Gas was 34 cents more expensive in Sidney that day, by the way, but car gasoline usage – whatever the price – is a huge environmentalist concern.

It's ironic that America invented Earth Day but it is also the country with the worst "planet Earth" habits. With only 5% of the world's population, for example, we consume 25% of the world's energy. Americans consume 11.4 kilowatts of energy per day – which compares to 6 kW for people from Japan and Germany and 1.6 kW for China. And 86% of the world's energy supply currently comes from fossil fuels. The use and abuse of fossil fuels (oil, gas and coal) is the greatest source of pollution to our planet earth. All of us, therefore, should try to conserve energy and practice "Earth friendly" habits. (Statistics from Wikipedia.com)

When I say we should "conserve energy" for the good of our planet that does not mean that we should lay around and watch TV all day, drink beverages out of disposable containers, eat ready-to-eat food, occasionally yell at the dog, and complain about tree-huggers. We (I really mean "I") should get up off our fat butt, turn off all the extra lights and radios in the house, adjust the thermostat (down in the winter and up in the summer), bike and/ or walk to do our errands, plant a tree, reuse or recycle our waste (most of it anyway) and do everything we can to be good to the planet earth. We should support industries that are using renewable sources of energy. And we should encourage countries of the world (including third world countries) to adopt "Earth friendly" habits whenever possible.

America is often criticized for fueling the "Industrial Revolution" of the 19th century with coal and igniting the 20th century "Age of the Automobile" with oil. Both of these fuels have caused excess atmospheric pollution. We now know more about pollution and green technology, though. It's time to adopt 21st century thinking on energy matters. Switching from incandescent lights to fluorescent or LED lights, for example, could save 70-90% off your light bill. Similar advances will help us in other areas as well. Automobiles could become more efficient. Factories could reduce their emissions. Paper and plastic packages could become less wasteful – and easier to recycle.

Technology will help us win many of these "good Earth" battles. But still there remains the problem that HUMAN BEINGS are too wasteful and harmful to their environment. That's why Earth Day is such a good idea – and should be practiced every day of the year. We all need to do our part. Start making better "good Earth" choices. We only have one planet earth, after all, so we should take better care of it.

National Debt

(6/16/2010)

On June 1, 2010, our national debt surpassed the $13 trillion mark. That's 13 followed by twelve zeroes. Each American's portion of that debt is $50,000. Fifty-six percent of that debt has been added in the last ten years. Our debt now equals 90% of our Gross Domestic Product. And two-thirds of our debt is owned by foreigners. Right now about 10% of our yearly budget is spent on the interest to service that debt; and it could go up if those who own our debt (the central banks of China, Japan, etc) decide to increase the interest rate they charge us.

During 2003 through 2007 the federal government spent about $1.20 for every dollar that they collected in tax revenue. In 2008 that went up to $1.40. In 2009 the government spent $1.90 for every $1.00 it collected in tax revenue. How much will it be in 2010? And how much longer will it be, I wonder, before we spend more on "loan interest" than we do on national defense, Social Security, and other essential programs?

If the United States was just one big family (and we are – if you think about it) then we are a family with "really screwed up" finances. We are spending more money than we are taking in. We have been "living in the red" for so long that we think it is normal – but it isn't! It is downright dangerous. The last time we were this much in debt (as a percentage of GDP) was in 1946, when we had just come through World War 2. It is true that we have recently had to finance several wars (Iraq and Afghanistan) but the biggest "extra" expenses we have are our entitlement programs and the recent bailouts of the banking and housing industries. Many experts question whether this money has been spent wisely. Many Americans are still unemployed. Many Americans have lost their retirement savings in the stock market. And 80% of Americans say that our country has serious economic problems. (Statistics from Wikipedia.com)

Some optimists have said that the U.S. can "grow its way" out of these fiscal challenges. Their argument is that economic growth will generate sufficient tax revenue to offset the increase in federal spending. Ben Bernanke and the General Accounting Office have said that the U.S. cannot realistically expect to grow its way out of this problem, however.

Any family that has responsibly looked at problems of this nature would conclude that there is only one way to improve this financial picture: spend less! And it's a conclusion that our national leaders do not want to accept. If a financial advisor was trying to help a family with these problems, he would say: "Live within your means! Plug the holes in your leaky boat!" And our nation needs to do the same thing.

I recently visited with Larry Tveit, Sr., who was a Republican Montana state senator for 16 years – and is now an oil consultant – and he had some important things to say about our "national debt" problem. He says that if our debt continues to grow at the present rate, then someday we will no longer even be able to pay the interest on our indebtedness. "Our nation will then be bankrupt," he says. National security would be compromised, and foreign policy decisions would be influenced by countries we owe money to.

Tveit also reminded me that when Barack Obama was in Congress, he was ranked the "most liberal" legislator. And now Obama is President. Tveit is concerned that Obama is getting way too many of his liberal programs turned into law, and that has aggravated our national debt problem.

"This fall's election is the most important one that people will ever vote in," says Tveit. He "can't believe" that some people don't even bother to vote. Tveit then says: "It is important that we restore a system of 'checks and balances' to our federal government." We need to elect some fiscal conservatives this fall – otherwise our national debt problem will certainly get worse.

Tea Party

(7/14/2010)

For many years I have teased my wife about her penchant for holding "tea parties" with her friends. And she does like to hold social gatherings where she and her friends discuss "girl things" while sipping flavored tea from fancy little cups. I have never been invited to any of these gatherings, however. But last Sunday – which was the 4th of July – my wife and I went to a tea party of a completely different kind … It was the local Tea Party's "Independence Day Rally," held at the fairgrounds, and it was a pleasant gathering where a variety of individuals spoke of their love for America, and spoke of their concerns for our country.

Fairview resident Russ Unruh, the chairman of the MonDak Tea Party, had this to say about the event: "There were over 200 people attending this rally. Food was served by the Richland Ranger Hockey Team. Music was provided. Children and families were encouraged to attend. Speeches were given by Jordan Hall, a local minister, Dan Hepple, a citizen of Pony, Montana, Curt Graham, from the Montana Policy Institute, and Alan Doane, a politician. Members of the local MonDak Tea Party, Williston Tea Party, and The Eastern Montana Patriots Organization also spoke. Everyday citizens were also invited to speak. Our rally, like other Tea party rallies held around the country, does not owe allegiance to any particular political party or organization. We are simply concerned Americans. We are individuals uniting together to voice our concerns about the country. We want to inform people about the issues. We want America to once again become the greatest, most powerful and richest nation on earth."

For those of you who may not know, the name "Tea Party" is a reference to the Boston Tea Party of 1773 – which is when the American colonists protested against unfair British taxes. "TEA" also stands for "Taxed Enough Already." And the central theme of the national Tea Party movement is that taxes have gotten out-of-hand. The Tea Party is also opposed to the increased size of government, its fiscal irresponsibility, and the burgeoning size of the national debt. Tea Party members also voice concerns about the continuing influx of illegal immigrants, recent bailouts of the banking and housing industries, the costly new national health care plan, out-of-control entitlement programs, and the federal government's increasing interference into our daily lives. The Tea Party wants us to return to what the Constitution says about individual and states' rights, and notes that it never intended for the word "God" to be prohibited from the public domain.

The Tea Party is opposed to President Obama's over reaching liberal agenda. While the Tea Party is opposed to many Democratic Party initiatives, it also opposes Republicans who have veered away from their conservative roots.

I saw people at the rally who are anything but radicals. They were all *regular* people – men, women, children and families. Ethnic minorities were also represented. One man joked that he was surprised to see so many of his law-abiding neighbors at an "anti-government" rally. That's why this rally was so unique. "Only in America," I thought … It's only in the good old U.S.A. that we can hold demonstrations against our existing government, oppose their policies, and plan peaceful protest action.

Other themes were also discussed at the rally: We "should pray" for God to bless our country. We should stand up for what the Bible says about government and fair policies. And we should exercise our God-given right to vote in the November elections … The message was as American as you can get. I'm glad I was there. And I'm glad I got to attend a modern-day "tea party" with my old-fashioned wife.

Here We Go Again

"On Your Mark, Get Set, Go!" The politicians are off and running. Mid-term elections are just two months away, so everyone should brace themselves for another bitter fight. Democrats say "their side" has accomplished much: the economic stimulus act saved the economy, health care reform was finally passed, and the financial industry is now subject to new guidelines. Republicans will respond by saying that the only thing the stimulus money did was increase the national deficit, the health care reform was unwanted and unneeded, and all the financial reform bill did was increase the size of the federal bureaucracy.

The national polls note that only 41 percent of those recently surveyed approve of how President Obama is handling our economy. And 61 percent say the economy has gotten worse or stayed the same on Obama's watch. Our dim view of the economy is mostly due to the fact that the unemployment rate is still near 10 percent. The summer-long mishandling of the Gulf oil spill also cost Obama some points. Obama's overall approval rating is now at 49 percent, but his recent support of the Muslim "victory mosque" near Ground Zero will probably cost him some more popularity points.

Republicans are enjoying Obama's drop in popularity – and are counting on voter frustration to help their cause in the November 2nd elections. Tea Party supporters are coming out of the woodwork, and their groundswell of anti-tax sentiment will likely "swing the pendulum" back to those who favor a reduction in the size of government.

The drumbeat of political haggling continues to beat. It's interesting that not too long ago liberals were making fun of President George W. Bush. Now conservatives are saying "I told you so" when they chastise President Obama. Politics always seems to go from one extreme to the other. These are the battles that continue to be fought: liberal versus conservative ideology, big government versus limited government, pro-choice versus pro-life, tax raises versus tax cuts, and so on, and so forth. These are the things we love to argue about. And sometimes I think we argue more for the sake of arguing than we do for the issues themselves.

Are you one of those people who love to argue politics? Or maybe you're okay with "discussing the issues" so long as you can avoid messy differences of opinion. As a child of the 1960's, the Vietnam War era, I'd have to say that "arguing politics" comes naturally to me. Growing up in Minnesota, I was inundated with the Democratic Party perspective. When I first moved to

Montana, however, I was exposed to "The Conservative" point of view. I was told that "as a young man, if you're not Liberal, then you have no heart. As you get older, you should become Conservative – unless you have no brains."

Differences in political opinion should never be taken too seriously. A friend recently pointed out that "it is invigorating to argue" regardless of what the argument is about. That's why politics is an interesting subject. It's also why I no longer wish to be labeled Democrat or Republican. I want to be regarded as an Independent. That way I get to argue with people from either side of the political aisle.

Section 6:
Sentimental Journey

Dad's Shoebox

(ca. 2004)

Teachers and historians politely discuss the causes of World War II. It was a time when Germany, Italy, and Japan were anxious to improve their status in the world. These countries formed the Axis alliance. The Allied forces, including the United States, fought to protect the world from totalitarianism. And experts have asked: "Would there have been world war if not for Hitler?" and "Would the U.S. have entered the war if Japan hadn't bombed Pearl Harbor?"

These are important historical questions. My dad might have given these ideas some thought. More likely than not, though, he went to war for the simple reason that all his friends were signing up; and he wanted to do the right thing. A teacher's son, Dad was a good student at a prestigious college. He was promised officers training when he enlisted. Dad joked that the army filled their quota for officers when they got to "H" in the alphabet, so he was put in the infantry.

This was just one of the things I learned about my dad after he died. In the summer of my 14th year (a few months after Dad died of a heart attack) I found a shoebox of his letters in the attic. These were letters he wrote home from World War II, and they captured my interest more than any school subject ever has. Psychologists say a young man should know his father in order to better know himself – and I certainly found that to be true for me.

As Dad crossed the Atlantic Ocean in 1943, he thanked God for taking care of him and his fellow soldiers. He expressed great faith that the U.S. would not only win the war, but would also take care of its soldiers. And after arriving in Northern Africa, he admired the beauty of the land. He was curious about the culture of the Arab people, and couldn't believe that their leaders lived in ridiculous luxury while the masses lived in utter poverty. His letters weren't allowed to say exactly where he was, or what his mission might be, but he never forgot to thank God and pray that he be protected from danger.

Dad's first and only combat experience was in January of 1944. It wasn't the grand and glorious experience he might have hoped for, though. His company was supposed to cross the ice-cold waters of the Rapido River in central Italy, secure a foothold, and fight the enemy. German soldiers were entrenched across the river, where they were hiding in and around the monastery of Mount Cassino. The German forces were almost insurmountable from this vantage point. Asking the Americans to dislodge this force was truly an impossible mission. The newspapers of the day reported that approximately 2000 Americans (of the 34th and 36th Divisions) were killed or captured that day. Only 17 of Dad's company of 184 men (the 143rd Regimental Combat Team) survived that battle.

The newspapers also reported that "these men did not die in vain." The attempted crossing of the Rapido River had been done to divert the enemy's attention away from the nearby campaign at Anzio beachhead. The main attack was led by Major General John Dahlquist, and his troops were able to advance 300 miles during the next month. This eventually allowed Allied forces to recapture Rome. Rather than complain about being used in a decoy mission, Dad, in his inimitable manner, thanked God that he "was one of the fortunate few" of his company to have survived the experience.

Dad suffered a shrapnel injury to his neck in that battle. This injury caused him neck pain and spasms for the rest of his life. He was captured by the Germans, and spent the next 30 months of his life in a German P.O.W. camp. Although he lost 50 pounds during his imprisonment, his postcards of the day express gratitude for the care he received from the Germans.

Mom says Dad had many girlfriends before he left for the war. She was surprised that his letters called her "my gal." As the tide of the war turned, and victory was at hand, Dad made a list of things he wanted to do. As he was processing out of the service, he wrote Mom this letter:

"I love you an awful lot," he wrote. "If you can ignore my ignorance, we'll get along just fine. I have a strong back and sturdy arms. I've been promised a job [in St. Paul, Minnesota] that pays $22.50 each and every week, sometimes with overtime pay, and soon it will pay all the way up to $30 per week. By the way, I've even arranged for a house. I've already arranged to buy a nice 4 room house on Western Street for $17,532. The payments are only $87 per month... As I said before, I really love you. I'm from a good family – with no insanity or syphilis – and everybody in my family lives a long life. Please meet me in Minnesota and give me a chance. If things work out – maybe, I hope, we can get married on October the 26th, 1946 – if that's okay with you." And it was signed, "Yours (if you want me), Jerome John Kessler, single, 28 yrs of age." P.S. also included: "Enclosed is a picture of me so you will recognize me at the train depot."

Mom must have liked what see saw at the train depot that day. They got married, right on Dad's schedule, and started a family. Dad had no interest in going back to college. He wanted to get on with his life. He was hired by the Post Office. As a letter carrier he got to wear a uniform, just like in the army – but nobody shot at him anymore. Sometime later, he was offered a supervisory position. After a month on this new job, however, he asked to get his old job back. He didn't like having to tell his friends what to do.

Mom had a baby every 18 months for the next 12 years. Eight hungry kids were quite a financial burden on a mailman's salary, so Mom got a job as well. The older girls took care of the younger kids while Mom was at work. Dad did a variety of part-time jobs: janitor during the winter, groundskeeper in the summer, and landscaper during the spring and fall. Dad needed help with his part-time jobs, and that's where I got involved with the family finances. I was Dad's helper for his part-time jobs. That was a duty I sometimes complained about as a kid, but now treasure the time I got to spend with Dad.

As a kid, I was occasionally embarrassed by Dad's rough hands and twitching neck. At the time, I didn't know anything about his war injuries. I also didn't know Dad had "Shell Shock" from seeing so many of his war buddies die. A lifetime of counseling and neck therapy didn't do much good. He had a small library of WW2 books, and spent many nights researching the war. He never spoke openly about these experiences, though.

Dad kept most of the promises he made to Mom. He was a good husband

and father. He almost went crazy thinking about the war, though. He was a hard worker, had many friends, and was admired for his honesty and gentle nature. He never lied – except to hide how many extra loans he had to take out in order to make ends meet. And he wasn't able to keep his promise to live a long life.

Dad was working especially hard in May of 1968. After delivering mail in the day, he was landscaping the local doctor's clinic building in the evenings. Dad complained of chest pain to that same doctor. He was told that "indigestion" was the cause of his chest pain, so he shouldn't worry about it. Dad resumed his work, and died of a heart attack the following morning.

At Dad's funeral, I was mad at God for having taken away my father. I was also mad at our family doctor for not recognizing that Dad's chest pain was a warning that he was about to have a heart attack. But it was 1968, after all, and heart problems were not treated as effectively back then as they are now. It was his heart attack that made me decide to become a doctor. Years later I said to myself "that could be your dad" when I took care of patients with chest pain. I didn't want to let them die. I didn't want their kids to be left without a father.

Lake Wobegon

(10/14/2009)

"It was a quiet day in Lake Wobegon," Garrison Keillor says, and then he goes on to describe the fictional events occurring in his fictional town … and he's been making up the news about this town since 1974. Garrison Keillor, for those of you who haven't heard of him, is an enormously successful author, humorist and performer. His books and radio show demonstrate that many people would rather hear about the everyday events in the lives of average people than hear about robberies, murders, shootings, etc.

Maybe you recognize some of Keillor's characters where you live. Our town, like Keillor's, is where "all the women are strong, all the men are good looking, and all the children are above average." It's where the Catholics (from Our Lady of Perpetual Responsibility Church) and the Lutherans (from the Lake Wobegon Lutheran Church) peacefully co-exist; they only occasionally claim that one group's sausage is superior to another's lutefisk; and the "uff-dahs" of one group harmoniously complement the "guzuntas" of another.

Keillor's radio show has several make-believe sponsors. Powdermilk Biscuits, for example, "give shy persons the strength to get up and do what needs to be done." And the motto for Ralph's Pretty Good Grocery is this: "if you can't find it at Ralph's, you can probably get along without it." It's good that small town people feel that way about their local stores and products – especially when they have to compete against the Megamalls and Wally Marts of the outside world.

Graduate students in American literature debate the exact location of Keillor's mythical town. Because he lived near St. Cloud, MN when he was going to college, most experts suspect Lake Wobegon is somewhere in central Minnesota. I too have wondered where he got his ideas from, and have explored the "Lake Wobegon Trail" – which includes the small Minnesota towns of Albany, Avon, Cold Spring, Freeport, Rockville, St. Joseph and St. Stephen. I have eaten at the legendary "Charlie's Café" in Freeport, which is where Keillor used to hang out. But Keillor could easily love our "M & M Cafe" or "Sunny's Family Restaurant," to name a few of our local establishments; and Lake Wobegon could just as easily have been Crane, Fairview, Lambert, Savage or Sidney.

Like most authors, Keillor's imaginary characters are based on people he actually knew. His most loveable characters are based on people he met in small towns – and not the "plastic" people he met when he subsequently moved to New York City.

The 35 year anniversary of Keillor's first show on Lake Wobegon was held this past 4th of July in Avon, MN. 10,000 visitors crowded into this town of 1200 people. The radio broadcast of the event was heard by four million people. Musical performances, speeches, and celebrity appearances helped make the occasion a success. It was not, as some people mistakenly think, a criticism of small town life. "It's all in good fun," said one fan. It's also about celebrating the American way of life. Everyday life, it seems, is something that people want to hear about.

Garrison Keillor has several best-selling books, including his 1985 *Lake Wobegon Days*. He has also been inducted into the Radio Hall of Fame. Last month Keillor had a minor stroke. I have great appreciation of Keillor's work, and hope he recovers without incident. I want to hear more about Lake Wobegon and its strong women, good looking men, and above average children. And maybe, just maybe, we have some of those same characters in our own small town.

Next Big Thing

(8/22/2007)

Do you ever wish you had been the one to invent Velcro? George de Mestral, a Swiss electrical engineer, patented the name "VELCRO" in 1941. He got the idea for Velcro by noticing how burrs stuck to his wool hunting pants. He made millions from his idea. Many inventors, however, never capitalize on their novel ideas. Sir John Harington's 1596 design for flush toilets was contained in a publication that criticized the British royalty. He was banished from the court, and never received the accolades his toilet design deserved … and indoor plumbing wasn't put into widespread use until the late 19th century.

Maybe I'm crazy, but I think my ideas are revolutionary. Sometimes I see new products that I swear are based on ideas I've had in the past, and kick myself for not having patented "my inventions." Perhaps these ideas are floating around in the air – many people have them – but then one person or company capitalizes on them. They say necessity is the mother of invention, but I don't believe that. I think boredom has resulted in more interesting ideas than dirty hands ever did.

More patents (for various inventions) come out of America than any other country in the world. We are a society that is fascinated by gimmicks. For example, my kids recently played 10 consecutive hours of video games on their X-box. Our cell phone bill shows how much they value talking to and text-messaging their friends. Our library card, on the other hand, doesn't get much use.

Your idea of "the greatest invention ever" depends on your perspective. My mother, a former seamstress, used to say the sewing machine (invented in 1836 by Josef Madersberger) deserves that recognition. Many people feel the telephone (invented by Alexander Graham Bell in 1876) is the greatest ever. Doctors often say penicillin (discovered by Sir Alexander Fleming in 1928) is the most important medical breakthrough of all time. Another famous person, Sidney's Chad Mueller (433-2504), who installs and fixes garage doors, says "automatic garage door openers" is an extremely useful invention, and "everyone should have one." As a landscaper, I couldn't survive without a lawn mower, which was invented in 1830 by Edwin Beard Budding. Which invention do you think is the most important? Interestingly enough, a MIT survey in 1995 revealed that Americans felt "the toothbrush" is the invention they value the most – surpassing the car, personal computer, cell phone, and microwave oven in necessity.

Inventions require advances in our understanding of things before mankind can develop practical application of those ideas. Chemistry and Physics came before Nuclear energy. And, of course, inventions can be used for bad as well as good purposes. The Atomic Bomb is an example of that. Scientists, engineers, politicians, and sociologists should work together to use our inventions in a safe and useful way.

My ideas, I suppose, are no more revolutionary than the concept of sliced bread – an idea that Otto Frederick Rohwedder came up with in 1912. It wasn't until 1928 that sliced bread was sold to the public, however. (historical details from Wikipedia.com) One idea I have is to have grass that doesn't need to be mowed. If this catches on, however, then my landscaping business will suffer. In the same way, if Americans had better preventive health practices, then doctors and dentists wouldn't be able to send their kids to expensive colleges. Economic interests often determine which ideas are pursued more than others. Perhaps that's why our nation spends more money on heart surgery (bypasses, stents, heart caths, etc.) than on preventing heart disease in the first place.

Some people say we should "put a lid" on controversial ideas. I think everyone has ideas that are both unique and useful, though. If you have an idea for my "Dr. Dirt" column – no matter how crazy – let me know, and I'll tell everyone how smart you are. In the meantime, just keep having those far-fetched ideas. Your spouse might think you're nuts, but I'll tell the world that there's a method to your madness.

Technology

(2/17/2010)

Do you have trouble figuring out how to operate your cell phone? I do. I never seem to be able to get to the call in time, and I haven't figured out how to silence the darn thing. And then I get untimely "reminders" on my cell phone about missed calls that continue to squawk at me until I attend to them.

I really don't get that many calls on my cell phone, but they always seem to occur at the wrong time: when I'm driving in heavy traffic, during meetings, etc. And most people spend twenty times more time on their cell phones than I do. Society, it seems, hasn't figured out that that cell phones can be rude – and even dangerous. Technology, it seems, has surpassed Society's ability to use it properly.

It's the same way with video games. I was once a big fan of Pac Man. It was fun to go out, have a few drinks, and challenge a friend to a friendly game. I could even beat my kids at the game. When home video games first became available, I was able to interact with my kids on our Nintendo game. But then the games and the machines all became more advanced. And the parade of machines (Super Nintendo, Play Station, Game Cube, Xbox, Wii, etc.) all cost money – and dads all over the world were "guilted" into buying "the latest and the greatest" new video game.

Technology is one of America's greatest strengths. We invent things, hype the demand for them, and then the world buys them up. And it's sometimes a good thing. It's good that we don't have to mess with "eight track" players anymore, for instance. Albums were once okay, but were easy to scratch and hard to store. CDs and CD players were definitely an improvement, but iPods (and other MP3 players) have left those technologies in the dust.

Remember VHS tapes? I still have hundreds of them in my library – both the educational and entertainment varieties. Do you want to buy them? I also have several VHS players that I still haven't figured out how to operate. Now everybody has switched to DVD players, Blu-Ray, and Digital video recorders.

I was recently introduced to the world of GPS devices. These devices (Garmin, TomTom, etc.) sit on your dashboard and tell you where you are, when to turn, etc. At first I couldn't stand it yapping at me (from a backseat driver's position) as I traversed an area I was familiar with. I thought it was rude. Then my wife bought me one of those GPS devices. For many months I refused to take it out of the box. More recently, though, I had to travel the convoluted roads of Missoula, and I would have gotten lost without my GPS to guide me.

What will be the next "must have" technology? A device that exercises for us might be nice. Just turn on the switch and melt off the pounds. An automatic learning device would also be nice. Just turn on the "hypnopedia device," go to sleep, and learn whatever it tells us to learn. It will be, in the words of Aldous Huxley, a "brave new world."

Technology makes everyone happy. It's fun and all-consuming. Technology is safer than drugs, and less controversial than religion. Just buy whatever new stuff the market tells you to buy, turn it on, and do what it tells you to do.

Hey Romeo

(9/11/2007)

"If you like to write so much," a friend asked, "why don't you write a *real book*?"

After punching him in the nose, I picked my well-meaning friend from the floor, apologized, and tried to make amends.

"As you may have noticed," I said plaintively, "I tend to be a little impulsive."

"I would've never known," he said sarcastically. "But what else have you got to do? You can't mow lawns in January."

Good point, I thought. Maybe I should do what my ex-friend suggested. I'm certainly not getting rich writing a weekly newspaper column. If I write a best seller, I'd get to go on "The David Letterman Show," meet some movie stars, go to Hollywood parties, and make lots of money. Piece of cake! I'll do it! Now all I have to do is decide what to write about, research the topic for 2 years, write the book the next 2 years, find a publisher, do re-writes, finagle a contract, go on tour for another year, and hope it sells enough copies to cover my expenses. Piece of cake? It's not as easy as it sounds. Maybe I'll just keep doing what I'm doing until I stop doing it. When my loyal base of readers – mostly former patients, I presume – all die off, then I'll be out of a job.

I have a thousand ideas for a novel. But I'm so used to writing these short columns that my novel might be a bit truncated. For example, whereas William Shakespeare has Romeo (in "Romeo and Juliet," Act 2, Scene 2) say to Juliet's window: "But soft, what light through yonder window breaks? It is the east, and Juliet is the sun. Arise, fair sun, and kill the envious moon, Who is already sick and pale with grief, That thou, her maid, art far more fair than she, Be not her maid, since she is sick and green, And none but fools do wear it; cast if off. It is my lady, O, it is my love! [100 words later] See how she leans her cheek upon her hand! O that I were a glove upon that hand, That I might touch that cheek!" I'm afraid I might skip a bit of this chit-chat, throw a rock at Juliet's window, and shout: "I like you – a whole lot!"

It's true: I'm no Romeo. One of my many nicknames in high school, though, was "Hey Romeo." That wasn't because I was suave and debonair. I took foreign language classes, and that's how my classmates mispronounced "Jerome" in Spanish.

My tendency to get to the point is well known. Tolstoy took 1474 pages to write "War and Peace." I could do it in 99 pages, or less. Being blunt occasionally gets me into trouble. Getting to the point is a habit I probably learned from my 25 years as a doctor.

Doctors tend to answer their own questions, and try not to listen any more than they have to … "How are you? Not good, right? You wouldn't be here otherwise, right? I'll bet you have a sore throat. Am I right? Huh? Okay, take this antibiotic. Pay the clerk as you go. And, oh yeah, have a nice day!"

So writing a novel is probably not for me. A novelette, maybe. I hope you guys (and gals) are around to buy my next book. Stay healthy! And, oh yeah, pay the clerk as you go.

Ninety Nine

(1/27/2009)

It's fun to look through my files. In 1985, before I moved to Sidney, I offered to write a "Doctor's Corner" column for the local newspaper. I was told it was a bad idea. It wouldn't be popular – and some people would definitely hate it.

I am now writing my 99th article. With a bit of luck, I'll make it to the century mark. I think it's interesting how this "medical advice" column evolved into a "landscaping advice" and "home improvement" column, and now it has evolved into something that is difficult to characterize. I write humorous anecdotes, childhood memories, and psychobabble. I also write about interesting books, specific people, and recent events. Other times I just make stuff up. And when I'm feeling really stupid, I write about dangerous topics like politics and religion.

Recently a critic told me my writing style is "argumentative and confrontational." Ouch! And here I thought I was just a sentimental old fart that nobody takes seriously. That doesn't mean I don't push the limits from time to time. I've always thought one controversial talk is worth two "how's the weather" talks. Even my wife gets upset with some of my columns, you know; but she knows I'm a barking dog on the outside, and just a pussycat on the inside.

Writing is something I do in between other projects – mowing lawns, landscaping, refinishing the laundry room, etc. My next project is the downstairs bathroom. It needs a new tile floor. Living in a house that was built in 1915 gives me a lot of potential home projects. It also gives me a lot of "non-controversial" topics to write about.

Well, I've almost made it. I've almost got through a column without irritating anyone. Hallelujah! Do I sometimes tread in dangerous waters? Perhaps. That depends on how sensitive you are. All I need to do now is keep a low profile, avoid topics like politics and religion, and try to get one more (just one more!) column completed – in order to get 100 articles under my belt. Wish me luck.

(Author's note: I have now written over 200 articles.)

Shelley, 1982

Life with Shelley

"What do you think of the latest chapter to my book?"

"Do you really want to know?" replied my wife.

"Yes."

"It's boring." Ouch! Feedback is important, but can be painful. But this was something I needed help with. I am trying to write a story about a scientist that is interesting – which is not an easy thing to do. And my life as an aspiring author (like the life of a scientist) is "try, try, and then try again." And never get disappointed if you get "rejection, rejection and more rejection" … even from your Mrs.

"Well," I said, fighting back the tears, "maybe I'll write a book about YOU … I'll call it 'Life with Shelley' … You'll see how it is to have everyone know your faults."

"Faults? What faults?" she says … and then I realize she is joking. That's how it is in our household. And it goes both ways. Shelley is somber when I tell a joke, and laughs when I try to be serious.

I suspect many marriages are like this. Comeuppances and role reversals are common. But the issue is particularly acute in our household. For several years after moving to Sidney, for example, my wife felt like she was living in my shadow. I was, after all, the new doctor in town. Small towns love their doctors, especially when they have a doctor shortage. That problem (with my wife feeling "less important" than me) didn't last long. She is very sociable, and quickly made friends in the workplace, at church, and around the community. It wasn't long, in fact, before I became "Shelley's husband" … and nobody really cared if I was a doctor or not.

Wives are more sociable than their husbands. *Men Are From Mars, Women Are From Venus* discusses this topic. It's an excellent book. Men are better at some things, of course, but that's rarely noticed …

I hate to imagine how life would be without my wife. I would eat lots of junk food, forget how to bathe, and dress in a slovenly manner. I already do those things. But worse yet, according to my wife, is that my clothes "would *never* match." If husbands did outlive their wives, our country would be in dire trouble: every toilet seat in the country would be left up, house lights would never be turned on, gift shops would go bankrupt, and – God forbid – Christmas would have to be cancelled.

Nobody knows if "Life with Shelley" will ever amount to anything. It could be a book, however, that describes how two twenty-something-year-olds meet and develop a relationship. When she proposes ("Are we gonna get married or what?") he agrees to the idea. But they don't really know what they are getting themselves into. They leave the comfort of their homes, move to a small town, and start a medical practice. They disagree, of course, on what is more important: cozy office furniture or modern medical equipment. He is a scientist at heart. She is more concerned about emotional than scientific matters. In the end, however, her way wins out. He has long known that a scientific perspective is important, but comes to realize that "matters of the heart" are more important.

Golden Oldies

(3/25/2008)

You might not care, but I've been gone for a while. Maybe you thought my column has "gone to the dogs" anyway. My son (Joel) and I went on a zigzag trip to California. In recent days, I also had another birthday. My wife wouldn't let this sneak by unnoticed, though. She gave me "Flower Power – the Music of the Love Generation," a ten CD music collection compiled by Time-Life Records (C. 2007). We enjoyed listening to these "golden oldies" on our car trip.

Listening to this music was like driving down memory lane. My son thought some of the lyrics were silly, though. That was sacrilege to me. You and I grew up with these words of wisdom, and people shouldn't make fun of us for living our lives to the beat of these tunes.

These songs tell the story of our soap opera lives. While gazing at the cloud-shrouded mountains of Utah, for example, I realize that Judy Collins' words are true: "I've looked at life from both sides now, from win and lose, and still somehow, it's life's illusions I recall. I really don't know life at all."

The Bee Gees band puts it more bluntly. Dr. Dirt, they imply, "told a joke that started the whole [town] laughing, but … didn't see, that the joke was on me." How could I have been so foolish? And now I'm *crying in my beer* with Billy Joel, who is "sharing a drink called loneliness – but it's better than drinking alone."

These tear-jerkers really know how to cheer a guy up. And now I also realize that my wife gave me Carly Simon's "You're So Vain" for a reason. But, as Joe Cocker puts it, "I'll get by with a little help from my friends." And even though I've been "through many dangers, toils and snares," the fact remains that "Amazing Grace" has saved "a wretch like me." So being a jerk isn't all bad.

These songs can be educational and insightful. Elton John warns that "Mars aint the kind of place to raise your kids; in fact, it's cold as hell" up there. Thank you, Elton, for that useful bit of information. Zager and Evans predict that in future years "your arms [will be] hanging limp at your side. Your legs got nothing to do; some machine [is] doing that for you." Jim Croce would like to "put time in a bottle," while the Chicago band asks the rhetorical question: "Does anyone really care what time it is?"

What would we do without pop music? The music can have foot-tapping appeal. And the lyrics put into words some of our unexpressed thoughts and feelings. You won't relate to some of these songs, of course; but others will touch you in a visceral way. I hope my "Dr Dirt" columns do the same thing. Stupid as they are, I try to tickle your funny bone and stimulate parts of your brain you haven't used for a while. I appreciate your support, and have tried to build a "relationship" with you, my faithful readers. In the immortal words of Mama Cass, I characterize our bond in this way:

"Believe it or not, there's something groovy and good about whatever we've got. And it's gettin better, growing stronger, warm and wilder … gettin better every day, gettin better every day, gettin better every day."

Bismarck or Bust

(9/30/2009)

The Heritage Center recently featured "Walking Jim Stoltz," who is a musician and story teller. It was an excellent show. Since 1976 Jim has gone on long walking trips. He has walked more than 27,000 miles on these trips. Most of his trips are about 500 miles long and take about 30 days to complete, but – as he puts it – are really just one step at a time. I was inspired by his words, and decided to go on an adventure of my own.

In my college days I went on long bicycle trips around Minnesota. I've also run marathons, canoed in the Boundary Waters, sailed in Lake Superior, and kayaked in Alaska. It has been a long time since I've done anything adventurous, though. I have become a bit of a couch potato, it seems; and my ever-expanding waistline confirms the fact that my current lifestyle is not that demanding.

For several years, I have been thinking about riding my bicycle to Bismarck. It's a "doable" project, I thought. It is about 260 miles on the back roads (highways 68, 85, 200, etc) and I could camp out along the way. Once I started telling people about it, I knew there was no backing out – or risk being called a failure. That's how a lot of goals are: don't say anything unless you plan on doing it.

Planning an adventure is half the fun … I shook the cobwebs off my bike, oiled it up, and make a practice run to Fairview. So far, so good, I thought. Then I dug out my old bike touring equipment. I loaded down my bike with a tent, sleeping roll, cook kit, food, water, spare tire, tool kit, candy, more water, rain gear, spare socks, toiletries, and, of course, more water. Things were a tad bulky. I weighed in (me, my bike and I) at 327 pounds. I did leave the kitchen sink at home, though. I also brought a camera, a book, and coffee. These were *nonessential* but *nice-to-have* accessories.

I started my trip last Tuesday. It's funny how a big trip starts the same as a little one. But it wasn't long before I had crossed the Yellowstone River and was struggling to climb the hills of western North Dakota. I had no idea there were so many hills! Seven hours later I arrived in Watford City. It looked like paradise to me. After a good meal, I was refreshed – and was able to bike another couple of hours to the north unit of Teddy Roosevelt National Park. The first day was history. I had survived 70-some miles of hills and more hills.

At the end of that day's ride, I was too tired to even eat. I set up my tent, drank lots of water, and went to bed. I heard the yelps of coyotes all around me, but was too tired to let them bother me. I slept for a few hours. After the sun went down, however, it got incredibly cold. My thermometer said mid 30's, which I wasn't prepared for. I had uncontrollable shivering. It's hard to be philosophical, I found out, when survival is at stake. Intermittent campfires and hot cocoa got me through the night.

The next morning seemed better. I welcomed the warmth of the morning sun. For breakfast I had freeze-dried eggs and bacon, coffee, water, and candy. My spirits were lifted. The road, however, turned out to be a heartbreaker. The uphill climb (out of the Little Missouri River bluffs) was horrendous. To make matters worse, highway 85 had little or no "shoulder" to bike on. Oil trucks and semis zipped by me at 75 mph. And the more I worried about keeping on a perfectly straight line, the more I trembled with terror. I pictured my blood and guts being splattered on the highway, being left to rot, and nobody ever hearing from me again. My grand and glorious adventure, I now realized, could turn out to be a bust …

I felt like quitting. I wanted to call my wife and tell her to come and get me. Just minutes after telling God I couldn't take it anymore, though, the roads dramatically improved. Finally I had a shoulder to bike on. Finally I was able to get a few feet away from the dangerous truck traffic.

I pulled into the tiny town of Grassy Butte, North Dakota. I had a nice lunch at Beicegel's country store, gas station, and post office. I was able to continue that day's journey on to Killdeer, where I camped in their city park.

That too seemed like an oasis. Their showers worked great. It's ironic that we don't appreciate little luxuries (like a hot shower) unless we are forced to go without them.

The next morning I was up bright and early. I wanted to make up for lost time. I wanted to get on the road at the first light – which was around 6 a.m. Highway 200 left a lot to be desired. It also had narrow shoulders – but wasn't as busy as Highway 85. I developed a strategy of listening carefully for traffic sounds behind me, deciding how big an approaching vehicle might be, and guessing if they were able to swing a path around me. Most car and truck drivers on my trip, by the way, were very thoughtful and considerate. They wanted to give me a bit of the road. There were other times, however, that I just rode my bike into the ditch to avoid *too close for comfort* encounters.

I was feeling pretty good about the trip, and the progress I was making, until I got near Zap, North Dakota. While zipping down a hill, I heard a sudden gush of air come out of my rear tire. "Is that a blowout?" I wondered. Of course it was. But I couldn't believe that I didn't fall or get hurt. The good Lord must be looking out for me, I thought. I changed the tire. My rear wheel was warped, though, and it didn't look like I could continue. I limped into Beulah. I was fortunate to find an "OK Best" hardware store where a nice young man named Zach was able to fix me up with a replacement tire. My bike wasn't quite the same, but I was able to go on; and I was able to make it to Hazen for the evening.

As I started on my 4th day of riding, I was still about 80 miles from my friend's house in Bismarck, North Dakota – which was my goal. The early morning ride went great. I enjoyed the scenery of the nearby Missouri River; the road was smooth sailing; and I was feeling invigorated that I might actually make it to Bismarck. I was advised not to take Highway 25, however, because of heavy truck traffic. I took the "no name" highway that heads south out of Hensler. The traffic was light, and the road was good, but the hills were very steep. I came to the realization that every road in life has advantages and disadvantages, and the only thing we can count on is that each road we are on will have "more hills." If I want to continue, I must accept the hills.

I took a recommended detour to Cross Ranch State Park. West River Road, I was told, was a "scenic" gravel highway, with "just a few" hills. I should have anticipated things better. It was very difficult to ride my weighted down bicycle on that desolate 20 mile stretch of road. And when I asked a local farmer for water, and told him what I was doing, he said: "What's the matter with you? Are you crazy?"

I said I was an author. "I understand," he said; and then he gave me two bottles of water … Water which, by the way, made it possible for me to continue on my seemingly endless trek on that lonely dusty road.

The gravel road eventually became a paved road, Highway 1806, which eventually brought me into Mandan, North Dakota. I struggled a bit through downtown traffic, crossed the Missouri River (on the new Memorial Highway Bridge) and rested at the "Welcome to Bismarck" sign. I made it, I thought. My friend's house was still a few miles away, but I had made it to Bismarck. My body was drenched with sweat, my legs were burning with pain, but I was happy – at least for a moment – that I had accomplished my goal. I knew I could not have done it without support from my wife in Sidney and my friends in Bismarck. I knew God had been looking out for me. This adventure, out of the many each of us takes in life, was now complete.

CANDISC

(8/11/2010)

Some writing assignments are harder than others. While many of you have been spending time at the local county fairs, Dr. Dirt has been doing "undercover work" on an activity that has increasing national and regional popularity. I'm referring to long-distance bicycle riding, and the recent week-long running of the CANDISC bicycle tour in Northwestern North Dakota. It was the 18th annual CANDISC tour. Each year they change their route somewhat, and this past year they took the "Northern Tier" route from Garrison to Crosby.

CANDISC stands for "Cycle around North Dakota in Sakakawea Country." It is a bicycle ride – not a race – but it is definitely not for the uninitiated. This was scheduled as a 458 mile bicycle trip, but many participants took side trips to push their mileage over 500 miles. We woke up each day at 5 a.m., took down our "city of tents," ate breakfast, and then hit the trunk highways and county roads to tackle each day's riding assignment.

We biked about 70 miles per day, usually on rolling hills, but also climbed a few "ginormous" hills along the way. We rode a few days in sweltering heat, and had to drink massive amounts of water to avoid dehydration. We also endured two tremendous rainstorms, including one on our final night that left me and everything in my tent soaking wet. We also had to fight a few 20 mph headwinds. Fortunately there were rest stops every 10-20 miles along the way. Another nice thing was that if the heat and hills got to you, the CANDISC support personnel would pick you up. They would escort your exhausted body and bike to the next campsite. It appeared to this reporter that about 20% of the riders "took the SAG truck" into camp – especially on the grueling 3rd day, 92 mile ride to Crosby. But there were no losers on this trip. Everyone who accepted the challenge of this ride was a winner.

The ride started at Fort Stevenson Park, in central North Dakota, and had nightly stops in the towns of Berthold, Kenmare, Crosby, Bowbells, Glenburn and Makoti. And on the seventh day we rested – providing we were able to make it to the finish line in Garrison, ND.

Each town greeted us like we were conquering heroes. They helped us with our gear, provided shower facilities, fed us, and made us feel like royalty. Most of the towns also had some type of entertainment. Glenburn offered a tour of a local elk farm; they also launched a hot air balloon later that evening. Many towns offered musical entertainment. Rachel Birdsall, a 9th grader in Berthold, sang like an angel – and seems like a "can't miss" star of the future. The "Treble Makers," a fivesome from Minot, put on an incredibly entertaining performance in Makoti. The rest stops also went all out to keep us happy and healthy. Literally hundreds of volunteers and support personnel made sure that all of our needs were attended to. They did so out of the goodness of their hearts, no doubt, but they also wanted to be voted the top site in their respective category – and receive the cash prizes that went along with that honor.

CANDISC certainly seems to have a winning formula for putting on an event of this nature. There were 305 bikers in this year's ride. Many of them had done CANDISC rides in the past. The bikers were from 29 states and 5 different countries. About 40% were female. The riders ranged from 9 to 82 years of age. The average age was 48.

Tom Ihde invited me to CANDISC in February. We were "Tom and Jerry" from eastern Montana. Tom also enjoyed the distinction of winning the "Porta Potty Rap Song Contest" at the pre-race festivities.

Tom is an avid biker, and trained at least twenty times harder for this event than I did. The difference in training was quickly evident. I struggled to keep up to him that first day – and a few hours later wondered if I had made a mistake by coming on this bicycle tour. Fortunately it was easy to meet people along the way, and a lady from Iowa made sure that I made it through the ride's hardships.

Biking long distance is an adventure and a challenge. It is full of rewards and satisfactions. It also has more than its share of aches and pains. And my aging body suffered from one malady after another: periodic dehydration, sore butt syndrome, foot blisters, a pulled leg muscle, a flare-up of my chronic knee arthritis, occasional sciatica, subluxing hip joints, more "sit bone" pain, stiffness from camping out, and – last but not least – a lot more butt pain. Even experienced riders, it seems, are bothered by "a sore seat" on these rides, and I was glad to know that I wasn't the only one to have suffered from this problem.

CANDISC is one of a growing number of fitness "participation" events that are being held around the country. There are many tricks to make something like this enjoyable. Tom and I are willing to discuss these with you or your civic group. These trips are also great for sponsoring communities, and I hope that CANDISC comes to our area in the future – as it did to Fairview some years ago. Shorter bike rides are also nice. We should, for example, support the upcoming "Duathlon" that the Richland Run and Bike Club is having on Saturday, August 21. That's all I have for now. I've got to get to work on my next assignment. I can't just "sit around" waiting for things to happen.

Costly Kids

(5/19/2010)

As the last of my three kids is finishing high school, I am thinking about sending him a bill for the expenses I have accrued in raising him. That sounds a bit extreme, but studies show that parents spend around a quarter of a million dollars raising "their little darling" from birth to age 18. And chances are they will be "asked" to provide another $20 to $150 thousand per kid to help pay for college expenses. Yikes! No wonder my hair is turning gray…

This is a topic I have occasionally researched: A few years ago "experts" said that it costs about $1 per hour to raise a kid from birth to age 18. That didn't seem too bad. I figured if I could get them to mow a few lawns I could recoup some of my losses. But the figure has gone up to $1.70 per hour. Inflation, or something like it, has taken its toll.

It shouldn't surprise you that rich people spend more on their children than "regular folks" do. If your annual family income is under forty thousand dollars, you spend an average of $7000 per kid per year. If your income is between 40 and 70 thousand, then you spend about $10,000 per kid per year. And if you make over 70 grand, then you spend $15,000 on each child every year. I'd venture to say that the sky is the limit in that regard.

The data I'm quoting comes from a 2004 survey by the U.S. Department of Agriculture, so it must be accurate. My thoughts on the subject were stimulated by a "MSN Money" primer on the subject. The cost of raising a kid is broken down into the following areas: housing, food, transportation, clothing, health care, education and miscellaneous expenses. I'm all for giving kids a roof over their heads, by the way, and also agree that we should provide them with food and clothing – but sometimes I think that we give kids "extras" that they don't really need.

Do seventeen year-old kids really need a new car, for instance? And should public school kids be competing to wear the coolest designer clothes? I think not. Why should kids have the latest iPod, iPhone, iPad, or other i-gadget? (Notice the emphasis on "I," by the way.) There's way too much pressure for kids to have "the latest and greatest" of everything, I think; and commercialization of this nature is teaching our children some bad lessons.

I agree that education is a worthy expenditure. Young minds are a sponge waiting for the opportunity to soak up new information. Getting a good education is the best way that I know of for a financially challenged young person to improve their lot in life. That's why we should support our school systems, and try to help our kids go to the college or trade school of their choice. And I don't think a young person needs to go to an Ivy League school to learn what they need in life.

There's no getting around the fact that raising kids is expensive. It would be less of a burden if we did without some of the excesses, though. Financing our children's upbringing is one of our greatest responsibilities. Good parents are more than willing to make sacrifices (financial and otherwise) to help their children become all that they can be. My wife says our kids are "worth their weight in gold." I suppose that's true. It's also true that I get a bit of satisfaction knowing that someday my kids will have to support children of their own.

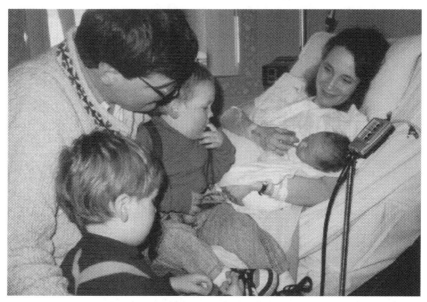

Kessler Family, 1991

Who's the Baby?

(8/18/2010)

"Come on, Dad, we've got to get going."

And so it is. The cars are packed. The plans are made. Now all we have to do is get in the car, start the ignition, and head down the road. Except this time it is different. We are leaving with "Baby On Board" but will be coming back as "Parents Only." We are sending our last kid to college, after all, and things will never be the same.

My wife and I have been blessed with three sons. One by one we have seen them head off to college. This week our youngest, Ian, is headed to Carroll College, and wants to become a math professor. Our middle child, Joel, is at Missoula, and plans to become an Elementary and Special Ed teacher – and landscaper on the side. Our oldest, Jerry John, is in Minnesota, a fifth year senior. He is a Physics major who plans to pick up an engineering degree in graduate school.

Long gone are the days of changing diapers, coaching little league and helping kids with their homework. Planning for college is not too distant a memory, but that pipedream has now become a reality. Thoughts of weddings and grandchildren do pop into my head – but that scenario seems too remote to provide much comfort.

It's a common situation, I realize, but the emotional impact of "Empty Nest Syndrome" doesn't really hit until it happens. After your kids are in college, some people ask, what is there to plan for? Your job is no longer interesting. You don't stand much chance of winning the lottery, so your "financial condition" isn't going to change. Your golf game sucks. Change the details (of your life story) if you must, but the end result is the same ... Eventually we all go through a period where the house seems empty, and we know life will never be the same.

I've been "emotional" for months ... It was our baby's last prom in March. Graduation was nice – but it was over in May. It was great that my son got a "real job" this summer, but it also meant he wouldn't be working for me anymore. I try to engage him in conversation, but he politely tells me he's got other things to do. He is still my son, and I'm his dad, but I must seem to him like a dinosaur – and I need to let him be his own person.

Where, I wonder, has my baby gone? I ponder this question, and then face the answer: Nowhere, really ... he's right in front of me, driving the car to his new destiny. So who is the baby now? Is it my youngest child, at 19 years of age, who seems to be living out his life as it is meant to be? I think not. The real baby is the one in the mirror, the image I barely recognize. It is me: retired doctor, small-time landscaper, and two-bit writer. Is that all there is? And will all of us come to a similar conclusion?

"I think therefore I am," the philosopher said, so I must still be in the car … but where am I going? I'm no longer needed as "father" to my adult children. My boys will make some mistakes – as we all did, but (God willing) will get over them. I'm still a husband, but more is needed. It's time to "re-invent" myself. I need to stop my blubbering and try to find out (with God's help, of course) what's in store for me. And I suspect that's how it is with all of us. The "kid chapter" of our life is nearly over. Now we need to see what "the rest of the story" is all about.

Retirement

(4/14/2010)

"You're lucky to be retired," said the man at the coffee shop.

"Retired? I don't feel retired when I've been mowing lawns all week."

Retirement, I've decided, is not for the faint of heart. If you received a gold watch and retired at a ripe old age it doesn't seem to matter. Even if you took an early retirement so you could "enjoy life" it also doesn't seem to matter. The fact is that there are stresses associated with retired life – just like there are during any other phase of your life.

A recent "Retirement Confidence Survey" from the Employee Benefit Research Institute reported that most people are not financially prepared for retirement, and the problem is getting worse. This private nonprofit institute interviewed 1,153 US workers and retirees in January, and discovered that just 16% of workers said they were "very confident" that they had saved enough for retirement. Only 69% have saved anything – which is down from 75% in 2009. In 2010, about 27% of workers had less than $1,000 stashed away, compared to 20% in 2009. Of those with some form of savings, 54% said they have less than $25,000. The same percentage said they need at least $500,000 for a comfortable retirement. But just 46% have actually calculated how much they need to be secure in retirement. (From the 3/10/10 edition of the "St. Paul Pioneer Press")

Retirement finances are only half the battle. Another major issue is how you structure your time. If you don't have a daily routine, you may get bored and fill the "commitment void" in your life with bad habits – like excesses of smoking, food and alcohol. So beware the evils of retirement! And in order to maintain your physical and mental health you should only consider retirement if you are "retiring to" a healthy new lifestyle rather than "retiring from" something you dislike.

Your physical health is bound to affect the quality of your retirement years. Heart disease, cancer and many other maladies are more common after we pass the "50 year" milestone. Take care of yourself. Some problems (like my knee arthritis) are more of a nuisance than anything – but can affect one's ability to enjoy retirement. And consider how you're going to pay for healthcare in your "golden years." Medicare is generally considered to be good health insurance, but you need a "Medigap" policy to pay for deductible and co-pay deficiencies.

In the final analysis, age is just a state of mind. Of course our bodies are fading! We've never been able to do as much as we've wanted to anyway. For most of us, wanting to be a scratch golfer in retirement is just as unrealistic as it was when we were young ... Deciding to enjoy your golf game "in spite of your scores" is the better choice.

It's okay to joke about your advanced age. As comedian George Carlin puts it: "You BECOME 21, TURN 30, PUSH 40, REACH 50 and MAKE IT to 60. [Then] you've built up so much speed that you HIT 70! After that it's a day-by-day thing; you HIT [Wednesday, April 14, 2010] ... You HIT lunch; you REACH bedtime ..." You get the idea. Life has never been about being just where you are. We're looking around the corner to see what's coming next. And that's the way it's always been. So plan your retirement with hopefulness and wisdom, and – if you're already there – live it in the same manner.

Hermits Don't Sing

(11/11/2009)

I noticed the old man at the café last year. He sat alone, sipping on his coffee, and didn't even look up when I said "Hi" to him – as I passed by, with my friends, on the way to our table.

Week by week I noticed him there, same time each week, always alone; and he never seemed to visit with anyone. The waitress would ask him a few questions; he would nod and whisper his order; and then he would eat his meal, quietly, before rising to pay his bill. Not that I was spying on him, or anything, but I noticed, as the year went by, that he and the waitress started to converse a bit. Once in a great while he would even smile. She brought a hint of happiness into his life, I thought, and I admired her for that.

Recently the local church has been trying to put together a Christmas choir. They needed more men, the director said, so I reluctantly agreed to join. And then I thought about the lonely old man at the café. Being a bit of a maverick, I asked the man to join our choir. He looked at me with sad eyes, and said: "Hermits don't sing."

He seemed perplexed when I continued: "That's okay. Most of us men can't sing worth a hoot anyway. We just fake it. I'll see you next Wednesday at choir practice."

I was pleased to see him behind the church the following week. He was pacing back and forth – apparently torn between entering the building or hightailing it for home. I went up to him, greeted him warmly, and coaxed him into entering the church.

I sat next to him in the Tenor section. The choir director told us when and what to sing. My voice was awful – and my misreading of the notes was even worse. Meanwhile my hermit friend barely whispered out the words to each song. He seemed to want to fade into the background of this mixed company of talented choir members. It was obvious that he was uncomfortable, and I felt bad for having invited him. Mysteriously enough, though, his voice gradually became bolder, and even beautiful, especially when we sang a song he was familiar with:

"O little town of Bethlehem, how still we see thee lie! Above the deep and dreamless sleep, the silent stars go by. Yet in thy dark streets shineth, the everlasting Light: The hopes and fears of all the years – are met in Thee tonight."

It was a miracle! My quiet hermit friend could sing like an angel. All he needed was a little practice – and an invitation to sing. Music, I later learned, was once a big part of his life. But many years ago his wife was killed in a car accident, his kids all moved away, and his life as a widower required less and less social interaction. He became the hermit I noticed at the café.

When choir practice was over, I gave my new friend a ride home. He told me how much he enjoyed singing. He and his wife used to sing in choirs together.

"Thank you," he said, "for wanting to be my friend; and thanks for rekindling in me the joy of singing."

Terrible Tenor

(12/9/2009)

Wanting to sing well, I've discovered, is a whole lot different than being able to do so. But I wish I knew that a few weeks ago … My wife and I were asked to join a choir recently. Everybody there was musically inclined – so I should have just politely declined. I do like to sing, though. I have sung in other choirs, but this group intended to do *four-part harmony*, which is something I have no experience with.

When a member of the choir said: "Give me a B flat followed by a C sharp," I thought she was joking. The pianist obliged, and told her (in music language) what she wanted to know. I never learned much about music in school, though, and I honestly don't know what I don't know – about music and other subjects.

"Maybe I shouldn't be in this choir," I told my wife.

"Nonsense; you're doing fine," she said. So I kept going to practice, and I kept struggling along.

"Should I sing louder?" I asked the director.

"I'd rather you didn't," he said … That should have been my clue that I wasn't hitting my notes, and I might be *throwing off* the Tenor section. That's a real concern, my middle son later told me. All three of my sons have had music education – courtesy of the Sidney Education System – so I appreciate their viewpoint on the subject. My wife told me not to worry about it … but she doesn't read music either.

"Who cares if you can't read music?" my wife said repeatedly. But what if I can't sing? Would that be a problem? And what if the experience is humiliating? Do I really want to make a fool of myself? These don't seem like profound philosophical questions, but – like other bumps in the road of life – they *can feel* like life and death. And maybe the expression "die of embarrassment" should be taken seriously …

"Just fake your way through the songs you don't know," my wife said.

My middle son offered a more sober appraisal: "Do whatever you think is best, Dad."

The choir's first public performance was two days later. As luck would have it, I came down with a case of laryngitis, and couldn't sing.

"Quitting was the right thing to do, Dad," my son said. "What you did was 'for the good of the choir.'" Thanks, I thought … but he was right. The choir sounded better without me – especially the Tenor Section.

The experience reminds me of the song by Harry Chapin (called *Mr.*

Tanner) where an amateur singer, a cleaner by trade, is talked into trying out music as a profession. His town hall debut goes poorly, and the critic lambasts him. "Full time consideration of another endeavor," the critic says, "might be in order." And so Mr. Tanner "never sang again … excepting very late at night, when the shop was dark and closed. He sang softly to himself, as he sorted through the clothes. Music was his life, it was not his livelihood, and it made him feel so happy, and it made him feel so good. He sang from his heart, and he sang from his soul. He did not know how well he sang; it just made him whole."

That's how it is with a lot of us would-be singers. But if we sing in public, we should do so as quietly as possible. When we sing in the privacy of our homes (in the shower and otherwise) we may sing as loudly as we want. Singing, they say, is good for the soul. If we sing badly, though, it *might not* be "good for the whole" – that is, for the music lovers around us.

Parent Shopping

(5/5/2008)

I remember shopping with my mom. It was something to do on rainy afternoons. As I was chasing after her in Piggly Wiggly, Mom was sharing her life philosophy with me. She said the store brands were usually a better deal than brand names. But she did like to buy Tide detergent, Cheerios, and Fig Newtons. I still buy these products. I can't help myself. I also look closely at store prices – just like Mom did. My wife and kids think I'm a dinosaur when it comes to shopping, but I think Mom was right on this issue.

Like it or not, my view on many topics reflects my mom's views. Maybe Dad had a philosophy on shopping – but I never knew what it was. He disliked being in debt, though, because he hid from the family how many times he remortgaged the house. When he died (40 years ago this week) he was still a stranger to me. I have spent many years trying to figure out what he was like – and what he wanted for me. He was always working. My mom, on the other hand, was always there. As little kids, we followed her like goslings follow their Mother Goose. During the course of her daily routine, she taught me the alphabet, to count, to tie my shoes, and to tell time. She also taught me "everything I need to know" about meat loaf, finances, politics and religion.

"Parental injuctives," the psychologists say, are the "lessons" that we learn from our parents. They are the slogans and commands we hear from Mom and Dad in our youth. Most of these messages have helped us through life. Some of the things parents say, however, can backfire.

"Do your homework before watching TV" sounded just as harsh to my kids as "Go weed the garden" sounded to me when I was a kid. But parents do the best they can – don't they? When my mom told me to "wash the dishes" and "clean the basement," she thought she was saying "Be Good" and "Try Hard." Those were appropriate messages, but sometimes they sounded like "Don't Mess Up" to me.

Eric Berne, the inventor of "Transactional Analysis," has had much to say on the topic of Parental Injunctives. What parents say is planted into the "Parent" side of our own nature. Our carefree and inventive side (our "Child") is often overwhelmed by all the "Do This" and "Don't Do That" statements we have heard, though. The third and most important part of our personality (the "Adult") is formed when we incorporate our genetics and our environmental lessons into a unique new person. The "Adult" is supposed to run the show, but sometimes is just a mirror image of what other people have told us to think and do.

Some experts say the "messages" we hear from our parents do more harm than good. In a similar way, the messages we give our own children are potentially harmful. God, I hope not! While there is no doubt that parents do make mistakes, I believe that 99% of the time parents really do "the best that they can," and the net result is that children realize they are loved *regardless* of what words are communicated. My mom, for example, taught me to do cost comparison when we went shopping together. And to this day I think that is what all people should do. I also watched as my parents *sacrificed everything* to provide for their children – and believe that's what all parents should do.

Kids can't shop for *Hollywood-perfect* parents. They are stuck with the ones they have been given. I have known for many years that my parents were not perfect. I also know that they loved me (and my siblings) more than life itself. I hope that someday my kids think the same thing about me.

The Great Depression

(2/3/2009)

Politicians are debating the causes and cures of our recent economic recession, and they look to "The Great Depression" for insight. The Great Depression, as many of you know, started with the Stock Market Crash on "Black Thursday," October 24th of 1929, and lasted throughout most of the 1930's. This decade-long period was characterized by high unemployment, poverty, and lost opportunities for personal growth. The purported causes of the Great Depression sound eerily reminiscent of our current situation: the false belief that the stock market would keep going up, inadequate regulatory oversight, tumbling real estate values, government bailout programs of dubious benefit, and – most importantly – a loss of confidence in our economic future.

There is a lot written about the Great Depression. Eighty years of analysis, however, has not solved the puzzle of what happened back then; nor do today's experts have a clear idea of what is going on now. For example, 49% of professional economists believe that Roosevelt's "New Deal" served to lengthen and deepen the Great Depression. And the Great Depression caused lifelong distress for some people. The stock market decline did not end until 1932, when the Dow closed at 41 on July 8, concluding an 89% decline from its peak. And "anyone who bought stocks in mid-1929 and held onto them saw most of his or her adult life pass by before getting back to even." (quote by Richard M. Salsman, and general information from Wikipedia.com.)

On a more personal level, the Great Depression affected my parents in ways that they never really talked about. My mother, for example, didn't hesitate to turn over her 1930's paychecks to her parents – in order to support the family. Think what kids would say if they were told to do that today! In the meantime, Adolf Hitler rose to power in a country that was also consumed by poverty, and his empty promises to the German people led to a war that affected many people. My father, for one, dropped out of college to fight Hitler, was injured and captured in his first combat action, and spent 30 months in prison hoping to someday marry my future mother. When the war was over, Mom and Dad took out a government loan to purchase a new home. Their house was one of 30 million built in the post-WW2 period. Like others of their generation, they also had a large family – which was part of the post-WW2 "baby boom." National and global news, as you can see, affected my family in a very personal way.

My mother smiles at news of the recent economic recession. She has seen it all before, and doesn't get too excited. "The most important thing," she says, "is family." She should know. She has eight children, 17 grandchildren and 9 great grand children. Born in 1920, she was a forerunner of the "women's liberation" movement. She worked from 18 to 26, then raised a family, and then went back to school at 48 years of age. After my dad's death in 1968, she had to "re-invent" herself. She became a medical transcriptionist, and worked until her retirement in 1988.

Last week my mom's baby sister died. Mom never expected to outlive her siblings. Her family pulled each other through the Great Depression, and has always been very close. They each had large families. Our family reunions are bigger than many small towns. Years ago, I used to bring whoever I was dating to these gatherings – to see what my family thought of them. They gave my current (and only) wife the highest rating.

There isn't anything that can tear our family apart. Our faith in God and love for each other has been the "super glue" that has held us together. Our parents lived through the Great Depression and World War II, after all, and have instilled in us the sense of *perseverance* that they learned in their youth.

God has a similar lesson for each person. Most of us learn that living *through* depression is more important than living *in* depression. Today's difficulty is just a bump in the road on our individual and collective journey to the hereafter. When we get there there's going to be a massive "family reunion" that you won't want to miss.

White Socks

(11/6/2007)

"Sorry, Dad, but you're not cool."

The words struck me like a dagger. Remarks like that only hurt if they're true. I hate to admit it, but my time has come and gone. Once I was cool (or thought I was) but now I'm *out of it*. It's not that I don't care, but I'm coming to realize that it's irrational to believe everything I do, think, and feel is going to be appreciated.

My attitude about *being cool* is changing. It's best to pretend you don't care what people think of you – when you really do. You need to know "how to jibe." Unfortunately, yesterday's slang is not "with it" anymore. That means you have to keep up with the latest trends. If you're going to be trendy, then you need to keep up with clothes fashions; which will require a complete change in wardrobe every six months.

I have never been overly concerned about what I wear, and that has become more obvious in recent years. I generally wear the clothes that are easiest to reach in my closet. It's an accident if my clothes ever match. Most of the time my choice of clothes does not meet my wife's approval. She cringes when she sees me emerge from the bedroom (on our way to a social gathering) with high-water pants, scuffed shoes, and a poorly fitting shirt. My color choices also bother her to no end. I've tried to tell her I'm color blind, but she says I'm just lazy.

When I was a kid, I used to care about my clothes. When I nonchalantly wore white socks with my blue pants and shirt to school one day, though, my classmates teased me to no end. Maybe white socks weren't an item of scorn in your grade school, but they were in mine. I suppose that's because we all wore navy blue uniforms, and any color deviation stuck out like a sore thumb.

My mom got a great deal on those white socks at Kmart. She never knew her cost consciousness would cause me to be ridiculed. In my school, white socks were as "uncool" as plastic pocket pencil holders. To an eleven year-old boy, being teased seemed like torture. Perhaps that psychological abuse is the reason I am messed up today. I defended my mom, of course, and hardened my attitude about clothes fashions.

As I got on with my life, I developed a perverse attachment to white socks. They certainly were good enough for sports. Why can't we wear them on other occasions? If they get dirty, you can just wear them *inside out*. And they're cheap. You can buy a *six pack* of white socks for less than you pay for six rolls of toilet paper. (No wonder so many public toilets are backed up.) And cotton socks are definitely more comfortable than synthetic dress socks.

In my doctoring days, I succumbed to protocol by wearing dress slacks, shirt, tie ... and matching socks. When I went to doctor social gatherings, I also did my best to look professional. Now that I'm a landscaper, I don't go to these "doctor functions" anymore. And now my choice of clothes is not based on fashion, but on function. And you can't beat white socks for flexibility and comfort.

Being cool has its disadvantages. It takes a lot of energy to keep up with fashions – and to always say and do the right thing. It seems superficial to pay too much attention to a person's clothing. When I wear *odd* clothes, you might think I'm *crazy*, but I prefer to regard myself as *eccentric*. If you agree with the premise of this article, throw away your dress socks ... It's possible that we could start a new trend. White socks could become the next big thing.

Everyday Heroes

(11/25/2009)

The VFW "Voice of Democracy" essay program asked the question: "Does America Still Have Heroes?" Since only one Sidney student bothered to enter this $175,000 scholarship contest, I will offer my opinion on the matter.

Nowadays, when we hear the word *hero*, we generally think of sports heroes. That's unfortunate. The New York Yankees, for example, just coasted to their 27th World Series championship. And why shouldn't they win? They spent $208 million on player salaries to have "the best team that money can buy." The Minnesota Twins, on the other hand, won their 5th division championship since 2002, but were deemed a failure because they lost to the Yankees in the playoffs. The Yankees spend 3 times more than the Twins on player salaries. Give the Twins credit for having a good team *year after year* despite having limited resources. They do it by playing good baseball and developing younger players to their full potential. And some of their best players, like Joe Mauer, are not only topnotch, but also realize there's more to life than being able to brag about how much money you make.

Some athletes will do anything to be regarded as the best. It has been claimed (by Jose Canseco and others) that many Major League Baseball players were using anabolic steroids in the 1990s. Barry Bonds, for example, was *suspiciously able* to increase his homerun production from 30 to 40 per year to 73 in 2001. Despite his denials, his urine has tested positive for banned substances. He amassed 762 dingers in his career, passed Babe Ruth and Hank Aaron on the all-time homer list, but will forever be suspected of using performance-enhancing drugs.

Maybe we should look outside the sports arena for our heroes. Barack Obama, for example, captured the imagination of our country last year by becoming the first black president in U.S. history. I did not vote for him, but I do give him credit for his accomplishment. His presidential agenda seems too ambitious for me. I do not think, however, that his presidency is "one continual mistake," as was stated in a recent editorial.

The media is quick to criticize people in the spotlight. "Bad news" and "muckraking" capture more headlines than the "millions points of light" good deeds that characterize our nation's people. America is a great country, and – in case you didn't know it – we are the most charitable nation in world history. Our country donates more than twice as much (as a percentage of

GNP) than the next-most charitable countries in the world (UK, Canada, Australia, etc).

I have met a few *everyday heroes* in my life. I have a neighbor, for example, who always helps people in need. My wife also donates her time and talents – to a variety of causes. My greatest heroes of all time, though, are my parents. Dad won a "Bronze Star Medal" for dragging a wounded buddy to safe ground in a treacherous World War II battle (the Rapido River campaign), was injured in the process, and spent the next 30 months in a German P.O.W. camp. He never talked about it, though. His greatest accomplishment, I think, was quietly working a variety of jobs to support his family of ten.

When Dad died in 1968, my mom took over the daunting task of leading our family. She went back to school to become a medical stenographer – in order to better support her large family. Mom and Dad never complained about their lot in life. They typify what many Americans do every day: they accept the hardships of their lives, labor away in jobs that aren't particularly easy, and do the best they can. Perhaps you are one of these people … In summary, I have this to say: The heck with sports heroes, politicians, and people who attract the media's attention. We should look around us to see what true heroes really look like.

Dr. Dirt With His Mom, 2004

Remembering Mom

(1/6/2010)

Dolores Kessler, my mom, died a few weeks ago. She was 89 years old. She died in her sleep on 12/19/09, in her own bed and in the home she loved – at 1868 Flandrau Street in Maplewood, a suburb of St. Paul, Minnesota.

I think my mom was the best mom of all time. She was, of course, the woman who gave me life. She also gave birth to seven other children. And not only that, but she took care of all 8 of us by herself – after my dad died (of a heart attack) at a young age.

Every kid should regard their parents as "the best" of all time. They probably also, at one time or another, reject their parents' values, and vow to avoid being anything like them. Then they get over it. That's just how it is.

For example: I now realize that Dad's neck twitch was caused by a war injury, but when I was a kid it embarrassed me. And I once thought Mom was cheap, but now know she had to be frugal in order to manage our family finances. It's all part of the package: when you're a kid you don't understand why your parents do the things they do, and then you find out they had a reason. And 99% of the time it is because they love you.

I'll never forget the day that Mom taught me to tie my shoes. I was frustrated, but then she taught me her "double loop technique." Then I got it. I was so proud of myself. And I'll never forget how she taught me how to count. "Look at the clock," she said. And so I counted the hours on the clock, got to ten, then started over (11, 12, etc), got to twenty, and then started *over again* (21, 22, etc). She made it seem easy. And then I counted (on paper) up to 13,000. I guess I've always been a bit compulsive – even as a kid.

My mom wasn't perfect, I realize, but she was a perfect mother for me. She was also perfect in her acceptance of the life that God gave her. Even though her life wasn't a "bed of roses," Mom said "Yes" to the burdens *and* the joys that God gave her.

Coming to Sidney MT meant moving 700 miles from my family home. During my busy doctoring years, I didn't get back to see my Minnesota family very often, but when I did get home it was like I had never left. My mom and I would sit at the kitchen table, drink coffee together, and talk about life. A few weeks before she died we did that very thing … We also made a recording of that visit – and it is something that my family and I will always treasure.

Mom was a great mother, grandmother and great-grandmother. Even when her kids did squabble – as kids always do – she loved all the parties involved, and she prayed that we would work things out.

Mom died in exactly the manner she wanted. I trust that she is now in heaven, looking down on me as I write this eulogy, smiling, and pleased that I am honoring her now.

And Mom can say, as it does in the Bible (2 Tim 4:7-8):

"I have fought the good fight, I have finished the race, I have kept the faith. Now there is in store for me the crown of righteousness, which the Lord, the righteous Judge, will award to me on that day – and not only to me, but also to all who have longed for his appearing."

And the Bible also says (1 Cor 15:55):

"Where, O death, is your victory? Where, O death, is your sting?"

So I bid you farewell, Mom. Thanks for everything. But it won't be long before we're all sitting around the table again, sipping on coffee, and talking about everything in the world – both on earth, and in heaven…

Flandrau Street

(3/17/2010)

Imagine, if you can, going to your home for the very last time. It has been your home for 56 years, and now it is being sold to the highest bidder. Any dollar value the house yields will certainly not equal the value – in your heart – that you attach to the place you've always called "home."

That's what it is has been like this past week. My mom died a few months ago, you see, and the "Kessler Kids" have been fixing up "the old homestead" for sale. The twenty year-old kitchen mural had to be stripped from the wall. This and other "sentimental stuff" made the house less sale-able, the realtor said, so it had to go. The spirit of my mother had already vacated the place, but the house itself still stored countless memories of my youth.

The upstairs bedroom is where I woke up each morning, looked out the window to check on the weather, and anticipated what kind of day it would be. During the school year I had trouble getting up. My mom had to yell a reminder to me. I would stumble downstairs, have a bowl of cereal, and lay on the floor (near the heat register) for a precious few minutes before I had to get going.

Our grade school was ½ mile away. The walk always woke me up – especially when I met friends along the way. I travelled that route again this morning, and couldn't believe this would be the last time I'd take this familiar route. And tonight my old school wants me to be the featured speaker at their "all year" reunion – which is a task I fear and also look forward to. I'll let you know how it goes …

My walk is over. I'm nearing home again. Walking across our front yard reminds me of the zillion times I've taken this shortcut. The front step is inviting, but I enter through the back door – as always. The house is empty. It seems to be full of ghosts (no, "spirits") from the past. It's still a simple, warm and loving place. It embraces me this one last time, knowing that soon I too will be just a memory.

I look at the kitchen table where I drank a thousand cups of coffee – with dear mom, of course – and remember the countless stories she told me of the past, her present concerns, and her plans for the future.

Mom made arrangements to have the kitchen remodeled before she died, and paid the carpenter in advance. "Just in case anything happens," she said … Oh, Mom, how did you know? How does anyone know when their time is coming to an end?

I'm sitting in her living room chair as I write this. Her favorite chair. Everyone has one of these. And chairs like this bond with their patrons so that other people do not fit as well. The image of her watching "The Golden Girls" on TV is burned in my memory. She loved that show. Although TV can sometimes be drivel, I'm glad she had shows like that to keep her company.

It's my final walk around the house. Tomorrow I will be gone. And the house is to be sold before I come again. The next owners (I hope they are nice!) will not likely want us to parade through their home to reminisce. "Goodbye walls," I say out loud. Goodbye also to this room and that. The pictures have already been taken down, so part of me has already left. But I can still hear the walls talk, and they remind me of how it was. They will miss me and my family too, I think. They loved us as much as we loved them.

Driving out the driveway I try not to look back. It is too sad. I must be on my way. I must get on with my life. I'm on the street now – Flandrau Street – and ready to head down the road. But the house beckons me, so I sneak one more look. "Goodbye," it says. And so I fight back the tears, and say out loud:

"Goodbye, my old friend. Thanks for everything."